Wicca &
Witchcraft
FOR
DUMMIES®

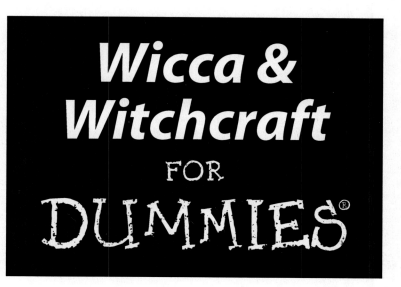

Wicca & Witchcraft
FOR DUMMIES®

by Diane Smith

John Wiley & Sons, Inc.

Wicca & Witchcraft For Dummies®

Published by
John Wiley & Sons, Inc.
111 River St.
Hoboken, NJ 07030-5774
www.wiley.com

Copyright © 2005 by John Wiley & Sons, Inc., Indianapolis, Indiana

Published by John Wiley & Sons, Inc., Indianapolis, Indiana

Published simultaneously in Canada

For general information on our other products and services, please contact our Customer Care Department within the U.S. at 877-762-2974, outside the U.S. at 317-572-3993, or fax 317-572-4002.

For technical support, please visit www.wiley.com/techsupport.

Wiley also publishes its books in a variety of electronic formats. Some content that appears in print may not be available in electronic books.

Library of Congress Control Number: 2005923742

ISBN 978-0-7645-7834-2 (pbk); ISBN 978-1-118-07161-8 (ebk); ISBN 978-1-118-07001-7 (ebk)

10 9 8 7 6 5 4

1O/RU/QX/QV/IN

About the Author

Diane Smith has been a Witch all of her life, but she realized the fact in 1987. She incorporates ideas from many diverse sources (including Shamanism, Bohmian physics, and String Theory) into her eclectic beliefs and practices. She has been a writer and an editor for more than 25 years, working in the fields of medicine, child advocacy, and book publishing.

Dedication

For my mother, Shirley Anne Smith, and my father, James Smith

Author's Acknowledgments

I want to thank Brian Kramer, the editor for this book. I can't begin to express in words my gratitude for his compassion, expertise, and professionalism. I deeply regret the unexpected challenges of this book project, and I appreciate his grace and good nature under extreme pressure. I wish him a Divine blessing on *all* his future endeavors.

I also want to thank Stacy Kennedy for her patience and compassion. I sincerely hope that she, too, is blessed and rewarded in the future.

I want to include a heartfelt thank you to Kristin Cocks, Kathy Cox, Diane Steele, and all the people at Wiley for their kindness.

I deeply appreciate the technical review of Debi Baker and her contribution and ongoing dedication to this project.

Thank you to Stuart Stuple and Bjoern Hartfvang for their invaluable input and assistance.

Publisher's Acknowledgments

We're proud of this book; please send us your comments through our Dummies online registration form located at www.dummies.com/register/.

Some of the people who helped bring this book to market include the following:

Acquisitions, Editorial, and Media Development

Project Editor: Brian Kramer

Acquisitions Editor: Stacy Kennedy

Copy Editor: Brian Kramer

Technical Editors: Debi Baker, Bjoern Hartfvang, Stuart Stuple

Editorial Manager: Michelle Hacker

Editorial Supervisor & Reprint Editor: Carmen Krikorian

Editorial Assistant: Hanna Scott

Cartoons: Rich Tennant (www.the5thwave.com)

Cover Image: © Steve Sant/Alamy

Composition Services

Project Coordinator: Adrienne Martinez

Layout and Graphics: Carl Byers, Andrea Dahl, Joyce Haughey

Proofreaders: Laura Albert, Leeann Harney, Jessica Kramer, Aptara

Indexer: Aptara

Publishing and Editorial for Consumer Dummies

Diane Graves Steele, Vice President and Publisher, Consumer Dummies

Joyce Pepple, Acquisitions Director, Consumer Dummies

Kristin A. Cocks, Product Development Director, Consumer Dummies

Michael Spring, Vice President and Publisher, Travel

Kelly Regan, Editorial Director, Travel

Publishing for Technology Dummies

Andy Cummings, Vice President and Publisher, Dummies Technology/General User

Composition Services

Gerry Fahey, Vice President of Production Services

Debbie Stailey, Director of Composition Services

Contents at a Glance

Table of Contents

Introduction

❖ ❖

*T*hank you for picking up this book. I hope it meets your need for reliable information. I didn't write the book in an effort to convert anyone but rather to dispel false stereotypes and to share the facts about the real Wicca and Witchcraft.

First and foremost, Wicca is a spiritual path of personal discovery and experience of the Divine. From Deity, Wiccans receive wisdom, strength, solace, and surprising synchronicities. The way that Wiccans perceive or experience Deity is unique to each individual, but for most, seeking relationship or union with the Divine is the heart of Wicca.

Nature flows from Deity. Wiccan ritual and celebration are timed to the rhythms and the cycles of the natural world, especially the Earth's journey around the Sun and the Moon's passage around the Earth. The Divine energy and the web of life are what real Wicca and Witchcraft are all about.

About This Book

This book is my attempt to provide a general reference about Wicca and Witchcraft. Unfortunately, such a book is impossible to write. Here's the problem: No author, including me, can write a book and claim that it definitively represents all of Wicca, because:

- ✔ Wicca is a spiritual path of personal discovery and communication with Deity. Each Wiccan decides what to believe and how to practice.
- ✔ Wicca doesn't have a doctrine or holy book that Wiccans must follow.
- ✔ Wicca doesn't have leaders who require that people worship or live a certain way. No central authority or hierarchy of clergy decides who is and is not a legitimate Wiccan.
- ✔ Wiccans differ wildly in their beliefs and practices. Most Wiccans happily respect each others' opinions and follow their own hearts.

In this book, I try to thoroughly explain the core beliefs, ethics, and practices that nearly all Wiccans accept.

For more controversial issues, I try to offer an inclusive look across Wicca, including many examples of different Wiccan ideas and opinions. Of course, no one really knows what the majority of Wiccans believe and how they practice.

No central organization collects such records, but I do my best to describe the predominant beliefs and practices.

Obviously, I can't include every single Wiccan's opinion about every single spiritual issue, and I had to make choices. The book undoubtedly contains some of my personal biases, but I made every effort to be fair and inclusive, and provide an accurate reflection of Wicca today.

You don't have to read this book from front cover to back. You are free to skip around and read about the subjects that interest you.

One bit of advice: Don't jump in and try to perform ritual or, especially, to work magic without first reading about Wiccan beliefs and ethics. Your practice will be more fulfilling, effective, and ethical if you understand Wiccan principles.

Conventions Used in This Book

Choosing the language to use in this book was a nightmare. Wiccans have no doctrine, and they are free to develop their own beliefs. They also define terms any way they darn well please. Many of the words or phrases commonly used in Wicca don't have clear, standard meanings. Two people may use the same term with totally different ideas in mind.

This section explains the definitions that I finally settled on. However, if you intend to study further, you need to know that the definitions of some terms are inconsistent throughout the Wiccan community.

Defining the Divine

In this book, I use the words *Deity, Divinity,* and *the Divine.* I know that these words are generic and vague, and I use them intentionally, although some Wiccans may find them aggravating.

Nearly all Wiccans believe in some form of a Creative Being, however, they have different ideas about the nature of the Divine. Deity may be the Goddess and the God in perfect duality. She may be the primal Great Goddess that is the source of all life. The Divine may be the Higher Self or a symbol emerging from the unconscious mind. Some Wiccans believe that Deity takes many forms or has many aspects.

I deliberately use vague words because I don't want to be disrespectful and assume that everyone perceives Deity in the same way. One alternative is to use *Goddess(es) and/or God(s).* That construction is far too unwieldy in the text, and even that awkward phrase discounts people who believe in a primal

Source or Creative Being without sex/gender. I apologize to all of those who think that I am dishonoring the Goddess, Goddesses, God, Gods, The All, The One, the Triple Goddess, Earth Mother, Source, Supreme Being, the Ancient Ones . . .

Defining Paganism, Witchcraft, and Wicca

Every time I thought I had acceptable working definitions for Paganism/Pagan, Witch/Witchcraft, and Wicca/Wiccan, further research made me change my mind. No one agrees on the use of these terms. The following sections describe their definitions for the purpose of this book.

Pagan originally meant peasant or country dweller. Pagan was a term of derision, sort of like the word "hick" today. *Heathen* originally meant a person who lived in the heaths (open wasteland covered in heather, low shrubs, and so on). *Paganism,* today, is a collective or umbrella term that encompasses any of the pre-Christian religions and cultures. It usually refers to a nature religion that defines Deity as immanent. *Immanence* means that the Divine energy is manifest in nature. Deity is right here, right now, and is all-present in the world. Pagan also refers to indigenous or tribal religions and cultures. Historically, pagans and heathens were the rural folk who were the last to be converted to Christianity.

A *Pagan* is someone who practices and/or holds the beliefs of Paganism. *Neo-Paganism* is a continuation, revival, or re-creation of an old Pagan religion. A *neo-Pagan* is someone who follows a new version of old Paganism.

Wicca, for the purposes of this book, is a continuation, a revival, or a recreation of pre-Christian, primarily European, nature religion or spirituality. Wicca is a type or sect of Witchcraft. Although Wicca has its roots in ancient spirituality, the modern Wiccan revival began in the 1950s.

Most Wiccans agree with one of the following definitions:

- ✔ Wicca is a continuation of a very old religion that has been passed down through families and groups since ancient times.

- ✔ Wicca is a return to or revival of an old, even ancient, form of religion. Because not a great deal is known about the original beliefs and practices, contemporary Wiccans must add to the old tradition.

- ✔ Wicca is a new form of spirituality that re-creates some very old practices and ideas. The modern form of Wicca began in the 1950s.

Put very simply, Wiccans generally accept two basic principles:

✔ A belief in immanent Deity: A Wiccan's main spiritual goal is to grow in his or her relationship with Divinity. Almost all Wiccans believe in a Creative Being. Many, but not all, Wiccans honor Deity in both the male and female aspects, the Goddess and the God. Most Wiccans believe that the Divine is *immanent* in the world, meaning that Deity is right here, right now, and is all-present in the world. People come from and are a part of the Divine energy, and Deity is within everyone.

✔ A belief in interconnection: All of life — everything that exists — comes from and is a part of the Divine energy, so everything is interconnected. All of existence is an unbroken web or circle of energy. Nature is a manifestation of the Deity. Wiccan spiritual practice is based on the cycles of nature.

A ***Wiccan,*** for the purposes of this book, is someone who practices and/or holds the beliefs of Wicca. Wicca is a type or sect of Witchcraft, and Wiccans are a type of Witch.

Note: Not all Wiccans consider themselves to be Witches. Some consider Wicca to be a separate system of beliefs and practices, different from all forms of traditional Witchcraft. Some Wiccans reject the Witch label simply because it has such a negative and evil connotation in the culture. They have abandoned the word, believing that Wiccans can never undo the centuries of propaganda and bad press that Witches have endured.

Witchcraft, for the purposes of this book, is an umbrella or collective term for the beliefs and practices of all Witches and Wiccans throughout history, beginning in ancient times, primarily in Europe. Witchcraft is a nature religion or spirituality. The term refers to both the spiritual practice (the honoring or worshipping of Deity) and the magical practice (healing, herbalism, midwifery, spellcasting, divination, and so on). I often use the word Witchcraft in references to history, because that is the word used in the documentation (for example, during the medieval and Renaissance Witch trials).

The word Witchcraft has many different meanings and contexts. The following are some of the — *sometimes contradictory* — definitions and usages for the word Witchcraft:

✔ Wicca refers to the spirituality (the relationship with or worship of Deity). Witchcraft refers to the magical practice (for example, spell casting, healing, divination, and so on). This is a very popular definition, and you may encounter it often.

✔ Witchcraft and Wicca are synonyms and are interchangeable.

✔ Witchcraft is an umbrella or collective term for the beliefs and practices of all Witches and Wiccans. Wicca is a sect or a specific form of Witchcraft.

✔ Witchcraft encompasses *all* the practices of Wicca, including rituals for worship and for magic. Generally, Wiccans create sacred space by casting a circle. Within that circle, they worship or honor Deity and they also work magic. Some Wiccans consider everything that happens in that sacred space to be Witchcraft. For them, Witchcraft is spiritual ritual and magical art.

✔ Wicca is the modern-day revival religion, and Witchcraft is the old, pre-Christian nature religion of Europe.

✔ Outside of Wicca and Witchcraft, there are a seemingly endless number of stereotypical and outlandishly inaccurate definitions for Witch and Witchcraft, even within credible sources (such as dictionaries). These definitions often characterize Witches and Witchcraft as evil or wicked and associate them with Satanism.

A **Witch,** for the purposes of this book, is someone who practices and/or holds the beliefs of Witchcraft.

Many Witches follow traditions that were in existence before — or are otherwise separate from — the traditions born during the Wiccan revival of the 1950s. The followers of these traditions commonly are called *traditional Witches* or sometimes *Hedgewitches*. Many traditional Witches focus on the oral teachings, literature, history, and folklore of a specific culture (for example, Celtic), and many traditional Witches have ancestry in their chosen tradition. Some Witches are from family (hereditary) backgrounds in Witchcraft. Some groups of Witches have well-defined spiritual beliefs, and others focus almost solely on practice (folk magic, healing, midwifery, and so on).

Note: Not all Witches are Wiccan; most traditional Witches don't consider themselves to be Wiccan at all.

What You're Not to Read

Wicca encourages independence and self-direction. If you don't want to work practical magic, you don't ever have to explore that topic. If you don't feel comfortable using divination, such as tarot cards, skip that chapter. If you aren't interested in dreams, pass up that information. However, before you engage in any practice (such as magic or trance), make sure that you read about the beliefs, ethics, and warnings that pertain to the practice.

Foolish Assumptions

I don't assume that the readers of this book are now or ever want to be Wiccan. My only assumption is that you want factual, reliable information about Wicca and Witchcraft, free of false stereotypes and sensationalism.

This book is not an effort to bring people into Wicca. Proselytizing, trying to convert others, violates Wiccan ethics. Wiccans assume that those who are meant to follow the Wiccan path will find it on their own.

In some of the more personal portions of the book, and especially in the how-to sections, I use the word "you." I use that word only to simplify the text. The use of the collective "you" doesn't mean that I want to encourage or pressure you to engage in any Wiccan activity.

If you do intend to pursue a deeper exploration of Wicca or you're moving toward making a commitment, I hope this book helps you on your journey.

I don't want to promote the stereotype that Wicca is scary, spooky, and dangerous. Wicca is a means for self-development and positive change. But please keep in mind that certain Wiccan practices may be intense (for example, ritual, magic, and trance work). If you experience emotional or mental problems of any kind, please seek competent and compassionate treatment before engaging in any type of rigorous spiritual or magical work.

How This Book Is Organized

This book is divided into parts devoted to the beliefs, the everyday lives, the spiritual journey, the ritual and worship, and the magical practices of Wiccans.

Part 1: Seeing the World through Wiccan Eyes: What Wiccans Believe

Many people think that Wicca is about casting love spells or using magic to come up with the winning lottery numbers. However, Wicca is a spiritual path, and the majority of Wiccans have thoughtfully developed and deeply held belief systems. Part I offers a description of the very different ideas about the nature of Deity. Read this part to explore the ideas and the elegance of Wiccan belief.

Part II: Looking at the Past, Present, and Future: How Wiccans Live

From the caves to the Internet, Part II looks at Wiccan lives. Explore mysteries of Wicca's past, realities of the present, and hopes for the future.

Part III: Coming Home: How Wiccans Become Wiccans

Part III is about the spiritual journey of Wiccans. How does one find and follow the Wiccan path? This part is about the spiritual journey of Wiccans, from the decision about whether to dedicate oneself to Wicca to the options for Wiccan practice (alone or in a group, an established tradition of practice or an individual path). Find out how Wiccans find their way home.

Part IV: Following the Sun and the Moon: How Wiccans Worship

Part IV describes how Wiccans develop and nurture their relationship to Deity. It's dedicated to the ritual and liturgy of Wicca. Here you can discover the Wiccan holy days (holidays) and explore the way that Wiccans celebrate the cycles and rhythms of the Earth.

Part V: Practicing the Craft: What Wiccans Do

Part V is optional. It describes practices that are not mandatory but are a part of most Wiccan's lives, including spellcasting; using candles, stones, herbs, and charms; reading tarot cards and other forms of divination; as well as trance and dream work. The part also shows you how to write down your experiences in a traditional *Book of Shadows*.

Part VI: The Part of Tens

Part VI offers the ten habits of effective Wiccans, ten principles that make up the unofficial Wiccan code of conduct, and ten warning signs of a scam or inappropriate behavior in Wicca (or any other group).

Appendixes

The Wicca FAQ appendix conveniently contains answers to the most frequently asked questions about Wicca in one handy location. I hope it helps readers separate the truth from the propaganda about Wicca and Witchcraft. A second appendix lists the magical properties of various herbs and stones.

Icons Used in This Book

Like all *For Dummies* books, this one includes helpful icons sprinkled throughout the text. The following interprets the icons used in this book.

 This icon marks text that clues you in to the history of the Craft. Text appearing with this icon explains major events in history or gives you the background information about a specific belief or practice. It usually signifies history that occurred before the modern Wiccan revival of the 1950s.

 The Remember icon flags key concepts. I use this icon to point out information that is critical to a basic understanding of Wicca — information that you need to know so that the rest of Wicca makes sense.

 The Tip icon signifies helpful information that makes Wiccan belief or practice more fulfilling, effective, or successful. Sometimes the icon marks an idea that makes the Wiccan path a little easier to travel. This icon gives you a heads up about an effective method or an acceptable course of action, or it points out a common challenge or pitfall of Wiccan life.

 This icon is important. It often flags something that can be physically or psychologically dangerous. I also use this icon to point out potential violations of Wiccan ethics, for example, activity that can draw harmful energy to you. Occasionally, I use this icon to alert you to some aspect of Wicca's unofficial code of conduct, so you don't commit a breach of protocol that can seriously offend the Wiccan community. Sometimes it denotes an area of conflict or disagreement within the Craft, or a major stereotype or myth held by non-Wiccans that people should avoid repeating.

Where to Go from Here

If you decide to pursue a deeper exploration of Wicca or you're moving toward making a commitment, remember that you are free to believe and practice as you see fit. Don't feel obligated to follow the instructions found in this book, or any other book or Web site. I encourage you to read and train, but think of your study sources as guides, not Bibles. Your own revelations from Deity are just as valid as someone else's. Follow your own heart.

Part I

Seeing the World through Wiccan Eyes: What Wiccans Believe

The 5th Wave   By Rich Tennant

"Charlie told me his coven is having a yard sale next weekend. Maybe we can pick up some Wicca furniture for the patio."

In this part . . .

*W*hen people are new to Wicca, they often want to jump into the practice of magic. Many are hoping to find a quick-fix cure-all for their lives — a spell to find love or to pay off their credit cards.

Before attempting to practice Wicca or before passing judgment on it, explore and understand the beliefs that underlie Wiccan practice. Wicca is based on personal discovery and direct experience of Deity, as well as reverence for nature and the web of life. This part reveals the foundation of the Wiccan path.

Chapter 1

Believing That Everything's Connected

Many people discover Wicca in bits and pieces. Perhaps Wiccan ritual empowers them. Or the Wiccan reverence for the rhythms and cycles of nature satisfies them. Or magic fascinates them. However, in order to fully understand and find meaning in Wicca, a person needs to grasp the big picture: the Wiccan worldview.

A few core ideas underlie all of Wicca, and if you understand these basic concepts about the world and the Divine, then Wiccan beliefs and practices make sense. This chapter provides the background to understand Wicca as a full-fledged spirituality and a specific way of experiencing and interpreting the world.

Swimming in a Divine Sea of Energy

You are about to discover one principle that is the key to much of Wiccan belief. Ready? Here it is: Everything is connected.

Everything that exists is part of an unbroken circle of vibrating energy. You may find it helpful to picture reality as a web of energy (like a spider's web), or as an energy grid (like an electrical grid). Some people refer to this idea as the *web of life* or *nature's web*.

Wiccans perceive Deity in vastly different ways (see Chapter 2), however, most believe in a Creative Being that is the source or creator of the web of life. Most Wiccans believe that Deity is *immanent* (is right here, right now, and all-present in the world), and also is *manifest in nature* (is evident and easily perceived). Most believe that the web of life — everything that exists — flows or unfolds from Deity. The Divine is the source of all life. Some Wiccans even believe that the entire cosmos is the living body of Deity.

The belief in Deity is a matter of faith. No one can prove that the cosmos has a Divine source; however, reality is one big, connected, infinite network — ask any Wiccan or any scientist.

Finding Kinship in the Cosmos

The Wiccan view of an interconnected world isn't just a mystical, spiritual notion. Modern science, especially cutting-edge ideas in quantum physics, supports the ideas of life's interconnection and interdependence. The following are some of the leading theories that blend perfectly with Wiccan belief.

Going quantum: Matter versus energy

People see the physical world as a bunch of independent and stable objects, but that's not exactly the truth. Modern science reveals that matter and energy are not separate.

Energy flows in waves that form patterns. What you see as a separate object (a dog, a bird, or a tree) is really just a pocket of reality where the energy is more dense, according to quantum physics.

Quantum physics

Physical matter is made up of molecules and atoms, which are made up of smaller components, called *subatomic particles*. In quantum physics, particles of matter and waves of energy are the same thing.

A subatomic particle isn't a little dot of matter that scientists can hold still and examine; it's more like a little dancing point of energy. These particles can't be understood as separate units. Scientists can describe subatomic particles only by talking about how they act with one another. The only way to meaningfully describe these particles is to explain the way that they interconnect.

Wicca meets quantum physics

Quantum physics clearly demonstrates the Wiccan belief that all reality is an integrated web of energy. Even at the subatomic level, life is interconnected.

Tuning up the strings and dancing with the universe

The preceding section describes subatomic particles as dancing points of energy. String theory suggests that they may not even be points, but strings.

String theory is bold and beautiful, but complicated. Read on to find out more, but if you start to feel a migraine coming on, take a break and watch a *Gilligan's Island* re-run. It's always satisfying to watch the Professor build complicated stuff out of coconuts.

String theory

A subatomic particle is not pointlike but is made of a tiny loop. Like a super-thin rubber band, each particle contains a vibrating, dancing *string*. Like a guitar string, each tiny string can vibrate. Every string is identical; the only difference is the way that it vibrates. Each string has a different vibration, like each guitar string creates a different musical note. The movements of the string — the "note" it creates — determine the kind of particle it will be. These itty-bitty vibrating strings make up everything in the universe — all physical matter and all forces (such as gravity). These strings vibrate throughout space-time.

We live in space-time. *Space-time* consists of three dimensions of space (length, width, and depth) and the dimension of time. All objects and all events exist in these four dimensions. Well, that's what scientists used to think. According to string theory, space-time can have up to nine dimensions of space, plus the dimension of time.

Wicca meets string theory

String theory unites matter and energy, and confirms the Wiccan view that the cosmos — from the smallest particles to the largest solar systems — operates by the same principles and is made from the same stuff. At all levels, life is interconnected.

Spreading chaos

String theory shows the interconnectedness of life at all levels, big and small. Chaos theory deals only with the big — and super-complicated.

Chaos theory

Chaos theory suggests that the weather and other huge, complex systems in nature have an underlying order, but they are chaotic and virtually unpredictable. The problem with predicting the weather and the behavior of other big systems is that nature is extremely sensitive to changing conditions. Very tiny changes can have major effects. Nature on a large scale can drive a scientist nuts!

Any small inaccuracy in evaluating the initial conditions leads to growing errors in the calculations. For example, the flapping of a butterfly's wings in one location may affect the weather on the other side of the Earth.

Wicca meets Chaos Theory

The important lesson here is that any action, no matter how small or insignificant, can affect everything else. Earth's ecology is a network of relationships. All the members of Earth's environment are interdependent. The success of the whole community depends on each living thing, and the success of each living thing depends on the success of the community. This idea forms the core of Wiccan ethics (see Chapter 4 for more explanation).

Gazing at Gaia

The universe appears to be made up of individual parts, and these parts may function on their own. However, the parts are all made of the same energy and are connected to form one giant whole. For example:

- An individual cell is a part of a human being.
- Human beings are part of life on Earth.
- Earth is part of the solar system.
- The solar system is part of the universe.

The point is that each part isn't separate and isolated from the others, even though it may function by itself. Small parts join together to form a living thing. That living thing joins others to create a bigger living thing. Bigger living things join into groups to form an even bigger living thing, and so on. Throughout reality, small parts join together to form an integrated whole.

The grand mystery is that the whole is always much greater than its parts. For example, a human being is so much more than just a collection of simple little cells. The human brain's cells work together in networks, and together, they create a brain that is so complex and sophisticated that the world's top scientists can't fully figure out how it works.

Some scientists believe that Earth as a whole is one big living system.

The Gaia hypothesis

Atmospheric chemist James Lovelock, microbiologist Lynn Margulis, and others have developed a theory termed the *Gaia hypothesis,* in honor of the

Greek Goddess of the Earth. This concept describes all of Planet Earth as a living system that organizes itself and keeps all its parts in balance.

The Gaia hypothesis links Earth's inanimate objects (rocks, oceans, gases, and so on) with living parts (plants and animals) and brings together all the planet's cycles and rhythms into one unified whole. The hypothesis links the evolution and survival of a species to the evolution and conditions of its environment.

Lovelock and Margulis never suggested that Earth is a sentient being (a conscious, creative being), but others have expanded the theory to arrive at this idea.

Wicca meets the Gaia hypothesis

Of course, the view of Earth as a living being isn't new. From Neolithic times, human cultures all over the globe have worshiped Mother Earth. This scientific theory reveals that life organizes itself into larger and larger networks that form one big integrated whole. If this is the model of the universe, then the idea of immanent Deity is rational and even probable. All reality may, indeed, arise from and be embedded in one creative source.

Unfolding and enfolding

Physicist David Bohm built an entire theory of physics on the idea that reality unfolds from one original, infinite source.

This concept is often called the holographic universe. Have you ever seen a hologram? A *hologram* is a three-dimensional image made with a laser. Many credit cards have these pictures. Each small piece of a hologram can reproduce the entire image. In other words, each part contains all the information about the whole. This structure is common in nature. A tiny seed contains all the information to grow a tall sunflower.

The holographic universe

Based on this model, Bohm (a former colleague of Einstein) suggested that the information for the entire universe is held in each of its parts. For Bohm, the *explicate order* is the separate parts of the world that we see. The *implicate order* enfolds all these parts into one whole. The implicate order is the original energy, the source of all reality.

According to the theory, this source is called the *Subtle Nonmanifest*. This holy intelligence gave rise to all space and time, all dimensions, and all planes of existence. All reality unfolds out from this primal source, and then enfolds back into the source, in a never-ending cycle.

All beings, including humans, are born from this source, are connected, and share consciousness. They continually have new experiences and grow in wisdom and knowledge. Then they enfold back into this source. This way, the source, the core energy that fuels the cosmos, is always advancing and evolving, along with everything that is a part of it.

Wicca meets the holographic universe

The relatively new model of the Holographic Universe reflects a worldview that Pagans have held since the most ancient times: We are all part of the Divine energy; we are all connected; and our fate is inexorably linked.

Human beings are a part of the Divine energy. They are a part of nature, not above it or separate from it. All parts of the Divine web of life are equal in value. This outlook profoundly impacts Wiccan religion, politics, and social relationships.

The next chapter explores more fully the diversity of Wiccan beliefs about the nature of the Divine, but the basic trust in immanence and interconnection is the heart of Wicca.

Nature flows from Deity, and Wiccan spirituality revolves around the celebration of our connection with nature, and the human place in the web of life. Much of Wiccan practice is devoted to developing relationship with the Divine energy, in which we are permanently embedded.

Chapter 2

Believing in Deity

· ·

· ·

Most, although not all, Wiccans believe in a creative being or force. However, the way that Wiccans perceive and experience the Divine is unique to each individual. Wiccans stretch the idea of Deity to the outer limits of diversity.

Two people may comfortably call themselves Wiccan. They may perform the same rituals, work the same magic, and happily practice side by side, but they may have radically different concepts of who, or what, Deity is. Most Wiccans would rather celebrate their differences than become a religion in which everyone must conform to the same belief or seek the same experience.

This chapter dares to explore the nature of the Divine . . . er . . . the Goddess, the God, the Gods, the Old Ones, the Great Mother, the Higher Self . . . you get the idea.

Honoring the Mysteries

You won't see an announcement like this on the 6:00 News: "The Goddess spoke to Jane Doe today and told her to quit her lousy job and join the Peace Corps. Film at 11:00." Jane may, indeed, have received a Divine nudge to write the letter of resignation and pack her bags, but no other person can likely verify the encounter.

You may be absolutely, positively convinced that you received guidance, insight, or comfort from Deity. But here's the thing about Divine revelation: It's personal. Your experience is yours alone. Others may see the results in your life, but feeling the presence of or interacting with Deity is an individual and a unique experience.

The following sections outline some ways that Wiccans define the Divine. It's an overall look at some common ways that people think about Deity. The information may help you understand the diversity of Wicca. However, you may not be able to pigeonhole your own experience according to these explanations. Don't try to intellectually choose one of these categories and then force your spiritual life to perfectly conform to one of these examples. Let your spiritual life reflect what is true for you, whether it reflects one, a combination, or none of the following examples.

Honoring The One

Many Wiccans believe in a Deity who is the source of the cosmos. The Wiccan names for this Divine power include, but certainly aren't limited to: The One, The All, the Ultimate Sacred, the Great Mystery, the Source, Creative or Supreme Being, the Life Force, and the All-Encompassing Unity.

Many believe that this Deity is too vast, too complex, too inscrutable, and too infinite (can something be *too* infinite?) for the human mind to ever comprehend. Although most Wiccans acknowledge this idea of Deity, they have many ways of defining, perceiving, or otherwise making the concept of the Divine more manageable. This section expands on the concept of a single Deity. Later sections deal with other perceptions.

Deity as life force

Deity, the Goddess (or the God), is the core energy of all that exists. All of reality is an unbroken web of vibrating energy, and that energy *is* the Goddess. The entire cosmos is the body of the Goddess (including physical and mental energy, as well as the forces of nature and the laws of physics).

The Goddess is *immanent,* meaning that She is right here, right now and is all-present in the world. She is *manifest* in nature; Her presence is evident and easily perceived. Everything that exists is the Goddess.

Deity as the primal Goddess

Deity is the primal Goddess. She is the source of all life, and the life force unfolds or flows from Her. Goddess is the only or the primary Deity, and She is a supernatural, creative being. If there is a God, He is the child, consort, or manifestation of the Great Goddess. Any other Deities that may exist come from Her. She is known chiefly in the Mother aspect, sometimes called Great Goddess or Earth Mother.

In addition to being immanent in nature, She also is *transcendent,* in the sense that She is a supernatural, thinking, creative being independent of the cosmos.

This theory is in keeping with the ideas of some early Paganism.

Deity as the Source

Although the outlook is not traditional, some Wiccans are reconciling their spiritual beliefs with the teachings of the new physics. Many scientists and philosophers have suggested this type of concept, but physicist David Bohm and scientist and paleontologist Pierre Teilhard de Chardin are largely responsible for the current popularity of this Deity theory.

According to this view, Deity is a being of pure, active, creative, holy intelligence. Bohm called it the *Subtle Nonmanifest.* Teilhard de Chardin and others have suggested many names, such as the Cosmic Apex, the Super-soul, the Hyper-personal, the Evolutionary All, and the Omega Point. Some people simply use the term, *Source,* because Deity, in this case, is the source energy for all that exists.

This holy intelligence existed before the cosmos was formed, and all reality comes from it. Everything is connected because all of reality flows from the Source. The Source encompasses all space and time, all dimensions, and all planes of existence.

Everything that exists unfolds out from the Source, and then everything enfolds back into the Source, in a never-ending cycle.

People continually have new experiences, and they gain wisdom and insight. All this new information becomes part of the Source energy, and the Source expands and evolves. People are part of the Source, so they also evolve and grow, reaching higher levels of consciousness. The Source, the core energy that fuels the cosmos, is always moving, advancing, and evolving. People are part of that evolution and even play a key role in the advancement.

Our own intelligence, our insight, allows us to perceive the Source. Our consciousness acts as the bridge between the regular world and this holy intelligence.

Through our consciousness, we take in information from our experiences in the world and share that information with the Source; and through our consciousness, we also can receive information from the Source for use in the world. In computer terminology, this is a *feedback loop* of information.

This view is consistent with modern physics. Although the language is contemporary, the theory isn't so different from the old Pagan idea of the primal Goddess as both life force and creative being.

Honoring the Two

Many Wiccans believe in The One, the Source of the cosmos, but they see it as an energy field with two poles. The Goddess and the God are opposite poles of the Divine, and Wiccans honor or worship both the male and the female aspect of Deity. The majority of Wiccans probably hold this view or a variation of it, but no one can say for sure.

A world in balance: Polarity and duality

In Wicca, especially in certain traditions, polarity or duality is a key principle. Much of Wiccan belief and practice hinges on this concept. Many Wiccans honor the polarity or duality in nature and have incorporated the idea into their spirituality.

Here's the idea: Energy flows in two opposite directions in nature; that's what creates the familiar cycles of the natural world, for example: life and death, light and dark, summer and winter, male and female, and so on. Many Wiccans see the Divine in the same way; the Goddess and the God are like two poles on the same battery. If they were truly separate beings, according to these Wiccans, confusion and chaos would reign in the universe.

The Goddess and the God, or the Lord and the Lady (as some Wiccans call them) are exactly equal energies, and while opposing each other, they are not in conflict with each other. They are in perfect balance.

The Goddess

The Goddess is the feminine aspect of the Divine. She is known as the Great Goddess, Earth Mother (or Mother Earth), the Universal Mother, the Great Mother, the Lady, and many other names. She has been worshipped by many cultures throughout time.

Maiden, Mother, and Crone

In many traditions of Wicca, the Goddess is closely associated with the Moon. She often is viewed as having three aspects that correspond with the phases of the Moon:

- The *Maiden* (the Waxing Moon) represents independence and youth. She is the virgin Goddess. She often is identified with a woman's wild nature and is shown as a forest Goddess in the company of animals.

- The *Mother* (the Full Moon) represents giving birth (not only to children, but to ideas, insight, and projects), and also nurturing, sexuality, sensuality, and creativity.

- The *Crone* (the Waning Moon) symbolizes age, maturity, wisdom, and the command for respect.

Over the course of the eight primary Wiccan holidays, the Goddess shifts in Her aspects from Maiden to Mother to Crone and back to Maiden. She gives birth to the Divine God child, nurtures Him to adulthood, unites with Him and becomes pregnant, and rebirths Him to begin the seasons again and turn the wheel of the year.

The importance of the Goddess for women

Many researchers surmise that the reason that Wicca is growing so fast is because it offers a powerful spiritual alternative to women. Unlike most religions, within a Wiccan circle, a woman can honor and worship the feminine Divine.

The importance of that fact can't be overestimated. In the doctrines of many religions, women are, at best, considered inferior to men and subject to their control. At worst, women are viewed as the source of sin in the world. This religious conditioning profoundly damages the psyches of women.

Within Wicca, women are equal; they are not "the other." Women have authority and autonomy equal to men. When women experience their own holiness and when they have the opportunity to direct their own spirituality, their lives can be transformed.

"The Charge of the Goddess"

"The Charge of the Goddess" is a prose poem that is very popular in the Craft and reflects the Wiccan view of the Goddess. An early version appeared in the book, *Aradia: Gospel of the Witches* by Charles G. Leland (1890). Gerald Gardner produced a later version of the poem. Doreen Valiente wrote a substantially different and very moving version, and many groups use her text today. Possibly the most popular is the version by Starhawk, from her book, *The Spiral Dance: A Rebirth of the Ancient Religion of the Great Goddess* (1979, 2nd revised edition 1989, 3rd revised edition 1999).

The God

In many Wiccan books and groups, the God is given less page count or time than the Goddess. In American culture, most people are familiar and even conditioned to view Deity as male. The Divine feminine is a more difficult concept for many people to get their minds around, so I devote more of this chapter to explaining the idea.

The God is the male aspect of the Divine. He often is represented as the Sun and is sometimes associated with forests and wild animals. He has been worshipped by many cultures throughout time. In most traditions of Wicca, the God is considered equal to the Goddess. The majority of Wiccan groups, traditions, and covens, consider men and women to be equal.

The God can be three-formed as the Hunter, Warrior, and Sage. In some beliefs, it is His travels to the Underworld to free His true love that cause the shift in the seasons. Some Wiccans believe that the God, like the Goddess, has always existed. Some see the God as having originated from or been born from the Goddess. He often is viewed as Her consort.

Over the course of the eight primary Wiccan holidays, the God progresses through a full life cycle. He is born, grows to manhood, marries and impregnates the Goddess, and dies. He is then reborn as the child of the Goddess. He once again grows from the Divine Child to the Sun God, and begins the entire cycle again.

Honoring the Many

Many Wiccans honor or worship multiple Deities. These beings may be different aspects or parts of the one Divine Source, or they may be separate entities. They may be supernatural beings, nature spirits, or something else. They may or may not have human characteristics. You may hear them called *The Old Ones, The Mighty Ones,* or *The Ancient Ones.*

Some Wiccans honor and worship the Goddess and/or the God and feel no pressure to choose a named Deity or Deities. Other Wiccans feel very strongly that people should choose one or more named Goddesses or Gods to honor, worship, or interact with. For example, you may be familiar with the Goddess Diana or the God Pan. Some traditions (sects or denominations) of Wicca have specific, named Deities that they honor or serve.

The Gods are all part of The One

Many Wiccans recognize Deity as The One — the infinite, unknowable Source of the cosmos. They believe that Deity is too complex and vast for humans to comprehend, so these Wiccans may choose to define limited aspects, forms, or parts of Deity as Gods and Goddesses. In other words, the many Goddesses and Gods are various aspects or parts of one Great Source. Wiccans gain access to that Source by communicating with their Deities.

Or, perhaps, that one all-encompassing Source chooses to take many different forms in order to be perceivable and understandable to humans.

The Gods are separate beings

The Goddesses and Gods are separate, distinct, and named Divinities. Many different Gods and Goddesses exist, and each has its own personality and realm. Some of these beings may be Gods (male) or Goddesses (female), and some may contain both sexes or be able to shift sex and gender.

Sometimes Wiccans choose or feel called by a Goddess and/or God from an old Pagan pantheon for whom they feel affinity. Others choose or feel called by Deities of a particular cultural ancestry (for example, Celtic) and may work with several different Deities from that pantheon.

Honoring the Self

For some Wiccans, Deity may be the Higher Self, Deep Self, or Soul Self (a person's spiritual essence), or a symbol arising from the unconscious mind.

The Higher Self

Some Wiccans honor, worship, or seek to communicate with their own Higher Self, Deep Self, or Soul Self. Some consider it to be the Divine energy emanating from within. Most Wiccans believe that people have a level of consciousness or some other part that transcends time and space. This consciousness is the essence of who we have been, who we are, and who we will always be, our own individual truth.

These Wiccans turn inward rather than outward for spiritual growth and fulfillment.

Truths, symbols, and archetypes

For some Wiccans, Deity and/or truth lie only within the human mind and imagination. Deity may be a truth or insight arising from the personal unconscious mind or the collective unconscious, shared by all human beings.

The unconscious mind has two parts:

- *The personal unconscious* is the location of everything that isn't presently conscious but can be, including memories that you can call up easily and those that you have buried deep in your mind.

- *The collective unconscious* holds the accumulated knowledge and experiences of all humankind (and possibly animals). It is the inherited part of the brain. It holds instincts, which are patterns of behavior. Instinct tells a bird to build a nest, and a turtle to go to water. Humans also have instinctive ways of behaving.

The unconscious mind doesn't have language to express these human behaviors and experiences. It communicates only in pictures. It uses symbols. A *symbol* is an image or object that represents something else. The collective unconscious uses archetypes, symbols that are common to all humans. An *archetype* is not an image, but a tendency for humans to represent certain ideas with a specific symbol.

These archetypal symbols appear in religions, dreams, myths, and fairytales. The Earth Mother is an example of an archetype. Some Wiccans believe that when they communicate with Deity, they are reaching this symbolic information in their own minds.

A person may be an agnostic or an atheist and still practice Wicca. Wicca is a very big tent. Each individual's perception and experience of Deity is unique. Although Wiccans debate the issue, most would rather preserve their own freedom to worship as the Spirit leads them, rather than conform to a common doctrine about Deity.

Wiccans aren't Satanists

Although Wiccans hold varying beliefs about Deity, Wiccans don't believe in or worship Satan. Satan, as the opponent of God and the embodiment of evil, is a Christian concept. Wicca is a revival of *pre*-Christian nature religion. Wiccan belief and practices are rooted in a time well before the Christian era.

Historically, the Catholic and Protestant churches regarded Witches as followers of the Christian Satan. During the widespread Witch hunts of medieval and Renaissance times, the churches falsely accused alleged Witches of consorting with and worshipping the Christian Devil. (Actually, most of the accused were Christians, not Witches.) The historical link between Wicca and Satanism is unfounded but remains deeply embedded in many cultures.

In addition, some Christian groups today believe that anyone who worships a God other than theirs is following Satan. It's true that Wiccans don't worship the Christian God, nor do people of many other religions all over the world.

Wicca and Satanism were and are separate and entirely different systems of beliefs, practices, and ethics.

Chapter 3

Believing in Magic: Where Science Meets the Craft

In This Chapter

▶ Using energy from the mind and the Divine
▶ Finding sources of power and strength
▶ Demystifying magic

*M*agic is a process of moving and directing energy to achieve a goal, so any explanation of magic has to begin with some talk about energy. That's what this chapter offers: a tidy little explanation of the different sources and types of energy.

This chapter demystifies magic. Here, you can find out what magic really is. It's powerful. It's profoundly beautiful. And it's a very real force that many Wiccans use to improve their lives and to help others. Additionally, magic is a means to honor and deepen the relationship with Deity and to help the Earth and her inhabitants.

Tapping into Different Kinds of Energy

Many different cultural traditions divide the self into three parts. Each part represents a different type of human energy and power. This division is prominent in modern psychology, in various types of Shamanism (especially the Hawaiian Huna tradition), in the teachings of Jewish Kabbalah, and in many traditions of Wicca and Witchcraft (especially in the Faery or Feri tradition).

In this chapter, I use the model of the Three Selves — the Spirit self, the conscious mind, and the unconscious mind — in order to clearly define the three types of energy and power that are important to Wiccans, especially in the working of magic.

Drawing from the Divine: Energy of the Spirit

The energy of the Spirit Self is called the Aumakua in Hawaiian Huna Shamanism and the Neshemah in Kabbalah. Various books on the Craft refer to this energy as Deep Self (in Starhawk's books), High Self, Divine Self, True Self, or Bird Spirit. Modern psychology doesn't have an equivalent idea, however, the Spirit Self is directly connected to the unconscious mind.

The Spirit Self is a person's deepest resource, the place that transcends pain and limitation. This is the part of the Self that shelters a person's essence, the true nature. It transcends time, existing before birth and after death.

Deity is present throughout all creation, within and without, but the Spirit Self is the place where the Divine spark kindles an individual's soul. It is the Divine within.

Thinking and talking: Energy of the conscious mind

The energy of the conscious mind is known as the ego in modern psychology, the Uhane in Hawaiian Huna Shamanism, and the Ruach in Kabbalah. In various books on the Craft, you may see it called Talking Self (in Starhawk's books), Middle Self, or Talker.

The conscious mind is the part of the mind that functions on an everyday level. The conscious mind experiences the world and communicates with language (words and numbers). It is the rational mind that analyzes and organizes. It also makes moral judgments and handles social relationships. It interprets and finds meaning for the unconscious mind's images, emotions, and sensations. The conscious mind enables a person to understand spiritual practice on a rational level. However, the unconscious mind is necessary, too, in order to connect the conscious mind with the Spirit Self or Divine Self.

Going deep: Energy of the unconscious mind

Did you know that the human embryo briefly develops structures that resemble the gills of a fish, as well as a noticeable tail? This short stage of human development dramatically reflects our animal ancestry and our long evolutionary journey. Along with the human body, the mind, too, contains a remarkable remnant of the ancient past: the collective unconscious, a part of the unconscious mind.

The energy of the unconscious mind is known as the id in modern psychology, the Unihipili in Hawaiian Huna Shamanism and the Nephesh in Kabbalah. In various books on the Craft, you may see it called Younger Self (in Starhawk's books), Low Self, Child Self, Young Self, Child Within, Inner Child, Animal Spirit, or Fetch.

The unconscious mind has two parts: the personal unconscious and the collective unconscious.

The personal unconscious

The personal unconscious is the location of personal information that is outside of current awareness or consciousness, including memories that a person can call up easily and those buried deep within the mind.

The collective unconscious

The collective unconscious is the inherited part of the brain. It holds the accumulated knowledge and experiences of all humankind (and possibly animals). The collective unconscious mind doesn't have many language skills. It experiences the world and expresses itself in images, emotions, sensations, and dreams. It uses symbols. A *symbol* is an image or object that represents something else.

The collective unconscious contains our *instincts,* which are patterns of behavior. Instinct tells a bird to build a nest, and a turtle to go to water. Humans also have instinctive ways of behaving. *Instincts* are ways of acting. The collective unconscious also contains *archetypes*, which are ways of perceiving. An archetype is a tendency for humans to represent certain ideas with a specific symbol. These archetypal symbols appear in religions, dreams, myths, and fairytales throughout all human history. The Earth Mother is an example of an archetype, and the Hero is another prime example.

So what does all this mind stuff have to do with Wicca? Everything! Most of the practices of Wiccan ritual — especially ritual conducted for the purpose of working magic — are done in order to activate the unconscious mind.

Ritual, especially the working of magic, is more successful, more effective, and more fulfilling when the unconscious mind is involved. The unconscious mind is very powerful, and the images, symbols, emotions, and other information hidden within it are a valuable resource for understanding the self and bringing about change.

Wiccans use primal images, smells, textures, and sounds to arouse the unconscious mind. Candle flames, incense, stones, and drumming are some examples of traditional elements of the Craft that are used for this purpose. Spells are made to rhyme in order to engage the unconscious in the magic. Wiccans often *raise power,* which means to induce a light trance state, in order to activate the unconscious mind for magical work.

Sources of power, strength, and guidance

In addition to Deity, some Wiccans may welcome the presence or help of other types of energy forms or beings. These may include:

✔ **Ancestors:** An actual family member or someone else who has passed on. Some Wiccans contact ancestors for advice or support, or to resolve outstanding emotional issues. Whether and when a person contacts ancestors depends on the person's outlook on the afterlife. Reincarnation is a commonly held belief in Wicca. However, if a soul has reincarnated, the ancestor may not be available for counsel.

✔ **Elementals or nature spirits:** *Definition 1.* A spirit of one of the four elements, for example: gnome for Earth, sylph for Air, undine for Water, and salamander for Fire. Wiccans consider the four elements and the beings that they manifest to be helpers, protectors, or allies. *Definition 2.* Nature elementals include a vast array of creatures and beings, including fairies (or faeries). Wiccans hold wildly different views on elementals and/or nature spirits. Some scoff and are adamant that these beings are mere superstition, and others look at you askance and shudder if you dare to even suggest that these creatures may not exist.

The Celtic peoples have much folklore about fairies and other such beings. Because of Wicca's deep Celtic roots, belief in elementals is common. Entire books are written about elementals and nature spirits, as well as their varying appearances, demeanors, and behaviors. Space is way too limited here to provide a meaningful discussion of all the possibilities and the historical context.

✔ **Familiars:** An animal with which one has a deep psychic or empathic bond. The animal is more than a companion; it offers magical, psychic, or spiritual support. A cat is most common, although other animals may be familiars. A familiar usually (although not always) is an actual animal, as opposed to a thought form that arises from the unconscious mind, or an animal that one meets on another plane of existence during a trance or an altered state.

✔ **Power animals or spirit animals:** In Shamanic tradition, a guardian spirit that provides power, help, and protection. This spirit is often perceived as an animal and is generally referred to as a *power animal.* Throughout time, many cultures have believed that humans and animals are related. Mythology reflecting this connectedness is common. Many people believe that animals and humans can still communicate when a human is in an altered or Shamanic state of consciousness.

✔ **Quarters or the Guardians of the Watchtowers:** Energy forms or beings who are called during ritual. During some or all rituals, some Wiccans *call the Quarters* or *call the Guardians of the Watchtowers.* Some believe that they are calling basic, archetypal forms of energy for use during the ritual. Other people believe that they are calling actual beings, spirits, or other energy forms who guard or watch the four directions. See Chapter 12 for more on this ritual practice.

✔ **Spirit guides:** May refer to an ancestor, a power animal, an evolved human with the mission of helping living humans, or some other being who provides guidance and assistance. This is an all-purpose term, and the meaning depends on the intention of the person using it.

Engaging the unconscious mind is important in the working of magic for the following reasons:

✔ Arousing the unconscious mind makes a person open to experiencing Deity because the Spirit Self or Divine Self communicates directly with the unconscious mind.

✔ The unconscious mind drives certain behaviors, as well as emotions. For example, the conscious mind may rationally know that a certain behavior is counterproductive or dangerous (for example, smoking, drinking, or excessive gambling), but altering a behavior may be very difficult unless the unconscious is aroused and motivated to play a role in personal change. Magic engages the unconscious mind, and then the unconscious mind influences the person to make the magic work. This is the power of suggestion.

✔ The unconscious mind can help generate power to shape and direct energy to change the Self or change the world. The collective unconscious also may provide a link to the joined consciousness of all humans, to the species as a whole. Subtly shifting the energy in the collective unconscious may create change in the world beyond the self.

Directing Energy: Why Magic Works

Magic is the process of moving and directing energy in order to achieve a desired result or outcome. By working magic, Wiccans hope to make positive changes in themselves and the world.

Wiccans work magic to achieve self-improvement or empowerment; to find solutions to problems; and to meet their own and others' physical, mental, or emotional needs. The purpose of a *religious ritual* is to understand, experience, or feel the connection to the Divine. Wiccans often choose to work magic during ritual and to invite the presence or participation of Deity in the magic. However, magic is a natural force, not a religious practice.

This is how and why magic works:

1. **Everything that exists is interconnected.**

   All reality is part of a grand circle or web of vibrating energy (see Chapter 1 for further explanation).

2. **The energy within the human mind is not separate from the energy in the physical world.**

3. **When a person visualizes an event (sees it as a detailed picture in the mind), he or she forms energy into patterns.**

4. **A person focuses mental power in order to move and direct the energy toward a desired outcome.**

5. **By moving and directing the energy, a person's mind can affect events or conditions in the physical world outside of the self. This process is called magic.**

Quantum physics and string theory, chaos theory, the holographic universe theory, and the Gaia principle support the fact that all life is interconnected (see Chapter 1).

Modern science also reveals that matter and energy are not separate. In quantum physics, particles of matter and waves of energy are actually the same thing. Scientists have found out that merely looking at these particles/waves changes their behavior. That's right. Observing them causes them to change. (This idea is called the Heisenberg Uncertainty Principle.)

The bottom line is that scientists changed reality just by observing it. So believing that a person can use mental power to move and direct energy isn't far-fetched at all. Shifts in energy affect the physical world.

When we focus our minds, we can make change in the world. That's why magic works!

Reading energy: The truth about divination

Divination often is considered to be a form of magic, although this practice revolves around *reading* energy more than actually *moving* it. Here's the important point about divination: Contrary to popular misconception, the practice of divination does not foretell the future — at least not a predestined, unchangeable future.

The practice of divination simply reads the current energy. This reading may point to the way that the future may enfold if steps are not taken to alter the course, by changing behavior or making new decisions.

The term divination encompasses a wide variety of techniques, including (but not limited to) the interpretation of astrology, dreams, lots (dice, runes, and so on), natural phenomena (such as the flight patterns of birds or the falling of meteors), pendulum use, scrying (staring into a reflective surface or flame), tarot cards, or trance work.

Divination may work because Deity is intervening and revealing the current path or pointing toward solutions or better options. Or, the symbols and activities involved in divination may activate or trigger the unconscious mind to react and help solve problems, resolve issues, or establish a new, more desirable course for the future. Chapter 19 offers more information about divination; Chapter 18 explains dreams and trance work.

Chapter 4

Believing in Ethics, Responsibility, and Personal Relationship with Deity

. . . .

In This Chapter

▶ Walking an individual path with the Divine
▶ Rejecting dogma and control
▶ Acting ethically, responsibly, and respectfully

. . . .

*W*icca is a spiritual path. The focus of Wicca is personal discovery and experience of the Divine.

Wicca has no holy book or written doctrine that has been passed down through the ages for all Wiccans to follow. Wiccans create their own holy books of teachings, practices, spiritual experiences, and their own understanding (Books of Shadows). Wicca has no hierarchy of leaders who counsel people on how to live and worship, and who enforce religious laws and obedience. Each Wiccan has a relationship with Deity, and each Wiccan serves as clergy.

Wiccans do have principles and ethics that guide their behavior, and their goal is to balance personal freedom with responsibility and respect for the sacredness of all life.

Trusting the Individual Relationship with the Divine

For people who are self-directed, Wicca is a liberating and joyous exploration. For people who want structure and direction in their spiritual lives, Wicca definitely is not a good personal choice. This section explores Wicca's lack of hierarchy and dogma and its encouragement of personal strength, individualism, self-determination, and self-reliance.

Sending dogma to the doghouse

The people of many religions believe that Deity, usually God, is *transcendent*. That means that God is over or above the world and humankind, separate from the physical world. A person's own nature, the Self, is separate from God. In this view, the Self can't be trusted. People need rules and laws to control their own nature and behavior. A person can't trust his or her own self and will, which are separate from God.

Because people can't trust their own natures, religious rules tell people what to do. Religious *dogma* spells out the laws, teachings, beliefs, and principles of a religion, as well as the consequences of breaking the laws. The laws and rules, like God, are elevated, separate from the world. They are unquestionable and infallible. People must follow the laws and rules, regardless of the human cost.

Religious dogma and authority relieve a person of the responsibility of deciding on his or her own actions. People comply with religious authority because they believe that the institution knows more, is stronger, and is less able to be corrupted than the individual. They accept that the leaders in the institution can be trusted to know God's will.

Wiccans don't see themselves as separate from Deity. Their Goddess and/or God is not only transcendent, but *immanent*. That means that Deity is all-present in the world. People come from and are a part of the Divine energy, and the Deity is within everyone. Deity is a supernatural being capable of creative thought and action, but also remains connected to that creation. Wiccans believe that they have a direct relationship with Divinity. They communicate with the Goddess and/or the God themselves, and they don't need dogma or religious authorities to control their inner nature or direct their will or behavior.

A Wiccan trusts his or her own spiritual experience and ability to interpret the will of Deity for his or her own life.

Saying no to hierarchy: You're not the boss of me!

Religious institutions give leaders various titles: Bishop, Minister, Rabbi, Pope, Imam, and so on. Religious leaders have various levels of authority and control, depending on the length of time of their study and service, as well as other leadership qualities.

Wicca differs from most of the mainstream religions because it doesn't have a central authority with levels of clergy who make rules for all of Wicca. Whether Wiccan clergy are recognized by the government varies by the local laws and whether the clergyperson seeks out such recognition. However, recognized clergy hold no special place as part of some centralized religious body that oversees the Craft. Instead, Wicca is made up of loosely connected and independent, small groups who define their own spiritual beliefs and practices.

Many of these small, independent groups do have leadership. The leaders provide guidance and direction, but they generally don't exercise control over members. Wiccans independently decide how to believe and practice.

Many small groups (called *covens*) have High Priestesses and/or Priests, or leaders with some other title, who offer their skills to the group and direct its activities. Many Wiccan groups have levels of initiation; people advance as they study and grow in the Craft. Some groups have a Council of Elders who are a source of ongoing wisdom gained during their long experience in the Craft. However, in Wicca, leaders do not have control over the others.

If a leader has proven experience, gives valuable advice, and provides needed skills, the group respects him or her and cooperates willingly, but no one in Wicca is beholden to follow the leader.

Because each Wiccan has direct access to Deity, each is considered to be clergy. Every Wiccan is a Priestess or Priest. Wiccans are expected to direct their own spiritual lives.

Doing the Right Thing: Ethics and Responsibility

One of the biggest charges against the Craft is that it has no morality. Wiccans sometimes are viewed as immature "if it feels good, do it" types who refuse to follow the traditions of good and decent folk. That's just not true. Wiccans have a strong sense of ethics, and a brief trip to most Wiccan Web sites shows that Wiccans spend a great deal of time quibbling about the nuances of ethics and personal responsibility. Wiccans care a lot about what is right and what is wrong, and why. They generally are good people, but the basis for their ethics is different from most mainstream religions.

Many Westerners view Deity as transcendent, as over and above the world. Humans are separate from God, and they are separate from each other. So humans turn to religious dogma and institutions to help them interpret and live God's will.

Wiccan belief is different. The following principles are central to Wicca:

- ✔ Wiccans view Deity as all-present in the world. All life comes from and is a part of the Divine energy. Each person is a direct manifestation of Deity. Humans have constant access to Deity for direction and guidance.

- ✔ People also are connected to each other in an interdependent circle or web of life. Because people are connected to each other, instead of separate, a Wiccan knows that doing harm to others eventually causes harm to his- or herself.

Those principles are the basis for the Wiccan Rede and the Threefold Law, which are the heart of Wiccan ethics.

Following the Wiccan Rede

"Eight words the Wiccan Rede fulfil,

An' it harm none, do what ye will."

— Doreen Valiente, Pentagram, Volume One, 1964 (published by Gerard Noel)

These words are the central ethic of Wicca, known as the *Wiccan Rede*. The word *rede* means counsel or advice. Some Wiccans believe that the Wiccan Rede has been passed down through history. Some believe that it originated with Gerald Gardner (the man widely acknowledged to be the founder of modern Wicca) and/or Doreen Valiente (a renowned writer and High Priestess in Gardner's coven). For more information about the history of modern Wicca, see Chapter 5.

Regardless of its origins, the majority of Wiccans try to follow the Wiccan Rede, sometimes called simply "the Rede," and consider it to be the guiding ethic for their lives.

Following the Rede means to carry out your own will, but act in ways that cause the least harm to yourself, others, the Earth, and all beings.

Wiccans generally interpret the Rede to mean that a Wiccan should live and let live, while respecting the sacredness of all life. They should think critically about the consequences of their actions, before they act. Many Wiccans have expanded the scope of the Rede. They think that apathy, neglect, and failure to act — to stop violence, abuse, suffering, or injustice — also violates the Rede.

Wiccans believe that all of life embodies Deity; Deity is all-present in the world. To cause harm to anything or anyone is to act against the Goddess and/or the God.

Following the Rede gets a little complicated, though. It instructs Wiccans to harm none. But what about situations when a Wiccan is in danger? Are Wiccans allowed to defend and protect themselves, even if they have to harm an attacker? Can a Wiccan defend or protect family, or community? Should a Wiccan harm one person to save someone else? What about cases when a grave injustice is causing many people to be hurt? Should a Wiccan step in and help, perhaps causing harm to one person or group for the greater good of the community? Or should the Wiccan refuse to harm anyone and let evil go unchecked? Do Wiccans violate the Rede if they eat (and, therefore, harm) animals? Ask these questions at a Wiccan gathering and watch the sparks fly.

Wicca isn't easy. People of the Craft deliberate seriously on these questions.

Accepting the consequences: The Threefold Law

You may be familiar with the science of chaos theory and the butterfly effect. The idea behind the theory is that all of life is a complex system. A small change at one place in the system can result in a big effect somewhere else. For example, a butterfly flapping its wings in the forests of the American Midwest *may* ultimately change the weather in Ireland or on Mount Kilimanjaro in Tanzania.

The science of the butterfly effect is consistent with Wicca. Wiccans believe that everything is interconnected. All of existence is an unbroken circle of energy, and everything is merged into one living organism. Human beings are not separate from the web of nature, but are a part of it. Everything that exists is linked together, and any action, no matter how small or insignificant, affects everything else.

The behavior of every member of the web of life affects every other member. Negative or harmful energy not only harms the target of the energy, but the negativity and damage remain in nature's web and impact all of life, including the sender. For example, if people pollute the Earth's water, eventually they have to drink polluted and toxic water.

A Wiccan believes that his or her own personal energy is never separate from the energy of the rest of life and the cosmos.

Paying attention to intention

This principle of interconnectedness is the basis for the other Wiccan ethic, the *Threefold Law*. Whatever a person sends out comes back threefold. In general, the law means that whatever you say or do — negative or positive, bad or good — will return to you with three times the intensity. Some Wiccans believe that this belief applies to words and actions only, but others include thoughts.

Everything that exists is part of one unbroken circle. So when a Wiccan sends out energy — especially intentional, powerfully directed energy during magic — that person's essence:

- ✔ Remains in the Self.
- ✔ Is a part of the energy being sent.
- ✔ Is in the outcome — the energy that travels through the circle of life, nature's web, and eventually returns to the sender.

That's why this ethic is called the *Three*fold Law. The idea is sometimes called the *Law of Return*. This principle is reflected in the old folk saying: What goes around, comes around.

Heeding the hex warning

If you read many beginning books on Wicca, you will undoubtedly run across texts that offer spells to aim directly at people who are unwilling or unaware, to change their attitudes or behavior according to the sender's wishes. You even will find books that provide hexes and curses to use as retaliation for grievances.

Non-Wiccan media and society tend to focus on hexing and cursing whenever the subject of Wicca or Witchcraft comes up. The truth is that most Wiccans don't engage in hexing, cursing, and other negative practices.

Some Wiccans do engage in binding and/or banishing. The definitions for these ideas follow:

- ✔ *Binding:* A Wiccan casts a spell designed to restrict or limit the actions of someone (or some energy).
- ✔ *Banishing:* A Wiccan orders someone (or some energy) to be gone. To banish means to send someone or something away — from the area, or possibly, back to the original source.

Many Wiccans avoid these practices because they are negative forms of magic. Some Wiccans use binding and banishing as last resorts, when someone or something poses a serious threat, usually to the community (for example, a group of Wiccans may decide to bind or banish a criminal who is preying on others).

The colors of magic

You may hear people describe various types of magic by using colors. The most common references are to white magic and black magic or light and dark magic. Presumably, the terms white and black or light and dark magic harken back to a time in early human history when the night, the dark, was associated with fear and danger. The daytime, the light, represented safety. These labels are from folklore, not modern Wicca, and many Wiccans don't use these characterizations today. Personally, I object to these labels for several reasons:

✔ The terminology smacks of racism (designating that white is good and positive and black is evil and negative reinforces racial stereotypes).

✔ The usage isn't accurate. Magic is a tool, like mathematics or computer technology. Magic follows natural law, like gravity. Magic just *is*; it can't be black or white or any other value judgment. The ethics of its use depend on the intention of the user.

✔ Use of these terms perpetuates stereotypes about the Craft. Using the terms black magic and white magic reinforces society's misinformation and fear about the nature of magic. In addition, when someone says that he or she is a "white" or "good" Witch or Wiccan, the distinction implies that others are "black" or "bad" Witches and Wiccans. Society doesn't label the followers of mainstream religions in this way. For example, Methodists aren't asked to declare whether they are white or good Methodists or black or bad Methodists.

These labels have been around for a long time, and if you continue to study Wicca, you will undoubtedly run into them. Here's a general description of the meanings for the colors of magic:

✔ **White magic** is performed for a positive purpose, a beneficial result, or spiritual growth (for example, healing or self-improvement). A person works magic for him/herself or for someone who has knowledge of the magic and has given consent, without any type of coercion. Some Wiccans may perform white magic for a person who is unaware (for example, someone who is seriously ill). However, in those cases, the practitioner makes a general request for the best possible outcome and then sends the magical energy to Deity or out into nature (rather than sending the magic directly to the unaware person). Most Wiccans practice white magic.

✔ **Black magic** is any magic that is performed to coerce someone into doing something; is aimed at someone against his or her will; is aimed at someone without his or her knowledge; or is used to produce a restrictive, unwanted, unethical, or objectionable outcome. Wiccans do not knowingly practice black magic.

✔ **Gray magic** is situational, and Wiccans differ about the ethics of its use. Gray magic encompasses all of the aspects of white magic (see the first bullet) with one addition: Gray magic includes magic for defense or protection of the Self or others from danger,

(continued)

(continued)

abuse, menace, or crisis. Sometimes it is magic done for the greater good. Many Wiccans believe that they have an obligation to stop evil, that they can't ethically ignore abuse, suffering, injustice, and so on. Gray magic allows for a response for the greater good.

↳ **Green magic** has several meanings. The term often describes magic performed on behalf of nature, or to help the Earth and its inhabitants. It can also mean magic for healing or to ensure health and wellness. In some cases, the term is used for magic done to produce prosperity and abundance.

Some Wiccans also refer to blue, red, yellow, orange, or purple magic, but the meanings of these terms vary.

Most Wiccans are extremely reluctant to engage in any form of negative magic, because they know that their own energy is never separate from the energy of other people, and causing harm to others eventually results in harm to the Self. However, they also are fully aware that the failure to act to stop violence, to alleviate suffering, and to halt injustice is a violation of ethical duty and a betrayal of community. So the use of personal power remains a constant challenge for the people of the Craft.

First and foremost, Wiccans believe that positive, loving energy sent out into the world helps to heal the Earth and community, and ultimately improves conditions for the sender, too.

Part II
Looking at the Past, Present, and Future: How Wiccans Live

The 5th Wave   By Rich Tennant

"People practicing Witchcraft lead pretty normal lives. Still, I keep a rubber toad and snake in my spice cabinet just to freak people out."

In this part . . .

Modern-day Wicca is nothing less than the beginning of a new epoch of human civilization, a new paradigm for viewing life, and a hope for saving the planet and for reshaping civilization. Or Wicca is nothing but a grand fraud embraced by gullible people desperate for an alternative to mainstream religions.

The answer depends on your interpretation of Wicca and its past, present, and future.

In the end, the major questions come down to these: Separate from any claim to historical continuity, is Wicca a legitimate religion as it stands today? Does it provide relationship with Deity? Does it meet personal needs? Does it nurture the individual soul and the community? The answers to these questions will ultimately determine Wicca's fate as a modern religion.

Chapter 5

Digging into the Past

*W*icca is the oldest religion, it's the newest, or it's both. Wicca is a continuation, a re-creation, or a revival of ancient spirituality, depending on your outlook.

This chapter offers a glimpse of Wiccan history, from ancient times to the present. Writing a brief history of Wicca is an exercise in frustration because, the truth is, much of this material is speculative. Historical records and scientific evidence are scant and subject to the interpretation of scholars, historians, anthropologists, and others (all of whom view this material through a lens of their own biases and agendas).

Going Way Back: The Birth of the Goddess

Some scientists suggest that the conscious mind has evolved to perceive reality as fixed and separate objects. The Self is independent, an identity separate from nature's web. People are rooted in physical reality, only able to see physical forms and not the energy that flows through the cosmos. However, according to some researchers, the mind may not have always been this way.

Speculating about Shamanism

In order to survive, ancient humans had to live attuned with the cycles of nature. They had to know when to follow the migrations of the animals, where fresh water flowed, when the fish spawned, and where the fresh berries grew. On a daily basis, the ancients felt their interconnection with the world around them, and its interdependence.

Ancient people interacted with the natural world. Because their minds weren't yet structured like modern humans', they may have been able to perceive the energy flowing among beings. They realized their connection with the plants and animals, not only the physical forms, but also the nonphysical energy.

Some people may have been able to shift their consciousness and step out of the physical world into the world of the unconscious mind. They could reach the collective unconscious — the inherited, deep part of the mind common to all living beings. Here they were linked to all of life, and they were free to interact and communicate with the nonphysical forms of animals and other beings.

Mythology is full of references to animals as relatives, brothers, and sisters. Ancient art also shows this kinship. A large cave lies in the Ardeche region of southern France. The cave, called Chauvet, is divided into underground chambers filled with more than 300 paintings of lions and other animals, often shown leaping and running. The paintings have been shown to be at least 30,000 years old, according to radiocarbon dating. One painting, deep in the inner part of the cave, shows a figure that is half human and half bison, perhaps representing this union of human and animal nature or spirit.

Numerous cultures have creation myths describing an event in which humans lost the ability to step away from ordinary consciousness and interact with other beings. In many of these myths, the power to do so is then granted to only a few individuals — the Shaman of the tribes.

Shifting from Shamanism to spirituality

Ancient Shamans, who were adept at the ability to shift consciousness, used it to try to control the world around them in order to improve the lives of their people, for example, by locating migrating animals. These Shamans sometimes joined together to combine their efforts for greater power over their destinies.

When humans stepped out of their physical world into connection with the natural world, they were open to feeling the presence of Deity, the Divine Source of the web of life. They saw the Earth as Mother and the sky as Father.

They gathered together in early rituals to appeal to the Mother and the Father for healing, food, or good weather. Shamanic understanding grew and transformed into spirituality, and this, perhaps, became the beginning of Wicca and Witchcraft.

Finding Witches and Wiccans in History

Did Wicca and Witchcraft exist throughout history? People in many fields of study have been debating this issue for decades. No definitive answers have surfaced. Wiccans and others usually believe and promote one of three explanations about Wicca:

✔ Wicca is a new form of spirituality that re-creates some older practices and ideas.

✔ Wicca is a return to or revival of an old, even ancient, form of religion. Because not a great deal is known about the old Craft, contemporary Wiccans must add to the old tradition.

✔ Wicca is a continuation of a very old religion that has been passed down through families and covens in an unbroken line since ancient times.

What you believe about Wicca and Witchcraft really comes down to how you define the terms and who you believe.

Deciding whether Wicca and Witchcraft were real

Determining whether Wicca and Witchcraft really existed depends on how you define those terms. Here is what researchers know:

✔ Historical and archeological evidence clearly shows that many groups throughout history did worship the Goddess or Goddesses. For example, hundreds of carvings of the fertility icon Sheela Na Gig, such as the one shown in Figure 5-1, date back to the Middle Ages or later. These startling similar representations are on display on buildings — even Christian churches — throughout Great Britain, Ireland, Wales, and Scotland and may be artistic representations of the Goddess.

✔ Many groups throughout history saw Deity in nature; they believed that Deity was all-present in the world, that people come from and are part of the Divine and that Deity is in everyone.

✔ Some people did practice herbalism, healing, divination, and magic.

✔ Throughout history, people attended agricultural and fertility rites, festivals, and celebrations that were timed to the cycles of nature.

Figure 5-1:
An ancient carving of Sheela Na Gig, a fertility icon and possible representation of the Goddess.

© Homer Sykes/CORBIS

So one definition of Wicca and Witchcraft is as a set of beliefs and practices that people followed but didn't label — a natural way of life, as opposed to a religion.

But was there an actual, organized religion called Wicca or Witchcraft? That's a more difficult question to answer.

Some researchers believe that Witchcraft was an organized religion that was invented by the Catholic Inquisition during the great Witch hunts of the Middle Ages and the Renaissance (see the following section for more details about the hunts). According to the Witch hunters, Witches worshipped and served Satan. Proponents of this theory believe that the invention of Witchcraft was either a mass delusion by members of the church, who fervently believed in Satan's power to deceive humankind, or a deliberate ploy by church and government to persecute people for political and social reasons.

Other people, including Margaret Murray, believed that Wicca and Witchcraft were organized, pre-Christian religions of Europe.

Defending or doubting Margaret Murray

Margaret Murray (1863–1963) was a British Egyptologist, folklorist, and anthropologist. She is also regarded by many to be a grandmother of modern Wicca, because her books so heavily influenced modern Wicca.

Murray's claims

In 1921, Murray published her book, *The Witch-Cult in Western Europe* (1921). In her book, Murray argued that Witchcraft was the universal, organized, pre-Christian religion of Europe. This ancient religion survived across Europe until early modern times. Murray based her argument on her examination of the Witch trial documents of the Middle Ages and the Renaissance.

Murray believed that the ancient Witches worshipped a horned God, which the Christians of the Inquisition claimed to be their Satan. That's why Witches were accused of Satan worship. She called the ancient religion the Dianic Cult, because the female form of this God was Diana, the Queen of the Witches. However, the male Deity dominated the religion. Murray's Witch cult had come from a British race of small people, now known as the Fairies. The Witch cult celebrated eight festivals every year (Sabbats) and minor events (Esbats). They organized themselves into small covens of 13 people.

Researchers have been attacking Murray's scholarship for decades. They say that she assumed that the confessions of the accused in the Witch trials were true, when in reality the victims of the trials were tortured until they would say anything to stop the pain.

Some researchers do accept that small pockets of the ancient pre-Christian religions did survive into modern times in various areas of Europe. They acknowledge that these isolated groups may have retained fragments of the old rituals and practices. However, they don't accept Murray's idea of an organized and widespread pre-Christian religion that remained intact throughout history. Murray also showed no documentation for her claims about the religion — the Sabbats, the covens, and so on. Again, scholars say that these terms were created by the Inquisition during the Witch trials.

Leland and Graves: Other voices

Charles Leland (1824–1903) was an American writer who believed that the Craft survived from ancient times. His works, like Murray's, had a big influence on the modern Wiccan revival, especially, *Aradia, Gospel of the Witches* (1890, and reprinted 1974). Leland was an author from the United States. Apparently, he led an adventurous life as a political radical, an abolitionist, and a folklorist.

Leland claimed that he knew a woman, Madellena, who was from an old Witch family of Italian heritage, and she provided him with the family's book of magic. The book tells the story of Diana, the Queen of the Witches and her union with Lucifer, the God of the Sun (not Lucifer, the Christian Satan). This mating produced a daughter, Aradia.

Aradia went to Earth to teach Witchcraft to the peasants, so they could use the magic against the ruling class and raise themselves out of poverty. *The Charge of the Goddess* is a very popular piece of poetic prose from this book. This passage has been rewritten often, and most traditions of modern Wicca use a version of it. The term "the Old Religion" probably originated with Leland's books. Leland maintained that women were treated equally with men in the old Craft, and he remains popular with many feminist Wiccans. He is not at all popular with scholars, however, and they have dismissed his books as bunk because he provides no documentation beyond his claim that Madellena was a practitioner who shared her knowledge with him.

Robert Graves (1895–1985) is a British writer who promoted the idea that the Craft existed in Britain from ancient times, and he claimed that several of the old covens survived. His book, *The White Goddess,* also influenced the modern Wiccan revival. Graves' writings about the Great Goddess are poetic and inspirational, but few people view the book as a work of scholarship.

Wiccans differ in their opinions of Murray, Leland, and Graves and about the historical timeline of the Craft. However, they take the period of the great Witch hunts very seriously.

Remembering the Burning Times

Witch hunt. The term is used today to mean the organized search for, investigation, harassment, and persecution of people who are perceived as a threat because of their unpopular views or behavior. Witch hunts are a form of societal hysteria, and during these times of panic, authorities violate human rights and perpetrate injustice, in the name of protecting the greater good.

The term Witch hunt comes from an actual time in history, a profoundly horrifying and tragic era that had an immeasurable effect on human development and continues to influence society today.

During the Middle Ages and the Renaissance, many thousands of people in Europe were accused of being Witches, and they were tortured and murdered. This time has been called the Great European Witch Hunt, the Great Hunt, and the Burning Times (the term used by many Wiccans today). You may hear Wiccans use the phrase, "Never again the burning." Although most of the accused were probably not Witches, Wiccans honor the victims of the Witch hunts, and many Wiccans feel a deep obligation to ensure that such persecution can never happen again.

The Burning Times is not an accurate term. Alleged Witches were tortured and executed in a variety of ways in addition to burning at the stake, including:

- beatings
- crushing with stones
- drowning
- hanging
- rape and sexual abuse
- sleep deprivation
- starvation
- stretching on the rack
- suffocation
- thumbscrews

The deaths include those who died as a result of their imprisonment and those who died as a result of the tests used to determine guilt or innocent (for example, when held under water, an innocent person drowns while a Witch is able to stay alive) as well as those actually executed.

Historians know that the Great Hunt did occur. That fact is indisputable. When, where, how, and why the Witch hunts happened are hotly debated among Wiccans themselves, among scholars, and between Wiccans and non-Wiccans. It's a subject that sparks strong emotions from many people. In recent years, the amount of available information about this brutal era in human history has grown substantially. This section offers some general theories about the Great European Witch Hunt.

Untangling the evidence

Researching the Witch hunts of Europe has always been a scholarly challenge. Many of the dead don't show up on official records; they died in prison, committed suicide, or in many cases, official documentation was not filed. Court records represent the opinions of the judges, not necessarily the facts. Torture very often was used to extract information and confessions, so the testimony of the accused always is questionable.

In general, researchers of the Witch hunts can draw information from three sources:

- **Official records.** These include the court records and reports of the accusations, arrests, investigations, court proceedings, confessions, verdicts, and punishments. These records often contain detailed information about age, gender, and occupation of the accused. These documents are preserved throughout Europe and in some locations in the United States. They pose problems for two reasons. No standard way of conducting and reporting Witch trials existed, and many of the details are open to interpretation. In addition, these Witch trial records are mixed in with all the other court records of the era. Finding and compiling information is painstaking work.

✔ **Literature.** Much of the popular knowledge about the Witch trials comes from literature of the time, including: literary prose and poetry, diaries, witch hunting manuals, records of sermons preached against Witchcraft, reports to church officials, writings of Witch hunters, and tabloid-style accounts of the most famous Witch trials. The source most commonly known today is the *Malleus Maleficarum* (*The Hammer of Witches* or *Women Who Commit Maleficia*), written by Inquisition Dominicans Heinrich Kramer (the main author) and Jacob Sprenger.

The problem with literature sources is that they are anecdotal and biased. They were often written with the purpose of promoting a specific view or just plain scaring the public. These sources don't give an accurate portrayal of Witch trials as a whole, only a compelling glimpse of the mind-set of one individual or group of people. Unfortunately, literature generally doesn't provide credible hard data.

✔ **Art.** These are visual portrayals of Witches and of the trials. Artwork, such as the example shown in Figure 5-2, has provided insight into attitudes and activities of the era, but like literature, it doesn't offer hard data.

Figure 5-2: A graphic depiction of the Burning Times.

© Bettmann/CORBIS

Today, researchers are doing more systematic and comprehensive studies of the court records of specific areas, so the data more clearly show who died and who was responsible for the deaths.

Although research in this area has revealed much new information in recent years, no one has definitively answered all the questions about the Burning Times.

Estimating the number of the dead

The European Witch trials spanned from 1300 to 1800, but were concentrated from the mid-1400s through the late 1600s. Witch trials occurred well before this time span, and the last legal executions happened in Europe as late as the 1790s.

Current scholarly research indicates that between 40,000 and 100,000 people were killed in the Great European Witch Hunt. The figure differs depending on the researcher and the method that he or she used. The number is usually based on investigation of court documents and on estimates of the numbers of lost records.

Many Pagan books continue to cite older statistics, often stating that as many as 9 million people were killed. The most current research indicates that this figure is too high, although many Pagans continue to stand by it.

Identifying Europe's hotbeds of hate

The European Witch trials can't be explained by geography. The Witch hunts were sporadic and spread out. Some of the areas of full-blown panic and extensive killing were next to areas where no trials were held at all.

Research indicates that the majority of the Witch trials were in central Europe: Germany, Switzerland, and France. However, Witch trials also occurred in the Baltics, Denmark, England, Finland, Hungary, Iceland, Ireland, Italy, Norway, Poland, Portugal, Russia, Spain, and Sweden. The most well-known trials in the United States, the Salem Witch Trials, occurred in 1692 and resulted in the deaths of 20 people accused of Witchcraft.

Recognizing the basis for the trials

Throughout history, humans have tried to improve their lives by using forces within themselves and forces outside of the ordinary physical world. For example, they tried to heal loved ones, to influence the weather, to boost harvests, and to protect livestock. Shamans, Witches, and others who were perceived to use these powers effectively (known as magic) have been honored and also feared. So being a Witch has always been risky.

Witch trials were rare before the 14th Century. Magic was punished when it was used in the commission of a crime. Magic used for good intent (for example, healing) generally was not a concern of the church or the government.

Beginning with the teachings of Thomas Aquinas in the 13th Century, Christianity began to focus on Satan's role in the fall from Eden and his ongoing efforts to deceive humankind and control human souls. According to theology, Satan and his hosts could tempt humans away from God. Satan and his demons could enter into contracts with humans, leave marks on their physical bodies, gather humans together to worship him, engage in sexual relations with humans, and give humans powers (including the ability to fly and change form). Over the course of time, these ideas continued to evolve and spread.

Beliefs and practices that were not approved by the church, including magic (even for healing or other good intent), became evidence of an alliance with Satan and his demons. The practitioner of magic was now perceived as a threat. People labeled as Witches (whether they were Pagan Witches, people who combined Christianity and Paganism, or falsely labeled Christians) were viewed as the agents of evil and misery in the world. In England, Exodus 22:18 of _The Holy Bible_ — _Thou shalt not suffer a witch to live_ — was interpreted literally.

This new perception of Witches as an organized and serious danger was the theological basis for the Witch trials.

Although church courts (the Catholic Inquisition and Protestant courts) tried many alleged Witches, the majority of the killings were ordered by civil (secular, government) courts. The dogma of the church was used to justify the arrests and the killings, both in church and in civil trials.

Most researchers believe that many motives and factors may have led to Witch hunts, and it's unlikely that religion is the only cause. Most of the victims were Christians or people who combined Christianity and Paganism.

Uncovering motives for the murders

The Witch trials were not all alike. Anyone could be accused of being a Witch. The alleged Witches didn't share any common characteristic. In other words, all the Witch trials that occurred in all locations don't represent an organized effort to exterminate any one type of person. However, much of the research shows that overall, approximately 80 percent of the accused were women, although the percentage shifted depending on the country.

Were the accused really Witches? Most research indicates that the majority of the victims were Christians. However, evidence suggests that some of the accused mixed Pagan beliefs and practices with Christianity. No one knows for sure how many were actually Pagan Witches, believing in and practicing pre-Christian ways.

In general, across all areas, the trials and the accompanying social panic don't appear to be a conspiracy solely against any one group. Even within a single area, those charged with Witchcraft are almost always diverse. However, members of the following groups often were accused:

✔ women, especially unmarried women and widows, who lived alone

✔ the poor

✔ the elderly

✔ people who were disliked or resented in the community

✔ the mentally or physically impaired

✔ healers and midwives

✔ people who owned property that others wanted

✔ people who were named by others during torture

Society was undergoing big changes at the time of the great Witch hunts. A number of conditions caused society to be unstable and may have contributed to the panics that gave rise to the Witch hunts. The following sections describe these conditions. None of these explanations can account for all the Witch trials. However, these conditions may have set the stage for Witch hunts in many areas across Europe. In times of rapid change and intense conflict, fear and desperation affect every aspect of people's lives and can drive people to commit acts that they ordinarily wouldn't do.

Economics

By the end of the Witch hunts, the economy of Europe was changing. The feudal system, which was based on agriculture and interdependent villages, was collapsing. Capitalism, which was based on industry and private property, was growing. Land shifted from communal property used by the whole village to private property reserved for use by a single person. During this time, illness and poverty were widespread.

Alleged Witches served as scapegoats for disease and famine that were rampant in these impoverished communities. Peasants blamed the alleged Witch for the illness or starvation of loved ones (frequently for failing to cure the illness if not causing it). The Witch trials discouraged peasant uprisings by breeding distrust in the community.

In some cases, the Witch trials may have been a direct result of the battle for private land. Under local laws, a Witch trial and execution sometimes allowed the Witch hunter or someone else to confiscate the victim's land.

Medicine and education

During the era of the Witch hunts, the church was taking control of medicine and medical treatment by institutionalizing training in medicine and regulating who was permitted to practice this new craft. Women traditionally had been responsible for healing, and many village wise women had vast knowledge of herbs, natural healing techniques, and midwifery.

One theory suggests that the newly church-sanctioned medical profession began to drive out traditional healers who were the only source of medical treatment for the majority of the population. The Witch hunts may have served to eliminate these wise women who were competition for modern physicians.

During this time, the church was also beginning to institutionalize education. The establishment of schools and universities (from which women were banned) meant that in many communities women were being forced out of jobs and positions of power that they had once held because they did not have the credentials that were now necessary. Men from the working class couldn't attend these elite schools, either, and the lack of opportunity ensured that the poor were forced to work in the early industries for inadequate wages.

Religion

At the peak of the Witch hunts, the formerly strong, central Roman Catholic Church was collapsing and fragmenting into different orders and sects. The Protestants separated from the Catholic Church and formed their own churches. This period of history, called the Reformation and Counter-Reformation (beginning in the early 16th Century), was a time of conflict and bloody warfare among rival religious groups. Both the old and the new churches were unstable.

In this time of instability, both the old and the new churches lashed out at anyone they perceived as a threat. The *Witch crazes* — widespread panic and intensified Witch hunting — swept across Europe.

The churches took over the peasant festivals and celebrations that had their roots in the old Paganism, which created an even greater distance between the common villagers and the practitioner of the old ways.

In addition to having stamped out the last remnants of Pagan belief and practice, the Witch Hunts may have stopped a resurgence of Paganism, except perhaps in areas such as the large forests of England, which are reported to have been filled with peasant squatters.

Centuries later, Gerald Gardner, the man widely regarded as the founder of modern Wicca, claimed to have met the members of a coven living on the edge of one of these forests in the 1930s. He reported that the coven had survived for hundreds of years, and he based his writings on the history that this group maintained.

Reviving Wicca

Gerald Gardner is often viewed as the grandfather of modern Wicca, and he is generally given credit for sparking the Wiccan revival, beginning in the 1950s. However, many people have played an integral role in the development of the modern Craft.

Gerald Gardner and the New Forest coven

If you ask a dozen Wiccans for their opinions of Gerald Gardner, you will almost certainly receive a dozen different responses. Depending on whom you ask, Gardner is either the savior or the scoundrel of the modern Craft. Whatever the truth is, his story isn't boring.

Gerald Brousseau Gardner (1884–1964) lived much of his life in the Far East, eventually becoming a British civil servant. Reportedly, Gardner was intensely interested in anthropology, folklore, religion, and magic, and he spent time studying the beliefs of many indigenous peoples, including the headhunters of Borneo. He retired and returned to England in the 1930s.

After returning to England, Gardner studied the occult. During this exploration, he encountered a coven that many claim had been in existence for centuries, possibly from ancient times, located on the edge of the New Forest. A hereditary witch, a woman called Old Dorothy and later reported to be Dorothy Clutterbuck, initiated him into the coven and into Wica (spelled with one "c" by Gardner, but now spelled Wicca).

Breaking the long silence

From his experience in the New Forest coven and his own research, Gardner created a system of Wica, which evolved into Gardnerian Wicca (for details on the beliefs and practices of this tradition, see Chapter 10).

Gardner was initiated in 1939, and he could not reveal or publish his experiences because of the anti-Witchcraft laws that remained on the books in Britain. These laws carried heavy penalties, and they are one of the key reasons that the Craft remained shrouded in secrecy throughout British history. But with the repeal of the laws in 1951, Gardner published two books, *Witchcraft Today* (1954) and *The Meaning of Witchcraft* (1959), which detailed the beliefs and practices of the Craft.

Gardner became a celebrity and appeared often in the media, touted as the "official Witch" of Britain. For many years, he ran a Witchcraft museum on the Isle of Man.

By publicizing Wicca, Gardner violated the Craft's long tradition of silence and secrecy, and he was widely criticized. Reports began to appear suggesting that the Craft had survived in pockets and fragments throughout Britain (and within immigrant groups in the United States), each with its own beliefs and practices. Members of hereditary (family) or traditionalist covens claimed that their traditions were as old or older than the New Forest coven. Many declared that Gardnerian Wicca was not representative of their own beliefs and practices. A key issue was the question of whether the Craft was a practice (focusing on influencing everyday events) or a religion (centered around belief in and worship of Deity).

As to his own reasons for publishing, the members of the New Forest coven were growing old, and Gardner believed that they were the last surviving members of the Craft. He was genuinely afraid that the Craft would die out, and all its beauty, mystery, and power would be lost to future generations.

Debating Gardner's historical account

Since his books were published, every aspect of Gardner's story has been challenged. Today, Wiccans and scholars still debate his account. Does Gardner's system of Wicca come from an ancient, European, Goddess-centered Pagan religion? Does the Craft really have a continuous, unbroken history back to ancient times? Did covens actually exist that predated Margaret Murray and Gerald Gardner? Did Gardner really encounter the New Forest coven or was the coven a literary ploy around which to center his books and his Wiccan system? Was he really initiated into such a group? How much of Gardner's version of Wicca is based on the beliefs and practices of the New Forest Coven?

Gardner himself is reported to have admitted that the old coven had retained only fragments of the original ritual and practice — not enough to form the basis of a full system of the Craft. No one knows how much of Gardner's system of Wicca is based on the historical Wica tradition. No proof exists to show the degree to which Gardner took material from other sources to build this version of Wicca. However, evidence suggests that Gardner may have used material from the following:

- ✔ **Prior works about the Craft.** These include the books of Margaret Murray, Charles Leland, and Robert Graves (see the preceding section).

- ✔ **Doreen Valiente (1922–1999).** Valiente is often credited with being a co-creator of modern Wicca. Gerald Gardner initiated her into Wicca in 1953, and she was one of the High Priestesses of the Gardner coven.

She co-created many of the rituals and she rewrote and edited much of Gardner's work. Most of the beauty, poetry, and lyricism of Gardnerian Wicca is attributable to Valiente. She was a widely published author and, during her lifetime, contributed immensely to the body of writings on Wicca and Paganism in general. She is the author of a popular and beautiful version of *The Charge of the Goddess.*

She produced evidence for many of Gardner's claims, and she was the one who validated that Dorothy Clutterbuck was the "Old Dorothy" of Gardner's account of the New Forest coven.

Valiente's contribution (in research, writing, editing, poetry, public lectures, and political advocacy) to Wicca and Paganism is enormous.

- **Aleister Crowley (1875–1947).** Crowley is a prominent figure in Ceremonial Magick. He was not Wiccan, and many of his ideas are not in keeping with contemporary Wicca. His books, the organizations with which he was associated, and his life were then and are now extremely controversial. However, some of Crowley's ideas may have influenced Gardner's Wicca. For example, Crowley's idea that magic is a science that manipulates natural forces is common in contemporary Wicca. He is also responsible for the quote, "Do what thou wilt shall be the whole of the law. Love is the Law. Love under will." The Wiccan Rede ("An ye harm none, do what ye will."), the central ethic of Wicca, may have evolved, in part, from this quote of Crowley's.

- **Dion Fortune (1890 or 1891–1946).** Fortune was a British Ceremonial Magician and author. She was introduced to the occult by the Hermetic Order of the Golden Dawn (an occult society), and then launched her own group, the Society of the Inner Light. Over the course of her life, she wrote a number of nonfiction and fiction books on the occult. She is the source of the often-quoted definition of magic, "the art of changing consciousness at will."

- **Fraternal orders, secret societies, and occult and mystery societies.** Much of Gardnerian Wicca's philosophy and structure (for example, the three degrees of initiation based on increased knowledge) seem to have come from several groups, including: Freemasonry, the Hermetic Order of the Golden Dawn, the Theosophical Society, and the Rosicrucians (Order of the Rosy Cross).

- **Gardner's own personal conception of what the Craft should be.**

Despite the controversy about its origins, Gardner's Wicca met a deep need within society, and the religion began to spread to many countries.

Coming to America

Raymond (1934) and Rosemary Buckland were initiates of Gerald Gardner. Many historians give them credit for the successful introduction of Wicca into the United States in the 1960s. Raymond Buckland has been a prolific writer and has produced many books on Wicca and related topics. He also developed his own tradition of the Craft, Seax Wicca.

In the United States, secrecy, hierarchy, and the dictates of formal ceremonial magic were rejected by many. Books of Shadows outlining the way to practice Wicca were published. Solitary practitioners challenged the traditional belief that Wicca should be practiced only with covens. The environmental and women's movements, and other ongoing social and political changes, shifted the direction of Wicca. Diverse traditions began to spring up, although many maintained elements of Gardner's system.

Gardnerian Wicca is one of the most widespread of Wiccan traditions, and perhaps the most influential. (A *tradition* is a denomination or sect of Wicca.) Many Gardnerian covens exist today, and many traditions of Wicca are offshoots of Gardnerian Wicca or borrow heavily from it.

Some Wiccans believe that Gardner hurt the Craft because of his lack of credibility, as well as his insistence on nudity, sexual symbolism, coven membership, and hierarchy.

Others feel that the Craft was and is valid, regardless of the historical accuracy of Gardner's account and his inconsistencies and eccentricities. They believe that Deity is the focus and center of Wicca.

Even if they don't find the works of Murray, Gardner, and other forerunners of the Wiccan revival fully credible, many Wiccans feel gratitude toward these pioneers for possibly saving Wicca from extinction, for sparking the re-emergence of the Goddess, for keeping an alternative worldview alive for new generations, and for providing the seed from which Wicca continues to grow and evolve.

A parallel path: Victor Anderson

Another Wiccan tradition developed parallel to Gardnerian Wicca and yet is different in many ways. Today, the tradition is known as Feri, Faerie, Faery, or Fairy. Victor Henry Anderson (1917–2001) is recognized as the founding teacher.

Victor became legally blind at 4 years old, and his physical sight was very limited for the rest of his life. His family moved to Oregon, where he attended a school for the blind. At age 9, he underwent a mystical experience, which he felt was his initiation into the magical world. During the 1930s in Oregon, Anderson belonged to the Harpy Coven, a pre-Gardnerian group who practiced the Craft in the 1920s and 1930s. He had many teachers and collaborators from diverse cultures and traditions throughout his life.

Anderson was self-taught in physics, chemistry, literature, and the world's indigenous spiritual traditions. He was an accomplished musician, playing the accordion professionally, and he spoke several languages. He wrote beautiful, lyrical poetry.

Victor Anderson's wife Cora was born in 1915 in Alabama, and her family practiced folk magic. She met Victor in person in 1944. Many reports say that they both claimed that they had met often on the astral plane and recognized each other when they met in person. They were married three days after their first meeting. Together, they had an immeasurable impact on the modern Craft.

From his already vast knowledge of spiritual traditions and practices and his early experiences in the Harpy Coven, Victor developed the early Feri tradition and began teaching it to others, although more informally than Gardner and others of British Wicca.

In the late 1950s, they began their long association with Tom DeLong, known as Gwydion Pendderwen (1946–1982), a friend of their son. Pendderwen was a major contributor to the tradition, and many consider him to be a co-founder.

The Andersons, Pendderwen and several others formed the Mahealani Coven in California in the early 1970s. The Feri tradition reached full fruition as this coven evolved. Feri is a tradition of power, mystery, ecstasy, and direct communication with Deity. The rituals and practices are extraordinarily diverse, incorporating African (especially Dahomean-Haitian), African American, Appalachian, Celtic, Hawaiian Huna, and Tibetan beliefs and practices. (See Chapter 10 for more information about the Feri tradition.)

In 1970, Victor Anderson published *Thorns of the Blood Rose,* a book of love poems and poetry rooted in the Feri tradition. In 1984, Cora Anderson's book, *Fifty Years in the Feri Tradition,* was published and serves as a definitive look at the tradition.

Currently, several different lines descend from the original coven, and because of the tradition's diversity, the Feri groups vary widely in ritual and practice.

The Andersons' and Pendderwen's impact on Wicca is more subtle than Gerald Gardner's, but it is profound. They trained and initiated many of the Craft's most influential people. Starhawk, the writer, activist, and co-founder of the Reclaiming tradition, is one of the most well-known initiates of the tradition. The Feri tradition has infused Wicca with poetry, daring, courage, honor, and wild spirit.

The Wiccan boom of the 1970s

In the 1970s, Wicca spread and evolved in the United States, becoming much more diverse. Books were published that outlined various forms of Wicca. These publications provided information that allowed more people to practice as solitaries (alone) instead of or until joining covens. The availability of these resources opened the door for more rapid growth in Wicca. Feminism and the women's movement also had a profound effect on Wicca.

A gathering of women

In the 1970s, a new tradition of Wicca was born out of feminism and the women's movement. Many women helped to launch this tradition, but Z. Budapest is widely considered to be the founder.

Zsuzsanna Budapest (1940), a hereditary Witch, came to the United States from Hungary when the Soviet Union invaded her country. By the early 1970s, she had developed a Goddess-centered, woman-centered tradition of Wicca. She based her tradition on feminist principles and the ritual, folk magic, and healing practices of her mother. She borrowed some elements from Gardner's tradition, as well as from Charles Leland's book, *Aradia, Gospel of the Witches* (1890, reprinted 1974). The Dianic tradition is named for the Goddess Diana, the Goddess of untamed nature (although Dianics celebrate the Goddess in all her aspects). See Chapter 10 for more on the feminist Dianic tradition.

A central theme of Gardnerian Wicca is polarity, the balancing of male and female energies. Gardnerians generally worship the Goddess and the God. The Budapest tradition rejects polarity and is Goddess-centered. Dianics practice the Craft with women only.

Budapest's early book, *The Feminist Book of Lights and Shadows* (1976), and later revision, *The Holy Book of Women's Mysteries* (1989), served as the foundation for the feminist Dianic Craft.

Many authors have played a critical role in the birth and growth of the Dianic tradition, including: Ruth Barrett, Carol P. Christ, Mary Daly, Riane Eisler, Marija Gimbutas, Susan Griffin, Hallie Iglehart (Austen), Diane Mariechild, Shekhinah Mountainwater, Charlene Spretnak, Starhawk, Diane Stein, Merlin Stone, and Barbara Walker.

In 1971, Zsuzsanna Budapest founded the Susan B. Anthony Coven #1 of Los Angeles, which served as a role model for many of the other Dianic covens.

Today, Dianic has become a collective term for any person or group that emphasizes the Goddess and whose spirituality and practice are woman-centered and/or based on feminist values and principles. Some are no longer women-only, as required by the original Budapest feminist Dianic tradition.

Wicca redefined

As feminism and the women's movement gained momentum, many women were searching for a spirituality of liberation, based on principles of equality. Starhawk and the other members of the Reclaiming collective founded a tradition that is inclusive of both women and men, and promotes liberation, equality, and justice for all people.

In 1979, Starhawk published her first book, *The Spiral Dance* (1979, 2nd revised edition 1989, 3rd revised edition 1999), which included information on belief, ritual, structure, and practice of the new tradition. (See Chapter 10 for a closer look at the Reclaiming tradition.)

Starhawk had been initiated into the Faery (Feri) tradition by Victor Anderson, and she has blended many elements of that tradition with the feminism and creativity of the Dianics. Reclaiming offers an alternative to the separatism of the Dianic movement and the traditionalism of the Gardnerians.

Over the years, Starhawk has produced many must-read books on the Craft. Her books have been widely read throughout the English-speaking world, and her impact on Wicca is boundless. She is also a courageous, insightful, and wise political activist, and a role model for many Wiccans.

In the same year that *The Spiral Dance* was published, another pivotal book helped to redefine Wicca and introduce it to the general public. Radio producer and journalist Margot Adler published her book, *Drawing Down the Moon: Witches, Druids, Goddess Worshippers, and Other Pagans in America Today* (1979, revised and expanded 1986, updated 1997). This book gave the general public the facts about Paganism and dispelled the stereotypes.

Adler's book has become the source book on the history, beliefs, and lifestyles of the new Paganism. Thanks to her diligent reporting, the public has a more accurate view of Paganism.

The publication of the books by Starhawk and Adler introduced Wicca to the general public and helped Wicca evolve from its predominantly Gardnerian roots. These books are responsible for much of the growth of Wicca since their publications.

Chapter 6

Living Wiccan Today

*W*iccans may have some unique practices, and they face some unique challenges, but the average Wiccan is a sharp contrast to the stereotypes that many people still hold.

This chapter gives you a glimpse into Wiccan lives and answers the question, "What's it really like to be Wiccan?"

Taking a Snapshot of Contemporary Wicca

Who are Wiccans? Media portrayals of Wiccans have become more sympathetic over the years, but the TV and movie images probably don't reflect the lives of average Wiccans.

The truth is that no one really knows how many Wiccans there are, who they are, and what kind of lives they lead. Wicca doesn't have large institutions that can provide this kind of collective information. Wicca is a spirituality of small, loosely connected groups (although the Internet may be changing that fact by strengthening the Wiccan community). Wicca does not have organized leadership or a centralized organization.

Many people claim that Wicca is the fastest growing religion in America, but no hard data exists to prove this claim. Surveys by several non-Wiccan groups, the expansion of the Wiccan presence on the World Wide Web, and the increase in Wicca-related book sales support the idea that the number of

Wiccans is increasing. In addition, records suggest that attendance at Pagan festivals is high and probably growing. *Festivals* are events that typically happen in a rural setting at the same time annually. They usually last for a weekend, or perhaps several days. Festivals vary in size, but some draw hundreds of people. They offer Pagans an opportunity to interact with one another socially and to exchange information about beliefs and practices.

Commonsense suggests that Wicca is changing in addition to growing. The early participants in the Wiccan revival are now middle-aged, and many have children. Dr. Helen Berger argues that the involvement of entire families encourages Wiccans to create organizations and churches that will help Wicca survive and expand as a religion. Dr. Berger suggests that Wiccan parents want the religion to be viewed as legitimate by society, so that their children won't suffer persecution for their beliefs. Dr. Berger and colleagues, Evan A. Leach and Leigh S. Shaffer, present the results of an in-depth survey of the Pagan population in the book, *Voices from the Pagan Census: A National Survey of Witches and Neo-Pagans in the United States.*

The book is profoundly important and provides insight on many aspects of Pagan life. However, keep in mind that the population of the Berger survey was small (approximately 2,000 people from several traditions, including Wicca) and *self-selected* (meaning that participants were not randomly selected, and they volunteered to respond). So these respondents may or may not represent Wicca as a whole.

Out of fear of persecution and desire for privacy, many Wiccans lead very low-profile lives. Many don't disclose their affiliation with Wicca to outsiders. They go to work or school. They come home, cook dinner, watch some TV, and go to bed. They attend PTA meetings and little league games. They go to the movies. They do read lots of books. The average Wiccan looks and lives pretty much like anyone else.

Keeping Silent or Telling the World: The Wiccan Dilemma

Some people cautiously hide their beliefs and never tell others about their involvement in Wicca — not their families, not their friends, and certainly not their employers. They hide their altars, keep their books hidden in drawers instead of displayed on shelves, and find an excuse to leave in a hurry when people start talking about religion. They only share their beliefs with like-minded Wiccans, and sometimes with no one at all.

Other people, from the moment they encounter Wicca, begin telling everyone they know about the wonderful new world that they have discovered. They heap books on their friends, they hang pentacles in their cubicles at work, and they wear bold T-shirts proudly displaying their devotion to Wicca. They're proud, and they want the world to know it.

Both of these positions have merit.

People who keep silent aren't just being paranoid. Most Wiccans are well versed in the long and brutal history of persecution against real and alleged Witches (see Chapter 5). Discrimination and persecution continue today around the world. In the United States, Wiccans are fired from jobs, lose custody of their children, are discriminated against in housing, or are forced to make other painful sacrifices because of their religion.

Some people want to keep silent because they worry about being put in a position where they are forced to divulge the names of fellow Wiccans. In addition, some Wiccans are alarmed by the escalating use of technology to collect and reveal very private information about individuals.

So, quite reasonably, some Wiccans choose to limit the number of people who know about their religion and could cause them trouble — or even put them in danger — now or in the future.

Keep in mind that you should never ask someone directly whether he or she is a Wiccan or a Witch. Wait until the information is volunteered. If a person mentions the subject in conversation, show that you are open minded and receptive, but wait for the person to confide in you. And this advice goes double if others can hear your conversation. Never, and I mean *never*, "out" anyone. Don't divulge to others that someone is Wiccan without first getting permission in private. Please respect that some people want to keep their religion to themselves.

In addition to concerns about discrimination or persecution, some Wiccans consider Wicca to be a mystery religion that should be kept secret. A *mystery religion* is one in which the Deity is revealed through individual, personal experience. These events are kept secret in order to preserve their power and significance. Also, according to this view, some things are best taught person to person and should not be made public. In addition, certain knowledge and techniques (magic, for example) may be dangerous if used by people who have not had proper training or who may intend to harm others.

People who choose to openly share their beliefs also have some very good reasons for doing so. Personal empowerment as well as physical, mental, and emotional strength are central to Wicca. Some Wiccans feel that living in fear of discrimination or conflict is contrary to their beliefs and limits their ability to practice their religion. Being open and honest about Wicca builds self-confidence, which in turn makes magical work more effective and makes ritual more fulfilling.

Some Wiccans believe that keeping their spirituality hidden encourages persecution and puts Wiccans in more danger, not less. Many feel that denying their religion dishonors the Goddess and the God. They also believe that silence dishonors the Witches and alleged Witches who have been killed in the name of Witchcraft.

Most Wiccans, though, find themselves at a happy medium between these two extremes. Most share their beliefs with family and friends. A smaller number are open about their religion in the workplace. Everyone has to determine his or her own level of comfort.

Many people find Wicca to be liberating and joyous. In their enthusiasm for their new religion, new Wiccans may be tempted to chatter on about their religion to anyone who will listen, without sizing up the person or the situation. If you are considering Wicca as your spiritual path, do some studying, get the facts, and make up your own mind about Wicca. Then, before you start moving that 50-pound pentacle into your cubicle at work, give some careful consideration to whom you want to tell and what you want to say about Wicca.

Some Wiccan traditions advise that newbies study and train for a year and a day before disclosing their participation in Wicca to their personal communities. (A year and a day is a traditional time period in Wicca. The year-and-a-day approach is to ensure that Wiccans prepare well and consider all consequences before making major changes in their lives.)

Spilling the magic beans to family and friends

Although Wicca has its roots in ancient times and is older than many of the world's religions, the Wiccan revival is a fairly recent phenomenon. Most people practicing Wicca today were not born into the religion. They come from the established mainstream religions, often from Christianity. When Wiccans break from their traditional religious roots, serious conflict can erupt.

Family members may feel disappointed, angry, betrayed, or frightened. In all fairness, these strong emotions are understandable. The family may believe that the new Wiccan has turned his or her back on God, and may now be in danger of going to Hell or suffering other exile from God, as well as being separated from the rest of the family after death and for all of eternity.

Certainly everyone has the right to practice whatever religion meets his or her needs, and no one should be bullied by family or friends. But new Wiccans can ease their own transition by thoughtfully considering the question of who to tell about their interest in — or devotion to — Wicca. Everyone's personal community is different, with varying degrees of tolerance. However, the following tips may be helpful to a Wiccan who wants to share his or her spirituality:

- ✔ **Be selective and use good judgment.** Telling your partner, your sister, and your best friend about your interest or participation in Wicca may be important to you, but do you really need to have the same conversation with your frail but very judgmental 91-year-old grandfather, with whom you visit once a year at the nursing home 1,100 miles away?

- ✔ **Be clear about your own motives.** Why are you telling a particular friend or family member? Do you want to be genuine and deepen your intimate bond with this person? Or are you just trying to shock or be rebellious? The former is a good reason; the latter is, perhaps, immature.

- ✔ **Be cautious.** People can be unpredictable. When I made my own change in spirituality, some of the people whom I thought would be fearful or hostile turned out to be remarkably tolerant. Others, sometimes the people I expected to be supportive — or at least *nice* — were uncomfortable, cynical, or downright nasty. Be aware that if you disclose your participation in Wicca, you run the risk of alienating people who are important to you.

Weigh the risks of disclosure against what you stand to gain. If you decide to talk about your spirituality, choose the moment wisely. Don't discuss the issue during a crisis. Pick a time when you are calm and unhurried. You may even want to write down what you want to say, so that you can present your beliefs clearly and without anxiety. Focus on the positive and try to allay the other person's fears and concerns. Be respectful of his or her beliefs, but remain clear about the fact that you have every right to choose your own religion.

Venturing out: Wicca in the workplace

Deciding whether to be open about Wicca in the workplace is a big decision that can have serious financial consequences. If you are exploring Wicca or have made a commitment, think about the pros and cons of disclosing your beliefs before you talk about your spirituality at your own work site. You will probably find that the novelty wears off quickly, and co-workers will treat you the same as they always have. But be aware of the potential downside of coming out of the broom closet at work. Here are some examples of bad stuff that can happen to good Wiccans:

- Well, this one is obvious: You can get fired. Even in places where laws and corporate policies protect freedom of religion in the workplace, an employer who has strong opinions against Wicca may terminate you and cite other reasons. Even if your immediate manager is open minded and tolerant, your manager's boss may not be. Or the boss's boss. . . . Or the discrimination may be more subtle. For example, you may be passed over for promotions or find your work under more scrutiny. In some cases, you could file a lawsuit, but legal recourse is expensive, time-consuming, and rarely successful. (See Chapter 7 for more about the legal rights of Wiccans in the United States.)

- If you are in a business or a profession that makes you dependent on customers or clients for your livelihood, be aware that any disclosure about Wicca may threaten your sales or your relationships with clients. Depending on the nature of your business and your location, you may become the target of a boycott.

- Be prepared to deal with co-workers who try to convert you. Other people may be genuinely interested and want to talk about your beliefs. Some of these conversations may be surprisingly pleasant. Others may not be.

- On the flipside, you may find that some of your co-workers avoid you, or even shun you. Colleagues may display hostility or fear. Depending on your workplace, the stigma may be temporary or permanent.

- Wiccans — especially women — have been stereotyped as being sexually promiscuous, uninhibited, and unrestrained. Whether this applies to you or not, the assumption can cause problems at work in the form of unwelcome advances or even harassment.

But the situation isn't all bad. The following are some of the advantages of being open about your spirituality:

- Some employers allow Wiccans the same privileges as people of other faiths. Your employer may let you take off time on Wiccan holy days. Or you can negotiate for important days off; for example, you can offer to cover for your co-worker on Good Friday if your co-worker takes your place on Beltane.

- You don't have to lie or avoid conversations that involve religion or spirituality. In a work environment where people are close and often share information about their personal lives, lying about or covering up your beliefs can get messy and tedious.

- When people actually know someone who is Wiccan, they are less likely to believe and foster stereotypes about Wiccans. Being open enables you to build good will for Wicca and pave the way for others if you behave ethically and honorably.

> ✔ Living outside of the mainstream requires courage. Having the integrity to be honest about your beliefs and face personal attack can be empowering. The strength and self-confidence that you develop can serve you well in other arenas of your life.

Wicca encourages people to live their lives with courage and integrity. The next section offers a look at the sometimes unique Wiccan approach to life and its passages.

Dancing the Circle of Life: Wiccan Passages

Like everyone else, Wiccan lives are distinguished by passages: birth, puberty, falling in love, aging, and death. Like people of every religion and culture, Wiccans engage in rites, rituals, and celebrations to mark these happy or solemn occasions. The following sections describe how Wiccans distinguish and come to terms with life's memorable moments.

Naming or Wiccaning of a child

When a child comes into a Wiccan household, by birth or adoption, Wiccans may hold a ceremony to name the child and place her or him under the protection of the Goddess and God, as well as the Wiccan community. The vast majority of Wiccans do not consider this to be a dedication or initiation of the child into Wicca. It is more of a welcoming celebration.

The ritual is usually short and simple, but it varies according to tradition. Non-Wiccans are usually free to attend. Typically, a Priestess or Priest presides over the ritual. Sometimes a circle is cast (see Chapter 17 for information on circle casting). The rite usually includes the following elements (the order may vary):

- ✔ The child is welcomed. He or she is presented or introduced to Deity and the community.
- ✔ The child is given his or her name.
- ✔ The chosen Deity is asked to protect and bless the child.
- ✔ The community is asked to protect and bless the child. Sometimes each witness to the rite gives a one-sentence blessing.
- ✔ The child may be shown pictures of the ancestors, and the ancestors may be asked to bless the child. The child may be introduced to the living relatives.
- ✔ All the guests enjoy wine (or juice) and cakes.

The rite ends, and the ceremony is often followed by a party with feasting and the opening of gifts for the child.

The Naming ceremony is to show love and support for the child and his or her family, and is usually a warm and happy occasion.

Marking puberty

Coming-of-age rites that mark puberty are not a universal practice in Wicca. As with the rest of society, not all Wiccan parents are completely comfortable with their children's advance into sexual maturity, and adolescents may be too shy or embarrassed to want this type of celebration.

The rite is becoming more common for girls. Some Wiccan women organize rites of passage for their daughters in an attempt to balance the negative cultural conditioning that young women receive about their bodies. For example, many young women are taught directly or indirectly that menstruation is a curse and a punishment for evil.

No set structure exists for these coming-of-age rites, but most have the following in common:

- For a girl, the rite usually occurs after she has her first menstrual cycle. For a boy, the time is less clearly defined, but is usually around the time his voice deepens and he begins to grow body hair.

- The rites aren't commonly viewed as a dedication or an initiation into Wicca. The age that children reach puberty generally is considered too young to make an informed life choice about religion.

- Guests are all of the same sex as the adolescent undergoing the rite.

- The young person knows about the rite ahead of time and understands the significance. Generally, he or she has the opportunity to participate in the planning.

- During the rite, the young woman or young man is welcomed into adulthood and presented to the Goddess and/or the God.

- Both pride and responsibility are stressed during the ceremony.

- Usually, individual attendees offer short bits of advice to the adolescent.

Sometimes the young person is asked to symbolically part with some item from childhood, and then he or she is given something to represent the entry into adulthood. For some Wiccan families, this ceremony is when the young adult gets his or her first ritual tools (see Chapter 11 for a description of these tools).

For these coming-of-age rites, a circle may be cast or not, depending on the location and preference (see Chapter 17 for information on circle casting). Feasting and gift-giving usually follow the ritual.

Coming-of-age rites are almost always fun, light-hearted events; they are less intense and structured than some other types of Wiccan rituals.

Handfasting: Love Wiccan style

Handfasting is the ritual joining of people in love into committed partnership before the Goddess and/or the God. Handfasting is not the exact equivalent of marriage, as Table 6-1 shows. Handfasting is a religious ceremony; it doesn't require a state-licensed official or a marriage license. Just like the people of other religions, a Wiccan may have a religious ceremony (a handfasting), may take steps to make the union legal (obtain and process a marriage license recognized by the state), or both.

Table 6-1	Traditional Marriage versus Wiccan Handfasting	
Legal Institution of Marriage (Requiring a Legal Marriage License)	*Marriage Ceremony*	*Handfasting*
A legal contract that can be dissolved	Lasts forever, until "death do us part"	Lasts for any pre-agreed length of time (traditionally a year and a day) or "until we part," which means by death or choice
Recognized by government	A ceremony that usually marks the processing of a legal marriage license; most people who have a marriage ceremony are also legally married.	With a few exceptions, not recognized by governments as a valid legal marriage; a person can be handfasted with or without obtaining a legal marriage license
Restricted to opposite-sex couples in most countries (at the time of this writing)	Varies by church, but generally restricted to opposite-sex couples	Generally unrestricted with ceremonies for opposite-sex or same-sex couples or for multiple partners

(continued)

Table 6-1 *(continued)*

Legal Institution of Marriage (Requiring a Legal Marriage License)	Marriage Ceremony	Handfasting
Can be ended only by legal divorce	Varies by church	Can be renewed or ended at the will of the parties involved
Publicly recorded document	Can be public or private	Can be public or private
Requires a state-licensed Minister, Justice of the Peace, or other official	Requires a duly ordained representative of the church	Can be performed by the participants themselves or presided over by a Wiccan Priestess and/or Priest

Handfastings are often elaborate rituals presided over by a Priestess and/or Priest, or other clergy. The form of the ritual varies widely, according to tradition and preferences. Generally, at some point in the ceremony, the couple is bound together with a wedding cord, and they jump a broom held by witnesses.

The vows or oaths should be mutually agreed upon before the ceremony, including the terms of the handfasting (the length of time, and so on).

A handfasting is a religious ceremony; it's also a magical bond between two people. Most Wiccans believe that, when the relationship ends, the partners should be magically unbound from one another, to cut the ties and provide closure. This usually involves binding with the wedding cord and then jumping the broom backward and in the opposite direction. The cord is then severed or untied. This ritual is called a *handparting*. If one partner is unwilling or unable to participate in the handparting, the other may conduct the ceremony alone or with a stand-in for the absent partner.

Aging with dignity: The wisdom of the Crone and Elder

One of the great tragedies of modern civilization is the way that we treat the old. In this culture, people are valued based on their productivity, that is, what they contribute to the system. The result is that children and the old are often devalued and disrespected. Wiccan values reach back to the ideals of an earlier time, when all people had inherent value, and the old were cherished and respected.

Wiccans perform Croning or Eldering rites to honor older members of the Craft who have gained wisdom, skill, and knowledge. To many in the Craft, an *Elder* is a man or a woman who has reached his or her late 50s or older. Many Wiccans consider retirement age to be the time for an Eldering ceremony. The term *Crone* usually applies to a woman who has reached menopause. Crone is a term of respect, not derision. It is also the term for the third aspect of the Goddess (Maiden, Mother, and Crone).

Croning or Eldering rituals are rare. The Wiccan revival wasn't fully underway until the 1950s, so the number of older people in the Craft is limited. As the Wiccan population ages, this ritual probably will become more commonplace.

Eldering and Croning are rites of celebration and recognition. The focus is not only on the past achievement, but also the future potential of the Elder or Crone.

Like coming-of-age rites, no set structure exists for this type of ritual. The celebration is geared to the individual. Usually a circle is cast, and a Priest, Priestess, or other member of the community escorts the Elder or Crone into the circle and presents him or her to the group of guests. The person's life and contributions are summarized. Often the Elder/Crone is given a gift symbolizing the occasion. Guests are invited to speak, and then the Elder/Crone addresses the group. Celebration and gift-giving often follow the ritual.

Dealing with death

All of life, everything in the cosmos, is made of one unbroken and unending circle of energy. Energy has no beginning and no end. It can be transformed but it cannot cease to exist. Reality is in perfect balance, a synchronous cycle of creation and destruction and re-creation, birth and death and rebirth. This pattern repeats throughout the natural world, from the tiniest of cells to the most massive of stars; everything is in an endless cycle of regeneration. Most Wiccans believe that the same principle holds true for human lives, and reincarnation is one of the most commonly held beliefs in Wicca.

Passing on to the beauty of the Summerland

Many Wiccans believe that when a person's physical body dies, the soul or the consciousness goes to a non-physical or non-ordinary reality, commonly called the Summerland or the Land of Eternal Youth, the Land of the Young, or the Shining Land.

Some Wiccans perceive the Summerland as a literal place of overwhelming natural beauty, unspoiled and pristine. Other Wiccans interpret it as the place where a person's essence or lifeforce re-joins with the energy of Deity.

Wiccans have differing views of what happens next.

Coming back: Ideas about reincarnation

Many Wiccans believe that the soul engages in a life review while resting in the Summerland. Most reject the idea of a punishment for sins committed in life. The review is to help the soul learn lessons and evolve.

After a time in the Summerland, the soul then has the opportunity to reincarnate. Some Wiccans believe that the soul has a choice about whether or not to return to physical life or to move on to some other plane of existence. Some believe that Deity may make the ultimate decision or play a role in determining a soul's next step.

After determining what type of experience will help the soul gain further wisdom and progress, the general conditions for the next life are arranged. The soul returns to a physical body, and life begins again. Each new lifetime is viewed as a gift and an opportunity from Deity, not a banishment into suffering and drudgery. Some Wiccans believe that the people of the Craft accompany each other during multiple lifetimes.

Some Wiccans believe that after sufficient lifetimes or *incarnations,* the soul will reach a state of perfection and return to the Divine Source.

Wiccans have varied ideas about the afterlife, and some are complex. Some philosophies take into account that time is not linear, and people may be living many lives at once. Some believe in *Oversouls* that branch off and manifest in many physical lives. Regardless of the nuances, most Wiccans do believe in reincarnation.

Wiccans see death as a new beginning. They grieve just like everyone else, but the sadness is from the pain of separation from the loved one. If a Wiccan was open about his or her spirituality, the rites and the funeral can be Wiccan, presided over by Wiccan clergy or a High Priestess or Priest. Wiccan memorial rites vary according to tradition, personal preference, and whether non-Wiccans are present. Generally, a circle is cast, and the deceased is remembered as in any respectful memorial service (see Chapter 17 for information on circle casting). Many Wiccans specify that they want to be cremated after death, but Wiccans may choose different burial options.

Ideally, the Wiccan has made arrangements for the disposal of his or her spiritual property, such as tools and the Book of Shadows. These personal items may be destroyed, buried with the Wiccan, or passed on to family or friends in the Craft. Fellow coveners or Craft friends should make sure that familiars and pets of the deceased receive a good home. (A *familiar* is an animal who has a psychic bond with a Wiccan.)

Chapter 7

Looking Back to the Future: The Rebirth of the Goddess

*T*he Goddess is re-emerging, and the Craft is growing and changing. Many Wiccans see this time in history as a new beginning. Humankind is on the brink of evolution.

But in this time of so much potential, some Wiccans are turning on each other. Witch Wars, name-calling, and the heavy hand of orthodoxy are plaguing Wicca. Are these the birth pangs of a new era of humankind? Or is Wicca simply following the same cycle of growth as other religions? This chapter explores the current and future trends of Wicca.

Coming Full Circle

Based on anthropological and archeological evidence, some Wiccans believe that humans began worshipping the Goddess around 10,000 BCE. Others believe that Goddess worship began around 8,000 BCE, and humans have been worshipping Her for 10,000 years. Wiccans differ on the measurement of these historical time periods, but "10,000 years of the Goddess" is a common expression in Wicca. Some Wiccans even add 10,000 years to the current year, to recognize that civilization has existed much longer than the 2,000+ years identified by the Christian calendar.

Many people believe that the old agricultural, Goddess-worshipping societies, which existed for thousands of years, were peaceful, egalitarian, and life-affirming. The dominance of God as Deity began around 5,000 years ago, and patriarchal, warrior cultures, which were based on the herding of animals instead of agriculture, replaced the older matrilineal civilizations. (*Matrilineal* means that kinship was established through the mother. At that time, people didn't realize the role of the father in reproduction.)

Scholars disagree about whether these old Goddess-centered civilizations ever existed, and this is an old and ongoing debate in Wicca. But here's the point of all this year counting: Some Wiccans firmly believe that humans are at the beginning of a new 5,000-year cycle. During this cycle, the Great Goddess will re-emerge throughout civilization. This re-awakening represents a big step in human evolution and a major change in human consciousness. Humankind will once again view Deity (Goddess *and* God) and the world as whole. This change in consciousness will evolve gradually and will result in a slow shift toward healing, renewal, and peace for Earth and her inhabitants.

This vision of the future shapes the present lives and spiritual practice of these Wiccans. However, throughout the world, cultural acceptance of the Goddess and Wiccan values appears to be a long way off, and even basic civil rights are not always honored.

Ending Discrimination and Persecution

Many groups are working to protect legal rights and ensure religious freedom for all Pagans, including Wiccans. Many are trying to end discrimination by improving public awareness and understanding of Wicca and other Earth religions. Some groups work at the international and national levels; others focus on local, grassroots issues.

All Wiccans need to know their basic civil rights in order to protect them. In the United States, these rights are based on the following:

✔ The First Amendment to the United States Constitution provides: "Congress shall pass no law respecting an establishment of religion, or prohibiting the free exercise thereof. . . ."

✔ The Fourteenth Amendment to the United States Constitution states: "No state shall . . . deny to any person within its jurisdiction the equal protection of the laws." The Fourteenth Amendment protects against discrimination by state and local governments on the basis of religious beliefs, sex, or ethnicity.

These amendments mean that the United States constitutionally guarantees freedom of religion. No religion has official support or preference from any governmental body or its agents. Discrimination on the grounds of religious preference is illegal.

The Civil Rights Act of 1964 states "To be a bona fide religious belief entitled to protection under either the First Amendment or Title VII, a belief must be sincerely held, and within the believer's own scheme of things religious." Title VII is a section of the Civil Rights Act of 1964, and it prohibits employment discrimination based on race, color, religion, sex, and national origin.

Several landmark court cases have declared that Wicca is clearly a religion, for First Amendment purposes. Wiccan and other Neo-Pagan groups have been recognized by governments in the United States and Canada and given tax-exempt status. United States Military Courts of Justice have also found Wicca to be a valid religion, deserving of protection under the First Amendment of the Constitution.

The information in this section does not constitute legal advice. For legal services, please see a licensed attorney who is knowledgeable about your local and national laws.

In the United States and many other places around the world, Wiccans, Witches, and other Pagans are fired from jobs, lose custody of their children, are discriminated against in housing, or are forced to make other painful sacrifices because of their religion. Many face persecution, threats, physical violence, and in some cases, death.

Wiccans have invested untold dollars, time, and other resources in order to win and protect their civil rights. Legal recourse is expensive, time-consuming, and often unsuccessful. However, Wiccan efforts in the courts have gone a long way to establish Wicca's legitimacy in American society.

Settling into the Big Comfy Couch of Legitimacy

Contemporary Wicca has been made up of individuals and loosely connected, very small groups (often called covens). Wicca has never had a central institution holding authority. Modern Wiccans usually have practiced alone or with their own independent covens, but they had little contact with the larger community. Wicca has a long tradition of secrecy and seclusion, in part because of concerns about persecution. Today, legal protection, public acceptance, and growth mean that the times they are a changin' for the Craft.

The following sections offer a summary of some of the current and future trends in Wicca.

Dr. Helen Berger and colleagues conducted a survey of Neo-Pagans in the United States. More than 2,000 people from several traditions, including Wicca, responded voluntarily. The book, *Voices from the Pagan Census: A National Survey of Witches and Neo-Pagans in the United States* (2003), provides the results of the survey and some data about the trends explored in the following sections, as well as the possible future direction of the Craft. Check out the book for the numbers from this small, but interesting survey.

Gaining acceptance

Wiccans are working hard to win and protect their civil rights, and in doing so they are confirming Wicca's legitimacy as a valid religion. In turn, the public's acceptance of Wicca as valid helps dispel negative stereotypes and discourages future discrimination and harassment.

With more secure legal rights and better public relations, some people in the Craft have been venturing out of the broom closet. This new openness allows dialogue among the Wiccan community as a whole. Wiccans are no longer limited to interaction with their own small covens. The Internet offers a means to communicate widely and instantaneously with the full Craft community, but still offers a measure of anonymity for those who want it. Wiccans have created a remarkable presence on the Web, and they are notorious for their use of technology for spiritual purposes.

Books by Wiccans are providing the public with a more realistic view of the Craft. Media — books, television, and movies — by non-Wiccans are portraying the Craft more favorably, although still not accurately, and increasing Wicca's popularity.

Some Wiccans could give a flying fig about public acceptance of the Craft. They would rather maintain the underground nature of Wicca and protect their beliefs, practices, and traditions from public scrutiny, from a bunch of untrained newcomers, and from outside pressure for change. In short, they'd rather be left alone.

Many other Wiccans welcome more mainstream acceptance. Wiccans don't try to convert others, but most would like to see their values, such as equality and environmentalism, spread through the culture. Wiccans can't have that impact if they are huddled in the broom closet.

With greater public acceptance, Wiccans may be less afraid of exposure of their religious affiliation in the workplace, at school, and with family and friends. They also may feel safer in their practice of Wicca. For example, they may be able to perform ritual outdoors with less fear of interruption and harassment from the public and authorities.

Most important, Wiccans don't want their children to suffer for their beliefs. Many Wiccans now instruct their kids to keep quiet about the family's religion. Increasing acceptance in the culture will make life easier for children.

Maturing Wiccans

The Wiccan revival began in the United States in the early 1960s and gained momentum in the 1970s. Many Wiccans are now mature adults, and those who were involved with the early movement are now aging. This evolution of the Craft introduces new issues for the community.

Unlike the early days of the Wiccan revival, today many Wiccans have children. They worry that their kids will suffer from taunting and threats in school and other areas hostile to Wicca. Wiccan parents often harbor deep fears that misguided authorities will try to take their kids away. Some Wiccans have lost custody of their children because local judges hold negative ideas and opinions of Wicca.

Wiccans are also dealing with the dilemma of how to raise these first generations of Craft kids. Should they raise their children in Wicca, teaching them age-appropriate practices? Or should they wait and let the kids decide — when they are old enough — whether they want to embrace the spirituality of their parents? Some parents want to impart the values of Wicca to their children while they are young. Others hold a strong belief in freedom of choice, and they don't introduce their offspring to Wicca until they are young adults.

As Wicca gains greater public acceptance, Wiccans face the issue of whether to establish Pagan or Wiccan schools for their children.

At the other end of the spectrum, Wiccans are aging, and the community needs to decide what role these elders should play in the Craft and how to care for them as they grow old. New rites and roles will likely evolve so that elders can continue to impart wisdom to the community, and Wiccans can treat elders with respect and allow them to age with the dignity they deserve.

Growing fast

Wicca is growing by leaps and bounds, according to surveys by several non-Wiccan groups, sales of Wiccan books, growth of Wiccan sites on the Internet, and other indications. This boom in Wicca is a double-edged sword for the community.

On the one hand, Wiccans often welcome the opportunity to offer their values — such as respect for and preservation of nature — to the larger society. On the other hand, some Wiccans don't want to see the Craft's beliefs and practices changed or watered down by newcomers who have not received competent training and solid information or may not have any interest at all in spiritual growth. Not enough Wiccan leaders are available to train an influx of people into the Craft. Wiccans are afraid that new people who are unfamiliar with practices and ethics will damage the image of Wicca or even hurt or exploit others.

With the growing popularity of the Craft, leaders are needed who can make a considerable investment of time and effort in training others. Many Wiccans believe that Wicca will never be accepted as fully legitimate until it has sufficient numbers of paid, ordained clergy. This is one of the biggest controversies in modern Wicca. Many traditions prohibit leaders from accepting money for the training and initiation of new Wiccans, and many people still object to this practice.

Currently, there are some legally recognized, full-time Wiccan clergy in the United States. They primarily conduct services, such as funerals or handfastings (the Wiccan version of a marriage ceremony) and they do impart knowledge to the community, but they don't interpret and enforce religious dogma like the clergy of other religions. (Most Wiccan clergy hold down other full-time jobs and have not sought out legal recognition for their religious status.)

Building community and reaching out to other faiths

Whether or not to support paid clergy is a big issue in contemporary Wicca. Wiccans generally have been unable or unwilling to maintain paid clergy or to build permanent buildings (churches) for worship and practice. Part of the reason is that, as a community, Wiccans just don't have the money. The other reason is that many Wiccans reject the notion of a hierarchy of clergy. Wiccans believe that they each have direct access to Deity. They all serve as Priestess or Priest, and they don't need anyone intervening for them. Wiccans like their independence.

Unlike other religions, Wicca doesn't show any sign of organizing into stable congregations and churches with hierarchical leadership. An exception is the Covenant of the Unitarian Universalist Pagans (CUUPs). These are groups of Pagans within the Unitarian Universalist Church. Whether these groups will continue to be a part of the UU Churches or will eventually split off and form their own Pagan branches of the UU Church remains to be seen.

Instead of settling down into formal denominations and churches, Wiccans tend to form umbrella organizations that sponsor festivals, produce newsletters, provide information, engage in legal advocacy, and offer credentials to ordained clergy. The Covenant of the Goddess is an old example of such a group. These organizations don't serve as central authorities, and they don't enforce rules or dogma for Wicca. They do give Wiccans a way to unite with others.

Umbrella organizations also allow Wiccans to reach out to other faiths and build coalitions for charity work, political advocacy, or other common goals.

Infighting in the Witch Wars

Wicca is in transition. It's gaining legitimacy in the eyes of the public. More Wiccans are venturing out of the broom closet and reaching out to one another. By all indications, Wicca is growing wildly. Wiccans are living in a time of growth and celebration, of dialogue and exchange. The Goddess is re-emerging, and the world is bright and rosy for the people of the Craft.

Well, not quite.

If you spend more than 10 minutes online visiting Wiccan or Pagan Web sites, you'll see references to the *Witch Wars*. The term is a little scary and encourages stereotypical images of Witches hurling curses and lightning bolts at one another — or Witches lined up on the field of battle, wearing medieval garb and wielding long, decorated swords. This is not the case. The current Witch Wars are wars of words, but they do get pretty ugly.

What are the Witch Wars?

In general, a *Witch War* is a verbal, and often an Internet, battle between two or more people who call themselves Wiccans or Witches.

Witch Wars usually begin small, between individuals or small groups. The dispute spreads by way of gossip through the community (this gossip is sometimes called *bitchcraft* or *bicca*). When the conflict reaches the media (most often the Internet) and involves others in the community, it gains momentum. Wiccans often are strong-minded people who think critically about issues. As a conflict gains public attention, others add their opinions to the fray, which draws more attention and greater media involvement, which sucks others into the argument, and so on, until the result is a full-blown Witch War.

Witch Wars begin in several ways, including the following scenarios:

✔ **One person or group questions the legitimacy of another person's or group's beliefs, practices, training, or motivations.**

These arguments usually begin with words such as, "You aren't a *real* Wiccan because. . . ." (See the following section for more on derogatory terms, such as *fluffbunny* and *whitelighter*.)

✔ **A person or group has a bad experience with another person or group.**

Many Witch Wars start with bad experiences in covens. In some cases, the reason is simply coven politics: arguments over belief and practice, struggles for power, and breakdowns of communication (the same problems that occur in other groups in society). Occasionally, the charge is more serious. One person accuses another (or the group) of violating Wiccan ethics, for example, accusing a member of sexual misconduct.

Whatever the issue, the concern gets vented in public, usually on the Internet, and people take sides. Participants exchange verbal fire until the controversy is resolved or burns out, one of the participants leaves the field, or cooler heads prevail.

One of the significant factors contributing to the environment that creates Witch Wars is that so few covens exist. Many people are so desperate to find a coven that they end up among people with whom they aren't compatible. People are thrown together who may have very different views about important issues, such as leadership, ritual nudity, and so on. From this mix comes a disagreement that becomes public and then spreads until another Witch War is in full swing.

✔ **A leader's integrity is perceived to be compromised.**

People view a particular leader to be in the Craft for his or her ego rather than spiritual reasons, for example, to wield power over others, to enjoy the adulation of followers, to get publicity, or to make money. The leader's followers defend him or her; others publicly attack; war begins.

✔ **Wiccans argue over money.**

Commonly, these disputes are about:

• The quality or legitimacy of goods, services, training, or causes is in question. For example, are the owners of the local Pagan bookstore supporting the community or exploiting it? (The vast majority are invaluable resources to the community, but some aren't.) Should a local coven charge people for Wiccan training? Should Wiccans claim that they can heal, and charge for this service?

- Rival Wiccan or Pagan organizations compete for donations. There are many beneficial organizations and not enough Pagan dollars to support them. (Before you donate, evaluate any Wiccan or other Pagan organization just as you would any other group. Request a financial statement and ask plenty of questions. Most are happy to accommodate your inquiries.)

- Wiccans disagree about an organization's agenda. For example, they may argue about whether or not to spend the community's money to take a local case of discrimination to court.

✔ **Wiccans are in conflict about what is and is not ethical behavior.**

This category encompasses a wide variety of issues. For example, when, if ever, should Wiccans use magic for protection or defense? Should a Wiccan make claims about his or her ability to heal? When, if ever, is attempting to heal someone without his or her knowledge and consent appropriate? Should Wiccans charge money for healing? Should Wiccans charge money to teach the Craft? What kind of magic is acceptable?

The Internet appears to be changing the way that Wiccans and other Pagans interact with one another. Communication on the Internet, in e-mail, chat rooms, newsgroups, Web sites, and so on, often is anonymous. People feel freer to vent their feelings directly, impulsively, and with less tact than they would use during an in-person encounter. Unfortunately for the Wiccan community, name-calling and conflict have become rampant on the Web.

Who are fluffbunnies and whitelighters?

Name-calling appears to have been raised to an art form on the Web. Names — such as fluffbunny, whitelighter, and playgan — are used with varying degrees of intensity, from light-hearted fun to deep hostility. The meanings of the terms depend on who uses them and in what context.

People new to the Craft go online and expect to find Wiccans who respect all beings and live by the Wiccan Rede "An' it harm none, do what ye will" (Doreen Valiente, *Pentagram,* Volume One, 1964, published by Gerard Noel). Instead, sometimes they find Wiccans demanding conformity and spitting venom at one another. I include this section, not to encourage or condone the use of these words, but so that newcomers aren't blindsided by this behavior and so they understand the various terms that are being bandied about.

Fluff and light

Fluffbunny and *whitelighter* are the most common terms that you may see on Wiccan Web sites and in publications.

Originally, these derogatory terms were used by Wiccans and other Pagans about the New Age community. New Agers sometimes were viewed as holding beliefs of little substance, and as being unrealistic, superficial, frivolous, and, in some cases, materialistic. The paths of the New Agers, Wiccans, and other Pagans often crossed, and some Wiccans and other Pagans rushed to separate themselves from what they viewed as New Age fad. That's when the name-calling began. The terms gradually evolved and were more often directed at Wiccans whom others in the community felt were being New Age in their beliefs or practices.

A *fluffbunny* or *fluffybunny* is someone who is exploring or embracing Wicca for the wrong reasons or in the wrong ways, according to his or her critics. The term generally refers to people who don't know or investigate the history, beliefs, or process that underlie the practice of Wicca. For some, Wicca is a fad, for others it's a form of rebellion against society, the government, parents, or a mainstream church. Some are attracted to the tools, clothes, jewelry, spells, public image, or media hype, but have little interest in spiritual growth. Some focus on specific myths or assumptions about Wicca, and hold simplistic or biased views about Wicca and its history. Some are blindly devoted to one author or leader, but never study and investigate further to get a deeper or broader perspective on the Craft. Some learned their Craft by watching popular television shows, such as *Charmed, Sabrina the Teenage Witch,* or *Buffy the Vampire Slayer.* All these folks are full of fluff, according to their detractors. (*Playgan*, rhymes with Pagan, is another term used for individuals who don't seem to take their Craft seriously.)

A w*hitelighter,* a term sometimes used interchangeably with fluffbunny, is someone for whom visualizing white light (thus the term, whitelighter) and sending out nice energy are sufficient for the practice of Wicca and the improvement of the world. Whitelighters don't want to take responsibility for accomplishing specific acts in the Craft, often because they don't want to risk doing any harm. They don't delve into how the Craft works. They focus on positive and blissful ritual, and largely ignore serious issues in the world. This term describes feel-good, happy Wicca blended with New Age philosophy and practiced by people who don't have clue, according to the critics who use this term.

The definitions of these terms vary, depending on the critic and the context, but they are rarely used as a positive or encouraging comment. (However, the negative meaning of whitelighter may be changing because of the popularity of the television show, *Charmed.* On that program, a whitelighter is a spiritual protector or guardian, and that definition is working its way into general use.)

Sticks and stones

The preceding are basic explanations for these disparaging words. However, their use has become much more widespread and isn't limited to those explanations. Wiccans often lash out with these words in the following scenarios:

✔ **More experienced members of the Craft judge the sincerity or integrity of new Wiccans or people exploring Wicca.**

Some Wiccans and other Pagans call every newcomer a fluffbunny. (A slightly nicer term for someone new to Wicca or Paganism is *newbie;* the more polite and respectful term is *seeker.*)

This division in the Craft is often fueled by the generation gap. Older Wiccans sometimes charge that the younger ones just don't know what times were like when Wicca was dangerous, secretive, and difficult to access. The older generation built modern Wicca in a world that was hostile to them, and some are fearful that the newer generation will make changes in the traditions that they worked so hard and risked so much to establish. Some don't believe that young Wiccans appreciate the seriousness of the path.

✔ **Members of covens (organized small groups) judge solitaries (Wiccans who practice alone).**

Many traditions (sects or denominations) of Wicca don't recognize as legitimate people who practice Wicca without joining a coven and being initiated into a formal tradition.

✔ **Members of traditions judge eclectics.**

Eclectic Wiccans don't follow one tradition, they build their own individual traditions, borrowing beliefs and practices from many different sources to meet their own needs. People in some formal traditions don't acknowledge eclectics as true Wiccans.

✔ **One tradition judges the beliefs or practices of another tradition.**

Some Pagans believe that *all* Wiccans are whitelighters. They think that Wiccan ethics and practices render Wiccans less than effective, and that Wiccans don't deal realistically with the realities of the world. They think that Wiccans can't cope with negative, destructive, or evil forces.

Some Pagans also call into the question the controversial claims of the man credited with founding modern Wicca, Gerald Gardner (see Chapter 5 for more information).

✔ **Members of the community judge the integrity, accuracy, or motivation of a Wiccan leader or author.**

Many authors have been labeled as fluffbunnies, as are the people who remain loyal to their books and their ideas. In some communities, one leader may become a figurehead. Others may object to the power that this person wields in the community as a result of media attention as well as large numbers of wide-eyed and devoted followers.

Who let the dogmas out?!?

Wicca has no dogma, encourages everybody to act according to his or her own free will, and discourages causing harm to others. It seems contradictory that some members of a group that supposedly hold these beliefs are waging verbal wars and engaging in name-calling. The explanation is in the timing.

This is a pivotal time for the Wiccan community. Public acceptance offers Wiccans greater protection from discrimination and persecution. Greater security allows for much more dialogue among the Wiccan community.

In this time of increasing openness, Wiccans are turning their attentions from themselves or their own groups to defining what they are, and what they are not, as a community. Wicca is growing rapidly, and decisions made now affect and direct the future of the entire Craft. Many Wiccans have strong ideas about what Wicca should look like, and what is and isn't valid. In this critical time, voices are growing shrill, and orthodoxy is rearing its ugly head.

People who have invested time and effort in Wicca want to protect the integrity of the practices and traditions that they have established. But with all the new people and ideas, Wicca is bound to evolve as it grows. Some people will resist change, others will demand it.

Ideally, the dialogue can be respectful, and the Craft can preserve its traditions of independence, self-direction, and autonomy. Name-calling and full-blown Witch Wars harm both individuals and the community. This behavior violates the Wiccan Rede, "An' it harm none, do what ye will.", the guiding ethic that most Wiccans follow. Infighting harms the Wiccan community by:

- ✔ Driving people away from Wicca. Wiccans don't proselytize, but most Wiccans would like to promote their values. Negative behavior and bad public relations make that goal less possible.

- ✔ Distracting Wiccans from the more constructive and positive work that they need to do for themselves and for the Wiccan community.

- ✔ Slowing Wicca's emergence as a spirituality that society recognizes as legitimate. Witch Wars and name-calling reinforce society's stereotypes of Wiccans as potentially dangerous people with no morals and ethics.

If such internal conflicts continue, efforts to gain acceptance for Wicca in the courts, the workplace, and other institutions will take longer. It also means that the children of Wicca are more likely to grow up facing persecution, discrimination, and public hostility rather than gradual acceptance.

The Wiccan community can, and does, work together to further shared goals. Most Wiccans welcome new practitioners and are more than willing to listen to others and discuss their own beliefs in a non-confrontational manner. The key for Wiccans is to channel the passion into furthering the Craft, not into defending individual positions or attacking those of others.

Part III
Coming Home: How Wiccans Become Wiccans

"There are a lot of spells in the Craft, but they don't all work. Believe me, if they did, there wouldn't be any bald witches."

In this part . . .

The first two parts of this book center on Wiccan beliefs and culture. However, this part — and the remainder of the book — focuses on the personal, spiritual journey of Wiccans. This is the how-to portion of the book. For those people who are moving toward deeper involvement in Wicca or toward affirming Wicca as their own spiritual path, this part gives you some insight into your options. If you are already Wiccan, this section may help you decide where to go from here.

This part of the book has a more personal tone, so I want to be very clear about one issue: Wiccans don't try to convert others to their religion. So please don't feel pressured to explore Wicca further, to participate in any Wiccan activities, or to make any kind of personal commitment to Wicca. If you are reading this book only to get some reliable information about Wicca and Witchcraft, that's great as well!

Chapter 8

Considering the Wiccan Path

Some Wiccans know intuitively that Wicca is right for them. From the beginning, they never question their choice of spiritual path. Others have a more analytical nature, and they think through their spiritual decisions. Prudence and skepticism are very welcome in Wicca. Wicca encourages self-direction and the questioning of authority.

This chapter describes the ways that people come to Wicca and offers some hints for a wise approach to this spiritual path.

Looking Inward

Many people are reading this book only because they want information about Wicca and Witchcraft. If that's true for you, this section does not personally apply. However, *if* you intend to pursue a deeper exploration of Wicca or you're moving toward making a commitment, make sure that you aren't drawn to Wicca for reasons that are unrelated to religion. The Wiccan path will not be rewarding or transforming if it is followed for reasons other than spiritual ones. If you answer yes to any of the following questions, take some time to reconsider your interest in Wicca:

1. **Is someone pressuring you to get involved in Wicca?**

   Wiccans encourage independence, free will, and personal strength. They don't try to convert others. If someone is trying to coerce you into taking part in Wiccan activities or study, that person is not a true Wiccan, and I recommend that you free yourself of this manipulation.

2. Are you angry at your past religion, and you think that Wicca is the "opposite" of your former faith?

Many injustices have been done in the name of or under the guise of religion. Understandably, some people feel betrayed by religious institutions. However, you will be more effective if you choose a religion for positive reasons (because you are comfortable with the religion's principles, beliefs, and practices).

You are not expected to repudiate or denounce your former religion if you make a personal commitment to Wicca.

3. Are you drawn to Wicca because you perceive it to be counter-cultural, underground, or subversive?

The truth is that Wicca can be considered worthy of all these labels (and I personally celebrate that fact). However, Wicca is first and foremost a spirituality, not merely a way to rebel against your family, the government, or mainstream society.

4. Do you feel lonely and think that Wicca, especially a coven, can serve as a family and fulfill your needs for companionship?

Many coveners do develop strong, close-knit bonds with one another. However, a reverence for Deity and a love of nature, not a desire to meet emotional needs, are the basis for a sound commitment to Wicca.

By the way, Wiccans do not cut their ties to family and friends when they dedicate themselves to Wicca. They continue to nurture their personal relationships with people outside of Wicca.

5. Are you really just looking for sex?

The idea that Wiccans and Witches engage in orgies as part of their rites is pervasive. However, this stereotype just isn't true; sexual activity is definitely not a part of typical Wiccan practice.

6. Are you attracted only to the image or the more dramatic aspects of Wicca, for example, the jewelry, robes, tools, or elaborate rituals?

The practice of Wicca *is* beautiful, but the basis for Wiccan activities is to honor the Deity and celebrate the natural world.

7. Do you think that Wicca can give you some secret power or information that can solve your problems, such as getting you out of debt, breaking an addiction, or healing your relationship with your partner?

Of course, most people realize that it's not possible to point a finger or wiggle a nose to immediately clean the house, attract a mate, or zap enemies. But some people do have the idea that Wicca can impart a secret power or reveal some unearthly ancient knowledge.

It is true that Wicca is a spirituality of profound wisdom; its roots are in the Old Religion, which reaches back thousands of years. Wicca can give you tools for transforming your life (for example, information about healing or rituals for growth and empowerment).

It is also true that the practice of magic directs energy, which could enable you to make changes in yourself and the world. But no one in Wicca can bestow upon you a word, charm, or spell that suddenly puts an end to all your troubles and challenges. I've always wished that I was able to wiggle my nose like Samantha Stevens and pay all my bills, but unfortunately, Witchcraft just doesn't work that way.

8. Speaking of TV Witches, are you buying into the media hype?

From Samantha to Sabrina to the sisters on *Charmed,* Witches have always been popular on TV, but be assured that real-life Wicca isn't anything like TV Witchland.

Although this section brings to light some nonreligious reasons that people may be attracted to Wicca and Witchcraft, the next section addresses some of the spiritual issues that people grapple with as they consider whether Wicca is right for them.

Asking the Big Questions

How do people choose their religions? Some are born into a faith and never question their devotion to their childhood religion. Some claim to know intuitively when they happen upon the religion or spirituality that is best for them. Others engage in a quest to find the ideal religious or spiritual path. They search their own core values and principles and then compare them to the teachings of different religions. The following are typical questions that people may ask themselves when they are trying to define their religious beliefs:

- How do I want to live? What is my purpose? What is most important to me?

- What kind of interpersonal relationships do I want to have?

- How do I want to raise my children? How do I want to treat my parents?

- How do I want to express my sexuality?

- How important is money in my life? What am I willing to do to get it?

- What happens to me when I die? How do I prepare for death? Am I afraid to die?

✔ How do I feel about the world? Do I want to live fully in it? Transform it? Escape it? Transcend it?

✔ How do I value other people? What are all people entitled to?

✔ How should people treat the Earth?

✔ What is morality? What is evil? Does evil exist?

✔ Do I believe in a holy book or other doctrine?

✔ Who or what do I turn to when I am suffering?

✔ Do I believe in Deity? How do I conceive of Deity?

Many religions spell out the answers to these questions in detail. They have at least one holy book that addresses these issues. They also have churches or other institutions with leaders who interpret doctrine and counsel people about how to live.

Ideally, a person's core values, principles, and beliefs are in harmony with the teachings of his or her chosen religion, meaning that he or she agrees with the religion's leaders and doctrine.

Wicca doesn't have a doctrine or holy book that Wiccans must follow, nor does it have leaders who require that people live a certain way. However, Wicca is a spiritual path with some core principles and goals that most Wiccans hold in common. When Wiccans answer these big life questions, their answers reflect the core principles of Wicca. Wiccans choose this spiritual path because they share the basic Wiccan ideas about life, the world, and Deity.

Wiccan principles

A Wiccan can reject one or more of the principles that most Wiccans hold in common. No authority decides who is and is not a legitimate Wiccan. However, it's very unlikely that someone can be happy or effective in Wicca if he or she rejects the majority of the following core principles. (See Part I for more information on Wiccan beliefs.)

Immanent Deity

Almost all Wiccans believe in a Creative Being. Wiccans can have radically different perceptions of Deity (see Chapter 4). Many, but not all, Wiccans define Deity in both the male and female aspects, that is the Goddess and the God. The concept of immanence is central to Wicca. *Immanence* means that Deity is right here, right now, and is all-present in the world, instead of transcendent (over or outside of the world). People come from and are a part of the Divine energy, and Deity is within everyone. A Wiccan's key spiritual intent is to grow in his or her relationship with Divinity.

Interconnection

Wiccans believe that everything is interconnected. All of existence is an unbroken circle of energy, and everything is merged into one living organism. Human beings are not separate from the web of nature, but are a part of it. Everything that exists is linked together, and any action, no matter how small or insignificant, affects everything else. Nature is a manifestation of Deity, and people have an obligation to respect, protect, and preserve the natural world.

Love for community

For Wiccans, the word "community" encompasses all the natural world, including all people. Wiccans feel a personal responsibility to respect and serve community because it is a manifestation of Deity. Doing harm, even by neglect or apathy, violates Wiccan ethics. Respecting and serving community means working to end any condition that causes harm, including poverty and injustice. Wealth should not be valued over people, the Earth, and its inhabitants. Sexuality is a manifestation of and a gift from Divinity, thus is should be celebrated, engaged in wisely, and never used to cause harm.

Because Deity is within everyone, all people are equal, and they should not be valued differently based on race, ethnicity, sex/gender, sexual orientation, class, education, or beliefs. Wiccans are not perfect, and prejudice exists in Wicca, as in every other segment of society, but prejudice violates Wiccan principles and ethics, as does any type of violence or abuse.

Life and afterlife

Wiccans believe that everything that exists is an unbroken circle of energy. Energy has no beginning and no end. Life is a cycle of birth, death, and rebirth. Based on this conception, most Wiccans believe in some form of reincarnation, although the details vary. Many believe that, upon death, the soul or the consciousness goes to the Summerland, a place of peace and natural beauty that is located in non-physical, non-ordinary reality. The soul or consciousness may rest in Summerland, review the life that has just passed, and decide whether to reincarnate or explore other possibilities.

Almost all Wiccans agree that life flows from the Deity, so life is not to be simply endured or, worse, suffered. The Wiccan intent is to honor Divinity by living life to its fullest potential — not to transcend life, but to revel in it.

Wiccan ethics

Wicca doesn't force people to abide by laws and commandments. But the Threefold Law and the Wiccan Rede are widely accepted in Wicca. They are guidelines by which each Wiccan builds his or her personal code of ethics. Wiccans quibble among themselves about the nuances, however, if someone objects in general to the ethical standards in this section, he or she probably would not be comfortable in Wicca. (See Part I for more details about Wiccan ethics.)

The Wiccan Rede

The Wiccan Rede declares, "An' it harm none, do what ye will" (Doreen Valiente, *Pentagram,* Volume One, 1964, published by Gerard Noel). This is the cornerstone of Wiccan ethics. The idea is to live and let live, but do no harm (to other people, the Earth and its inhabitants, or yourself). Wiccans generally take the Rede to mean that they should consider the consequences of their actions, and act in a way that causes the least harm.

The Threefold Law

Whatever a person sends out comes back threefold. In general, the law means that if you say or do something negative, that negative energy will return to you with three times the intensity. Some Wiccans believe that this law applies to words and actions, but others include thoughts.

Self-direction and personal responsibility

Wicca is a spirituality, not a religion. It is based on experience, not doctrine. No holy book or leader tells people what to do and when, or provides forgiveness for sin. Wiccans decide on an individual basis how to live, how to worship, and how to practice Wicca. Many people find this lack of structure liberating; others may feel insecure and directionless.

Protection of privacy and prohibition on proselytizing (say that five times fast!)

Privacy and confidentiality are important in Wicca. The individual decides whether to be open about his or her spirituality and if and when to disclose such information. No one may expose the identity of another Wiccan. To do so could jeopardize the person's friendships, career, child custody, and so on.

Wiccans do not proselytize (meaning that they don't try to convert others to the religion). They feel that proselytizing is unnecessary; people who are drawn to Wicca seek out and find others of like mind.

Knowing for Sure

How does someone know for sure whether he or she is really Wiccan? If you ask Wiccans this question, you may get responses like these:

"I just *know.*"

"I felt like I was coming home."

"I feel the presence of the Goddess."

"I received a sign from nature."

These are all honest responses, but they aren't very helpful to someone who is evaluating Wicca from the outside.

Wicca is difficult to get a handle on because it is based on personal experience. Wicca is a spirituality of exploration and discovery, rather than church services and doctrine. Wiccans *discover* their personal connection to Deity. They feel the presence of or they communicate with the Goddess and/or the God. They begin to feel a deep kinship with the universe. They may start to pay attention to and find meaning in synchronicities (coincidental events that appear to be related) occurring in their lives. Their perceptions change, and they become aware of nature's cycles and patterns. They often find themselves gaining wisdom from the natural world, including animals.

Here's an example of a lesson from nature. I was once in a challenging career situation. I felt that I had to act quickly, but none of my options seemed good. One day, I was overwhelmed with uncertainty. I looked outside, and a great blue heron landed on the small lake outside of my window. The bird stared up at my open window for several moments, looking at me without agitation. Then she stepped gingerly into the water and began watching for fish. She calmly kept her eyes on the water, with unwavering concentration and eminent patience for more than 30 minutes. Suddenly, with great precision, she lunged into the water and caught a fish. She watched me as she ate it. When she departed, she flew gracefully toward me and once again made eye contact.

I felt that I had been given a valuable lesson in patience and wise action. I took my cue from the heron, and I was just as patient, focused, and precise in narrowing down my own options and waiting for the right moment to act. The results were far better than I had dared to hope.

Most non-Wiccans would say that the heron's visit was merely a coincidence, or that I had read way too much into a chance encounter. Wiccans generally don't believe in coincidence. They live their lives open to communication from Deity and in tune with nature. Feeling the presence of Divinity and the bond with the natural world affirms their choice of Wicca as their spiritual path.

Taking the First Step

If you feel drawn to Wicca, most Wiccans would recommend that you don't rush headlong into it. Your spiritual journey will be much more fulfilling and transforming if you take some time and work out your feelings and beliefs. Start slowly. Begin by deciding how you conceive of Deity. Do you believe in the Goddess and the God? Begin praying regularly and nurture the Divine relationship.

Don't get caught up in trying to work magic right away. You may not get the desired outcome if you don't build a foundation of understanding first. Read some credible books about Wicca. The following are good, classic books that have helped many Wiccans on their spiritual journeys:

- *The Spiral Dance: A Rebirth of the Ancient Religion of the Great Goddess* by Starhawk (1979, 2nd revised edition 1989, 3rd revised edition 1999)

- *Drawing Down the Moon: Witches, Druids, Goddess Worshippers, and Other Pagans in America Today* by Margot Adler (1979, revised and expanded 1986, updated 1997)

- *Wicca: A Guide for the Solitary Practitioner* by Scott Cunningham (1988)

- *Living Wicca: A Further Guide for the Solitary Practitioner* by Scott Cunningham (1993)

After you have prayed and studied, try performing some simple rituals (see Chapter 12 for more information about rituals).

Begin keeping track of the phases of the Moon. Celebrate the Wiccan holy days (see Chapter 14). Pay attention to natural phenomena, such as solar and lunar eclipses. Spend some time in nature and let yourself be fully present and open. Put mundane worries about career or family aside for a time, and focus on your surroundings. Feel the interconnection of all living things and the presence of the Goddess and the God. That is the best possible introduction to Wicca.

Chapter 9

Going Solo or Joining a Coven: Wiccan Options

A Wiccan has the option of practicing Wicca alone or with a group, called a coven. Experiencing both ways of life is best, because a person can find out how he or she is happiest and most effective. People new to Wicca don't have to make a decision about coven membership as soon as they decide that they want to seriously explore the Wiccan path. Anyone is free to practice alone indefinitely, or to join a coven at any time.

Wiccans don't need to sacrifice their individual religious experience if they do join a coven. Coven members may continue to have rich and productive spiritual lives on their own, independent of their coven mates.

Understand, though, that joining a coven is a serious commitment. Wiccans generally make this decision with the same thoughtfulness that they devote to other major life decisions. Many Wiccans believe that the deep bond among coveners continues even after death. And that's a *long, long* time.

Exploring the Choices

A *solitary* or *solitaire* is someone who declares himself or herself to be Wiccan and practices Wicca alone, without belonging to a coven. Many Wiccans are solitaries because they want to practice alone for good and valid reasons. Others are solitaries because no compatible coven is accessible, or they haven't found one yet.

A *coven* (rhymes with *oven*) is a group of Wiccans who gather together to study, perform ritual, work magic, or accomplish other goals related to their spirituality. A coven is usually small; 13 members are considered ideal, and three is the minimum. What the coven does depends on the desires and needs of the members.

Here are some common activities of Wiccan covens:

- ✔ Establish a structure for group activities.
- ✔ Choose a High Priestess and sometimes a High Priest for leadership and/or direction.
- ✔ Engage in rituals and work magic.
- ✔ Celebrate the Wiccan holy days.
- ✔ Exchange knowledge and provide training to members and/or the community.
- ✔ Encourage each other in personal transformation and provide each other with emotional support.

Sometimes coven activity goes beyond the religious — for example, the members may engage in political activism, create art, or specialize in healing — but these outside interests are not a requirement for covens.

Covens are autonomous; they operate independently, but they may elect to follow the structured rituals and practices of a *tradition* (a Wiccan sect or denomination). Sometimes covens band together to form a Wiccan church or confederation, but when they do, they don't sacrifice their independence. Incorporation as a church allows Wiccans to have clergy recognized by government bodies, and to more effectively fight for legal rights and protection.

The members of a coven may be mixed-sex or same-sex. Covens universally require that the members be adults. Covens generally meet on the nights of the full moon; some also meet during the new moon. Coveners also come together for the Sabbats, the Wiccan holy days (see Chapter 13). The place where a coven meets is called a *covenstead,* but not all covens have a regular covenstead.

Some larger covens have a *covenant,* a written contract that states the rules of the coven and governs the membership, but covens generally are small, close-knit groups that operate by informal communication, rather than reliance on a written document.

Most Wiccan covens have some form of leadership, often called a High Priestess (the female leader of a coven) and/or a High Priest (the male leader of a coven). The leaders coordinate group activities but do not enjoy absolute power. They usually hold their positions by the consensus of the group; most groups democratically elect leaders. Many covens today rotate leadership, so each person has the opportunity to develop leadership abilities. In some covens, the term of office is set (often it is a year and a day).

Some covens have *hived* or spun off daughter covens. In those cases, the High Priestess of the original coven is sometimes called the *Queen;* however, some Wiccans strongly object to the term.

In covens, the goal is to interact with love and with mutual trust. People perform ritual together. They work magic together. They share secrets. They make themselves open and vulnerable. The result can be a bond of almost overwhelming joy and power. Or not. The quality of coven experience depends on the wisdom, devotion, and intention of those involved. The quality of solitary experience depends on the same things.

Getting real

Some Wiccans maintain that you can't be a "real" Wiccan unless you belong to a coven. In the early days of the Wiccan revival, the goal was to join a coven, partly because covens were the only sources of education and training. Today, solitary Wicca is more accepted, and more people are practicing Wicca as solitaries than as coveners. But you may still run into some bias in favor of coven membership.

Many people assume that from ancient times up to the modern age, the Craft has been practiced primarily within covens. Some Wiccans believe that coven membership is better than solitary practice because covens are a re-creation or a revival of the Old Ways. However, the assumption that the Craft was mainly a group practice may not reflect the reality of early times.

Of course, the early Pagans came together for spiritual rites and festivals. If you could look back through history, you would undoubtedly see stirring images of followers of the Old Religion gathering around bonfires or under the full moons. However, in the past, people who made their living from farming often lived far from one another. Even in areas where people of the Craft were scattered around towns or villages, in proximity by today's standards, travel was slow by foot or horse. Early Pagans certainly couldn't communicate with one another by phone or the Internet; few could write. In addition, during most of human history, the common people have led brutally hard lives, laboring from sun up to sun down in order to survive. Pagans would not have had the leisure time or the means to assemble with great frequency for religious activities, even in small groups. So logic suggests that the spiritual life of the early Pagan was mostly solitary, simple, and self-directed.

The ancestors probably performed acts of worship, ritual, and magic as they worked in the fields and gathered berries in the forest, as they ladled soup from the hearth and dropped nets from boats on the ocean. In private moments, they called upon the Goddess and the God, The All and The One, for healing for sick parents and for blessings on cherished children, for good weather and for bountiful harvests, for strong backs and for calm seas. They thanked the Deity for their triumphs and reached out in their suffering.

In the hardship and the joys of their everyday lives, the early people of the Craft nurtured their connections to the Deity. And that is what all *real* Wiccans do — coveners and solitaries alike — even today.

Staying focused

The decision to join a coven or not isn't just a matter of how a person wants to practice Wicca. The choice also depends on what kind of Wiccan he or she wants to be. Covens often follow a particular tradition (an organized sub-group, like a denomination) of Wicca (see Chapter 10 for details about the traditions). Some traditions require coven membership; others recognize solitaries as well as coveners.

You can find information about solitary Wicca in the next section. For information on coven membership, see the section "Considering Coven Membership," later in this chapter.

The focus of Wicca is to grow in relationship with the Goddess and/or the God. If you decide to pursue Wicca as your spiritual path, practice in whatever way helps you fulfill that purpose. Whether you are a covener or a solitary, you study, train, worship, and pray. You embrace nature, advance your knowledge, and hone your skills. No one can do that work for you.

Sizing Up Solitary Life

Wicca is a religion of free will. If you decide to embrace Wicca, you can join a coven, or you are free to be a solitary (someone who declares herself or himself to be Wiccan and practices Wicca alone, without belonging to a coven).

You can practice alone for a period of time, and when you feel you are ready, you can choose to work with a partner or an informal group, or you can join or start a coven. Or you may decide that you are happiest and most effective as a solitary, and decide to stay that way. The following sections offer some insight into solitary Wicca.

Weighing the pros and cons

As with most life choices, being a solitary has its ups and downs. The following are some of the advantages of being a solitary Wiccan:

✔ You can worship the way that you want to. You can design your rituals to meet your own individual needs. Coven rituals are sometimes elaborate, but as a solitary, you can decide to make your rituals short and simple, if that's your preference. You can select the tools or other objects that you want to use. You also can pick your own style of dress (or undress). (See Chapter 16 for information on rituals.)

✔ You can do religious work (ritual, magic, and so on) whenever you want to, so you can choose the times when you are physically stronger, are especially motivated, or feel empowered. Covens must meet at times that are convenient for the entire group.

✔ Your religion can evolve with you. You can change your rituals and other practices as your age, your circumstances, and your beliefs change. The rules, structure, and practice of a coven are often firmly established and can only be changed with the agreement of the group.

✔ You can read, study, and train in the ways that are most effective for you. Covens often have prescribed training and learning. (In the past, oral teaching was the primary way that Wiccans could get information, so people could only explore Wicca within a coven. Today's technology and greater access to information enables solitaries to study and learn outside of a coven structure.)

✔ You are free to focus on the actual spiritual work. As a solitary, your time and energy aren't diverted by group disagreements and conflict. Loyalty and trust are necessary within a coven, and problems among members have to be addressed within the coven. This group process can build a satisfying bond among coven members, but it also requires effort from each individual and can divert time and energy away from the actual spiritual work.

✔ You may feel safer practicing alone. If you live in an area where the residents are intolerant or you have other concerns about your security, you may find life as a solitary less stressful.

The solitary life also has its challenges. Here are a few of the disadvantages of being a solitary Wiccan rather than a covener:

✔ You may feel alienated and lonely in your religion without a coven for companionship and emotional support. Isolation is the worst part of solitary life. If you live in an area with a sizable Wiccan population (in a big city or a college town, for example), you may have opportunities to attend gatherings of like-minded people and befriend other Wiccans. But for many people, meeting other Wiccans in person is infrequent.

✔ You must handle all aspects of ritual. During rituals, a solitary doesn't have the help of a group to raise energy (see Chapter 16). Solitary rituals can't be as elaborate or expansive as those of a coven. In a coven, the members all play different roles in a ritual. A High Priestess and sometimes a High Priest may provide direction. A solitary must perform all parts of a ritual.

✔ You often must rely on your own experience and intuition as you perform ritual, pray, work magic, and engage in other aspects of Wiccan life. Solitaries have less opportunity than coveners to learn from others' experiences or ask questions about specific situations or practices.

> ✔ You may have difficulty accessing materials of a more advanced nature, or in-depth information about the beliefs and practices of specific traditions. Some traditions don't recognize solitaries at all, and many keep their main rites a secret. (However, general resources for study and training in Wicca are readily available today.)

The sidebar, "Finding the Wiccan community" offers advice for fighting isolation and getting information. The suggestions may help a solitary find other Wiccans outside of a coven structure. Someone who wants to join a coven may find the list helpful for finding coveners.

Entering as a solitary: A doorway to Wicca

Wicca is a spirituality of revelation and self-discovery. Wicca blooms in the soul. A Wiccan may evolve spiritually, in attunement with Deity and in harmony with nature, and feel no need for ceremony to mark this inner development. Any person is allowed to practice Wicca and never make a formal commitment, perform a dedication ritual, or undergo an initiation.

People also have the opportunity to mark the passage into the Wiccan Way. Beliefs and traditions vary about how this ceremony should happen, and the process differs for solitaries and coveners.

The following is an example of the way a solitary may come to Wicca.

1. **The person dedicates himself or herself to Wicca.**

    A person feels drawn to Wicca and decides to devote himself or herself to a serious exploration of this spirituality. The person dedicates his or her life to the serious study of the beliefs, principles, ethics, and practices of Wicca, and especially to nurture his or her relationship with the Deity. The time period for this commitment usually is clearly defined, often a year and a day. This promise to deeply explore Wicca is called a *dedication,* or in the case of a solitary, a *self-dedication.* The person is called a *dedicant* or *dedicate.*

    Dedication does not mean that the dedicant is now a Wiccan, and it doesn't mean that he or she can't leave Wicca.

    The form of the dedication is individual and personal. It can be as simple as the dedicant saying, "I dedicate myself to the Goddess and the God." Or the dedicant may choose to perform a self-dedication ritual (see Chapter 11 for an example of a self-dedication ritual).

    The dedicant's goals during the dedication period include establishing a relationship with Deity, successfully performing ritual, and gaining a full understanding of the principles and ethics of Wicca.

2. The dedicant may choose initiation into Wicca.

After the dedication period is complete, the dedicant may decide to seek initiation into Wicca. A Wiccan *initiation* or *self-initiation* is a spiritual rebirth into Wicca, and a complete commitment to the Wiccan path. (See Chapter 11 for an example of a self-initiation ritual.) At this time, the dedicant decides whether to continue as a solitary or to join a coven. If the dedicant continues in solitary practice, he or she may perform a self-initiation, which is done alone.

During initiation, a Wiccan adopts a Craft name, which is different from his or her legal name. The name helps distinguish between a person's everyday life and his or her spiritual and magical life. Craft names also help protect the identity of Wiccans from outsiders. The initiate usually takes an oath of loyalty to the Craft and swears to protect the secrets, including the identities of people in the Craft.

Some Wiccans combine dedication and initiation for solitary practice. In this view, dedication and initiation are the same thing, rather than a two-step process occurring over time.

In fact, many Wiccans don't believe that *self*-initiation is possible at all. They consider initiation rites to be reserved for someone who is joining a coven because a person needs someone else to perform the initiation and channel power from the Deity.

The perspective on dedication and initiation depends on the tradition, book, or teaching that an individual Wiccan is following.

Some Wiccans believe that initiation into Wicca can happen spontaneously, but many traditions teach that a person must undergo the rite of initiation in order to finally be a true Wiccan. Many traditions don't acknowledge coven initiations performed outside of their own specific tradition, and they don't recognize self-initiation by solitaries.

Scott Cunningham (in *Wicca: A Guide for the Solitary Practitioner,* Llewellyn Publications, 2003, pages 74–76) proposes an alternative to the rigid view held by the members of some traditions:

Initiation is a process, gradual or instantaneous, of the individual's attunement with the Goddess and the God. Many of the Wicca readily admit that the ritual initiation is the outer form only. True initiation will often occur weeks or months later, or prior to, the physical ritual. . . . Rest assured, it's quite possible to experience a true Wiccan initiation without ever meeting another soul involved in the religion. . . . When you feel an insurmountable joy in watching the sunset or the moon rise, when you see the Goddess and the God in trees marching along mountains or streams meandering through fields, when you feel the pulsating energies of the Earth amidst a noisy city, you have received true initiation and are linked with the ancient powers and ways of the deities. Some say, "Only a Wiccan can make a Wiccan." I say only the Goddess and the God can make a Wiccan. Who's better qualified?

Finding the Wiccan community

In the past, information about Wicca was unavailable to most people. Knowledge could be gained only through oral tradition within a coven. However, in the last couple of decades, an explosion of printed and electronic Wiccan resources have become available. Solitaries and coveners alike can tap into a wealth of information, if they are motivated to do so.

Meeting other Wiccans in person may take a little effort even today, but as Wiccans become more "out" in their communities, making contact and meeting directly to exchange information and support are becoming easier.

Here are some ways to get information and reach out to the Wiccan community:

✔ Go online. Many sites on the Web are dedicated to Wicca and Paganism. Also, Wiccan and Pagan publications are available online. The following are a couple of good starting points:

The Witches Voice: www.witchvox.com. This site has been in existence for a long time. It is an international clearinghouse of news and information for the Pagan community, and it offers local and regional information.

The Covenant of the Goddess: www.cog. org. According to the Web site, "It is a confederation of covens and solitaires of various traditions, who share in the worship of the Goddess and the Old Gods and subscribe to a common code of ethics." The Covenant is an international organization, with a national board of directors and regional councils in the United States. The group:

   publishes a newsletter

   issues ministerial credentials to qualified persons; these clergy may perform legal marriages and preside over funerals, as well as provide counseling for military and other Wiccans

   holds an annual national conference open to the Wiccan community, as well as regional conferences

   takes part in spiritual and educational conferences, interfaith outreach, large public rituals, environmental activism, community projects and social action, as well as efforts to correct negative stereotypes and promote accurate media portrayals

   works to ensure that Pagans have the same legal rights and protections as people in other religions

✔ Go to a Unitarian Universalist Church that has a CUUPS (Coven of Unitarian Universalist Pagans) group. These groups offer a great way to meet other Wiccans in a safe, undemanding environment.

✔ Go to classes and workshops about Wicca.

✔ Go to lectures or book signings by Pagan authors. These are offered by universities, colleges, large bookstores, and so on.

✔ Go to Pagan festivals or gatherings. These are usually advertised in local newspapers or online.

✔ Go to a local, reputable store specializing in metaphysical books or goods. Some cities have shops dedicated to Wicca. Talk to the owners or look for a bulletin board with notices of local Pagan events. Think critically, though, and evaluate the ethics of individuals or groups before becoming deeply involved with them.

✔ Go to a library or coffee shop and look through the local free magazines and newspapers. Many cities, even smaller ones, have newspapers dedicated to metaphysical issues. Sometimes politically progressive newspapers and magazines carry advertising or articles related to Pagan events.

Another option is to wear a pentacle or jewelry with other Wiccan themes. Be aware, though, that this outward display may lead to questions and even confrontation with non-Wiccans. Many Wiccans aren't comfortable with this level of public expression.

Considering Coven Membership

Some people who want to join a Wiccan coven have trouble finding one. The sidebar, "Finding the Wiccan community," earlier in this chapter, offers some tips for meeting up with local Wiccans, which is the first step in finding a compatible coven.

Asking coven questions

Many covens are closed or are very difficult to join; others are open and inviting.

When evaluating a coven, a prospective member is wise to ask lots of questions. What tradition does the coven follow, if any? What are the principles and practices of the tradition? Is the coven's emphasis on spirituality or magic, or both? How are leaders chosen? How is ritual performed? Do members worship skyclad (nude)? Does the coven have a particular focus, for example, political action?

Prospective coven members should be on the look out for unsafe groups or leaders. Do the leaders of the coven exercise inappropriate authority or too much control? Are there any hints of sexual manipulation or exploitation? A coven should not charge fees for initiation or coven training. It is acceptable for coven members to pay their share for the rental of rooms, the copying of documents, and other incidental expenses. It's also fine for coven leaders to offer classes or workshops to the public for a fee. Any coven that doesn't follow the basic ethics of Wicca (see Chapter 4) should be avoided. (See Chapter 23 for the warning signs of scams or inappropriate behavior.)

Wiccans don't recruit. The prospective member must approach the coven and ask for initiation. Covens gain new members in a variety of ways. Some hold public classes and workshops where coveners may meet compatible people. Some coven members may bring apprentices into the coven. (An apprentice is a prospective initiate who is assigned to an experienced coven member for training.) Some covens meet new members through political action or other work. Some covens focus on people who can contribute needed skills (writing, sewing, herb gardening, and so on).

Coveners try to build a coven in which the members have good chemistry together, although they don't have to be best friends in order to be effective. Spiritual and magical practice does require mutual respect and trust, in order to create an environment in which people are fully empowered. Even friendly, nice, mature people may not be right for each other in a coven setting. When coven members meet to perform ritual or work magic, their individual energies merge. Ideally, the result is positive and productive, but sometimes coveners must work to find just the right group of people.

Entering as a covener: A doorway to Wicca

Many Wiccans want the exchange of knowledge, support, and inspiration that a coven can provide. A new and eager Wiccan may experience frustration, though, because many established covens require that a person study and practice alone for at least a year and a day before he or she can even consider joining the group.

Coping with coven politics

When a coven is working together in harmony, with love and mutual trust, they can achieve extraordinary results. But if the bond among coveners begins to unravel, the result can be stagnation, hurt feelings, and unproductive effort. Covens usually contain 13 people or fewer. In small groups, everyone's presence affects the rest of the group, and everyone has a role in the outcome of any effort. The following are some obstacles to effective coven work:

- A big difference in ages may make bonding difficult in some covens.

- Romantic liaisons or sexual tension among coveners can introduce stress and fragment the group's energy.

- Most of the group may bond tightly, but one or two people may feel left out.

- A leader may go on a bit of an ego trip and become domineering or inflexible.

- All coven members may not have the same level of commitment or the same goals.

- Coveners may begin to treat the coven as a therapy group, instead of a spiritual endeavor.

Wise guidance and direction from the coven leadership may help to resolve internal conflict. The best coven leaders can help facilitate discussion, resolve disputes, and clarify goals for the group. Covens must allocate time for working out personal and group problems. Sometimes talking is not the best solution for handling issues. For example, a visualization exercise may be more helpful than a yelling match in some situations.

Sometimes an increase in the number of disputes or other problems indicates that someone needs to leave the coven, or some members need to begin their own coven.

Dedication and initiation

The process of dedication and initiation differ depending on the practices of the individual coven, as well as the tradition that the coven follows.

Some covens require potential members to have undergone a self-dedication. *Self-dedication* means that the person (the *dedicant*) devotes his or her life to the Deity and the study of Wicca's principles, ethics, and practices for a clearly defined period of time, usually a year and a day. Self-dedication does not make one a Wiccan, but it is a personal vow to engage in serious exploration of the Wicca Way. The dedicant's goals during the dedication period are to establish a relationship with Deity, successfully perform ritual, and gain understanding of the principles and ethics of Wicca.

(See the section, "Entering as a solitary: A doorway to Wicca," earlier in this chapter for more information on self-dedication and initiation, and see Chapter 12 for an example of a self-dedication ritual.)

Other covens accept people new to Wicca into the fold, and the dedication ritual is performed within the group, instead of as a self-dedication. The dedicant is still expected to meet the same goals and engage in intense study for the year and a day (or other defined time period). Sometimes the new person is assigned to a specific coven member to serve as an apprentice and receive training and teaching in Wicca and the coven's specific tradition.

After the dedicant meets the requirements for study and training, he or she may request initiation into Wicca and the coven — but this is a matter of personal choice, not a requirement. A Wiccan *initiation* is a spiritual rebirth into Wicca, and a full commitment to the Wiccan path.

Acceptance into a coven is rarely automatic. Most prospective members must prove that they have begun their own Book of Shadows (see Chapter 20 for more information on these magical diaries and sourcebooks). Some covens require an oral or written exam or proof that the person has studied and trained as an apprentice to someone else.

In most covens, the membership votes upon the request for initiation. Acceptance must be unanimous, and the *Celebrant* (the High Priest or High Priestess) asks for coven acknowledgement of this acceptance.

The initiation rite

Each coven has its own rites, but in general the initiation rite is a very formal affair. As with the basic ritual, the altar is laid, the leaders light candles, the circle is cast, and the Deity is invoked (see Chapter 12 for information about basic ritual design). During the initiation, power is passed from the Deity to the person receiving initiation, the Most Wiccans believe that the High Priestess, or whoever performs the initiation rite, channels the power.

Most Wiccan traditions have three degrees of initiation. To achieve the First Degree, someone must study for the traditional year and a day and understand the fundamental principles and ethics of Wicca. A Second Degree requires another period of study of at least another year and a day and more knowledge and proficiency in practice. The Third Degree requires more devotion to study and practice (usually lasting longer than a year and a day). The Third Degree is the highest level of advancement in most traditions. Many High Priestesses and High Priests are Third Degree Wiccans.

Generally, only someone already holding the degree can initiate someone into that degree. Only the High Priest or High Priestess can initiate into the highest degree. Again, this varies from tradition to tradition. In some traditions, a male must initiate a female and vice versa. Other traditions hold that the High Priestess or High Priest must initiate all who aspire to the coven. More democratic groups share the responsibilities through the entire group.

In some covens, the whole coven attends the event; in others only the initiate, High Priest, and High Priestess are present.

The coveners design the ritual for the initiation. Almost all coven initiations require that the initiate experience the following during the ritual:

- A challenge that must be faced and overcome
- An oath of loyalty and secrecy
- A conveying of knowledge
- A symbolic death and rebirth

During initiation, a Wiccan adopts a Craft name, which is different from his or her legal name. The name helps distinguish between a person's everyday life, and his or her spiritual, magical life. Craft names also help protect the identity of Wiccans from outsiders. The secrets of the coven and the tradition are shared. The initiate takes an oath of loyalty to the coven and to Wicca and swears to protect the coven's secrets, including the identity of the members.

Most covens expect the new initiate's life to be transformed in some way by the initiation rite, otherwise it is not considered a success.

Chapter 10

Making Room for Everyone: Craft Traditions

In This Chapter

▶ Appreciating Wiccan diversity

▶ Taking a look at Wiccan traditions

▶ Figuring out how folk magic fits into Wicca

▶ Piecing together a unique practice

*W*icca is a spirituality of choices. Wiccans can choose to practice their spirituality alone or with a tightly knit group called a coven. They also can decide which type of Wicca they want to practice. There are more kinds of Wicca and Witchcraft than you can shake a wand at. The different types are called traditions.

To fully cover all of the old and modern traditions would require thousands of pages — more than the publisher could stuff into this book. So this chapter introduces a few of the traditions that serve as the roots of Wicca and Witchcraft, and it shows how the Craft grows from this base.

Taking a Look at Trads

In general, a *tradition* is a particular sect, subgroup, or denomination of Wicca. Specifically, a *tradition* is a system of Wicca, a framework for practicing Wicca, which usually includes spiritual principles, ethics, rituals, and magical practices. In other words, a tradition is someone's version of Wicca.

The term *tradition* applies both to the system of Wicca and to the group of covens that practice the system. A coven is a local branch of a tradition, just like your local bank is one branch of a larger corporation. All the covens together make up the tradition.

By the way, sometimes tradition is abbreviated *trad* in Wicca, especially in conversation or e-mails.

Finding no McWicca

Wicca offers great diversity. Unfortunately, though, not every community has a coven in every tradition. Wiccans who want to join a coven must pick from the traditions available in their areas.

Also, a coven in one city may practice a tradition differently from a coven in another city, because covens are autonomous. Coveners may or may not choose to follow their tradition exactly. They may adapt the tradition's practices to their own needs. Even if covens follow the same tradition, they may not practice alike coast to coast; covens aren't like chain restaurants or mall stores.

Many Wiccans find that the details of worship and magical practice, which are spelled out by the tradition, are less important than the personal relationships and the chemistry among coveners. The trust, support, and love within a coven are greater priorities than niggling details like the wording of rituals or the way that tools are placed on the altar.

Many Wiccans reject all traditions and choose to be *eclectic.* They build their own personal traditions, taking bits of beliefs and pieces of practice from many different sources.

Giving birth to a tradition

Traditions are as different as the people who invent them. They don't all begin and operate in the same ways. Here are some of the ways that traditions are born or spread:

- Today, most traditions begin when the founder writes a book introducing his or her particular version of Wicca. Sometimes an author doesn't intend for the book to become the basis for a tradition, but the readers find the material so compelling that they use the book as the foundation for their own covens or solitary practices.

- A single coven may develop a system of Wicca. The coven grows too large, and members *hive off* (split off or spin off) to form their own coven. Then a new group hives off from that coven and so on, producing a chain of associated covens, sometimes called *daughter covens.*

✔ People may come to a coven for classes or other training, and then return to their own areas to begin covens in the tradition. (A coven who offers this outreach is called a *training coven.*) Sometimes coven members go out to the community to teach classes or workshops.

✔ Some traditions are off-shoots of other traditions. For example, a coven member may like the basic structure but object to a few of the practices, so he or she may develop a new tradition with similarities to the old one.

✔ Some traditions are hereditary. A family develops the tradition over generations. Members are born into the tradition or initiated into it by family members. Sometimes someone from the outside gets access to a hereditary tradition, and it becomes open to members outside of the family.

Some traditions are public, and some are secret. Some are open to anyone, and some are closed to everyone (people may enter only by invitation). Some traditions provide basic information in a book, but someone must take training and/or hook up with a coven to get advanced information or receive formal initiation into the tradition. Some traditions acknowledge solitaries (people who practice the Craft but don't belong to a coven), and others do not. The next section offers some examples of specific Wiccan and Witchcraft traditions.

Choosing a Paved Path: The Traditions

Wicca is divided into dozens of traditions, and this section describes some of the largest or more influential ones. You may want to get the definitions for a few key words before you leap headlong into traditions. The following may be helpful:

✔ *Initiation* is the way that people are officially acknowledged as part of a tradition. Some traditions recognize solitary practitioners who self-initiate. Others only accept people who undergo a coven initiation.

✔ A *degree* is a level of initiation. Most Wiccan traditions have three degrees of initiation. To achieve the First Degree, someone must study for the traditional year and a day and understand the fundamental principles and ethics of Wicca. A Second Degree requires another period of study of at least another year and a day and more knowledge and proficiency in practice. The Third Degree requires more devotion to study and practice (usually lasting longer than a year and a day). The Third Degree is the highest level of advancement in most traditions. Many High Priestesses and High Priests are Third Degree Wiccans.

Generally, only someone already holding the degree can initiate someone into that degree. In some traditions, a male must initiate a female and vice versa. Other traditions hold that the High Priestess or High Priest must initiate everyone who enters the coven. Democratic groups share the responsibilities through the entire group.

- ✔ *Lineage* refers to a person's magical ancestors. Initiates in some traditions have a family tree, not based on birth, but initiation. For example, a High Priestess in Gerald Gardner's original coven initiates someone. That person initiates someone else in a Gardnerian coven, that person initiates another Gardnerian, and so on. Lineages are remembered, although the legal names are never written down. Some traditions keep lineages only for Third Degrees, but some have them for Second Degrees or even First Degrees. Some lineages have been lost, broken, or forgotten.

- ✔ *Oathbound* means that an initiate swears to keep the coven's secrets. This may refer to the identities of the members and/or the tradition's secrets of practice.

- ✔ A *Book of Shadows* contains a tradition's history, rituals, and practices. (Most Wiccans also have personal Books of Shadows in which they record the details of their own Wiccan lives.) The Books of Shadows for many traditions can be purchased or accessed on the Web.

- ✔ A *Sabbat* is a Wiccan holy day. Traditions vary on the dates that they celebrate Sabbats. The covens of almost all traditions meet on the Sabbats.

Traditional Witchcraft

Many people in the Craft today follow traditions that existed before — or are otherwise separate from — the traditions born during the Wiccan revival of the mid-20th Century. The followers of these distinct traditions commonly are called *traditional Witches* or sometimes *Hedgewitches*.

The beliefs and practices of traditional Witches vary and are often kept within the individual group and not disclosed to the public. Some groups have well-defined spiritual beliefs, and others place more emphasis on practice (magic, healing, midwifery, and so on). Some traditions require coven membership; for others, solitary practice is customary.

Many traditional Witches focus on the oral teachings, literature, history, and folklore of a specific culture. For example, a tradition may be Appalachian, Celtic, Cretan, Egyptian, Greek, Irish, Italian, Minoan, Pictish, Scottish, or Welsh (to name just a few). Some of these traditions restrict membership to people within the culture or ethnicity, but others accept anyone who has a sincere devotion to the tradition. Many traditional Witches do have ancestry in their chosen tradition, so they are returning to their cultural roots.

All people have the right to study and celebrate their heritage, as well as to adopt the spiritual practices of their ancestors. However, people in the Craft should avoid any group that its culture, race, or ethnicity is superior to others'. That claim violates the ethics and the true spirit of Wicca and Witchcraft. Personally, I would avoid any group that excludes people on the basis of ethnicity, race, or culture.

Don't assume that traditional Witches believe, practice, and celebrate in exactly the same ways as Wiccans of the modern revival traditions. Most traditional Witches have their own strong codes of ethics, although they usually don't acknowledge the Wiccan Rede or the specific Threefold Law. (See Chapter 3 for information about these Wiccan concepts.) Traditional Witches may have different ideas — about Deity, reincarnation, holy days, magical works, the roles of the sexes, and so on — than Wiccans who follow the traditions of the Wiccan revival.

A few traditional Witches belong to family traditions, and coven members are all relatives, by blood or sometimes by marriage.

Hereditary Witchcraft: Fam trads

A *hereditary Witch* is one who follows a family tradition of Witchcraft. These family traditions are sometimes referred to as *fam trads*. Many family traditions focus on magical practice, but some may include spirituality.

Fam trads are almost always very secretive, so little is known about their beliefs and practices. The actual number of fam trad witches is debated. Some people believe that only a few, if any, hereditary Witches are alive today. The truth is that no one really knows, given the secrecy of these traditions.

Fam trad Witches are taught by one or more living relatives, but reportedly, many fam trads can trace their Craft lineage back to a time well before the modern era. These claims are controversial today. (During the early days of the Wiccan revival, some Wiccans boldly exaggerated the involvement of their ancestors or relatives in the Craft. Having a hereditary, historical connection gave Wiccans credibility. These claims aren't as prevalent now that Wicca is gaining acceptance and legitimacy as a contemporary religion, apart from its historical roots.)

Fam trad Witches are born into the Craft or are initiated into it by a family member. Relatives may teach all the children basic knowledge about the tradition, and then offer advanced training to those who show interest or skill. Or they may teach only one or two children in each generation.

Folk magic and the Craft

In the past (and continuing today in many rural areas), people practiced folk magic and held beliefs that were rooted in the old nature-focused religions. *Folk magic* is an attempt to affect natural or chance events by using herbs, charms, stones, spells, rituals, healing techniques, and other knowledge. These traditions were passed down informally through generations but were not given a label — not "Witchcraft" or anything else. The wisdom and practices were just a part of people's everyday lives.

My own great grandmother, who lived in the rural Midwest, practiced and taught all manner of herbalism, healing, and magic, but she probably would have ranted at anyone who called her a Witch.

Today, many people hold onto remnants of these practices. For example, I know an urban software developer who returns to her family's small farm every April. She and her sisters gather very specific herbs and roots, and then carefully prepare the spring tonic that — because of its magical properties — the women in their family have made on the last Saturday in April for generations.

Growing up in these traditions, people know that their beliefs and practices are different from the surrounding modern culture's, but they don't know how to talk about that difference and often are embarrassed or uncomfortable doing so. They are afraid of being viewed as uneducated, superstitious, poor, peasant, or threatening to others. If asked about a particular practice, a woman from this background might say, "We follow the old ways" or "My family is old time" and then change the subject.

Some of the people raised in these traditions do find their way into Neo-Paganism and immediately feel like they've come home.

Even if these people of the "old ways" never embrace the words Witch, Wiccan, or Witchcraft, the knowledge and wisdom gained from them is often incorporated into modern Craft practices, so the line between folk magic and the Craft is blurry.

Some of the family traditions are closed to all but blood relatives. Some fam trads accept people who marry into the family, and a few accept people outside of the family, if they show sufficient interest and conviction.

The term hereditary sometimes has a more casual meaning. A Wiccan may call himself or herself a *hereditary* to indicate only that he or she was brought up in the Craft, but not necessarily within a family tradition. This term will probably become more common as Wicca ages and grows, resulting in more children being raised in the Craft.

Gardnerian

Wiccans generally credit Gerald Gardner with beginning the modern revival of Wicca. Gardner claimed that his tradition is based on the practices of a coven that had existed since ancient times. People argue about whether any of the old covens survived through the ages, and they argue even more hotly about Gardner's tradition.

Gerald Gardner (1884–1964) was a British civil servant. He lived much of his life in the Far East, and then he retired and returned to England. On the edge of the New Forest, he met the Wica, members of a surviving coven that had been in existence since ancient times. He was initiated into the coven and into Wica (then spelled with one "c") by a woman called "Old Dorothy," who was later reported to be Dorothy Clutterbuck. Gardner was initiated in 1939, but he could not reveal or publish his experiences because of the anti-Witchcraft laws that remained on the books in Britain. With the repeal of the laws in 1951, Gardner published two books, *Witchcraft Today* (1954) and *The Meaning of Witchcraft* (1959) because he had decided that it was time for Witchcraft to be revealed. He also brought Wicca to the attention of the media. Although he has been widely criticized for breaking the tradition of silence and secrecy, Gardner reportedly feared that Witchcraft was in danger of dying out. From the fragments of ritual and practice that Gardner learned from the New Forest coven, he developed his own version of Wicca.

Today, Wiccans and scholars outside of Wicca debate every aspect of Gardner's accounts. Was Gardner initiated into a genuine coven that had survived from ancient times? How much of his tradition of Wicca is based on what was left of the old coven's rituals and practices? How much is his own blend of ceremonial magic, Freemasonry, Eastern philosophies, ideas from other books, and his conception of the Craft? If the account is false, what does that mean for the tradition and all of Wicca today?

Despite the questions about its origins, Gardnerian Wicca is one of the most widespread of Wiccan traditions, and perhaps the most influential. Many non-Gardnerian groups have borrowed from Gardner in the development of their own traditions. The term *English Traditionalist* is often used to describe those groups that descend from Gardner's original group or borrow from it.

Gardnerian Wicca remains largely intact as Gerald Gardner taught it and passed on from his original coven. In addition to Gerald Gardner's books, the following book contains the rituals and practices of Gardnerian Wicca: *The Witches' Way* by Janet and Stewart Farrar (1984), which was published in the United States as *A Witches Bible, Volumes I and II* (1985).

Here are some characteristics of Gardnerian Wicca:

- **Deity and beliefs:** Gardnerians worship the Goddess and the God; many covens are more Goddess-oriented.

- **Covens and solitaries:** Gardnerians worship in covens. Solitary Wiccans are not recognized by Gardnerian tradition. Each coven is independent and can worship and practice in any way that meets the group's needs. However, Gardnerians follow their handed down Books of Shadows carefully. Gardnerian practices are detailed and precise, and the tradition is more rigid and strict than many others in Wicca. Almost all Gardnerians also keep a personal Book of Shadows.

✔ **Leadership:** Covens usually are led by a High Priestess. Leadership passes through successive Priestesses. Gardnerian Wicca is sometimes criticized for being hierarchical, rather than democratic.

✔ **Degrees:** Gardnerians follow a lengthy course of study and magical practice. Coveners can achieve three degrees of initiation. After completing the Third Degree, a Gardnerian can hive off from his or her coven and begin a new one. This continuous line of covens preserves the tradition and heritage.

✔ **Ethics:** The details of their practices are protected by oath and are not revealed to outsiders. Membership is also kept in strict secrecy, so Gardnerian covens are difficult to find.

Most people in the tradition follow the Craft laws set down by Gerald Gardner.

✔ **Practice:** Gardnerians cast a 9-foot circle in which to do ritual (see Chapter 12 for more information on circle casting).

Gardnerians usually worship skyclad (nude), and the tradition includes controversial practices, such as binding and scourging (although most covens no longer scourge). A scourge is a small ritual whip, usually made of silk, and used to heighten awareness and alter consciousness, not used in a sexual context. Gardnerian covens use sexual symbolism in their rituals, although sexual activity is not a part of worship.

The term *Gardnerian* can have several meanings. Strictly speaking, a Gardnerian coven is one that descends directly from Gardner's coven on the Isle of Man. All Gardnerians can trace their lineage back to someone who was initiated by a High Priestess of Gardner's coven.

Sometimes Wiccans use the term *Gardnerian* to describe any coven that has adopted Gardner's framework and rituals but may have no link to the original coven. These groups are sometimes called Neo-Gardnerians.

Many of the modern traditions of Wicca are offshoots of Gardnerian Wicca. The following brief sections mention a few of the most prominent.

Alexandrian

The Alexandrian tradition was started by Alex and Maxine Sanders in Britain in the early 1960s. It came to the United States shortly after its founding. Like Gardner, the Sanders helped bring Wicca to the attention of the media. Alex Sanders was very controversial and proclaimed himself to be the "King of the Witches." He often posed for lurid photographs with female Witches. Many in the Craft questioned his motivations and criticized him for publicizing Wicca. Sanders initiated Stewart and Janet Farrar, who have authored many popular books on Wicca. Their book *What Witches Do* (1971) describes this tradition.

Alex Sanders was briefly a member of a Gardnerian coven, and Alexandrian Wicca is very similar to Gardnerian. Generally, Alexandrian covens emphasize training. Some of the strict rules of Gardnerian Wicca have been discarded. The rituals and practice include more ceremonial magic than do Gardnerian. Alexandrian covens typically have a hierarchical structure. Most covens work skyclad, but the tradition does not require ritual nudity. They meet on the new moons, full moons, and Sabbats.

The tradition is named for the ancient city of Alexandria, not the founder of the tradition.

Georgian

Georgian Wicca is named after one of the founders, the late George "Pat" Patterson (also known as Lord Scorpio), who started the tradition in Bakersfield, California, around 1970. Lady Persephone and Lady Tanith were also founders. The Georgian church serves as the umbrella for all the covens in the tradition. Georgian Wicca is an eclectic combination of Gardnerian, Alexandrian, and British Traditional Wicca, as well as original ideas and Celtic influences.

Here are some characteristics of Georgian Wicca:

- **Deity and beliefs:** Georgians worship both the Goddess and the God, with perhaps more emphasis on the Goddess.
- **Covens and solitaries:** Georgians worship in covens.
- **Leadership:** The tradition is taught and passed through covens by people who have been initiated and elevated into the priesthood; the priesthood is passed male to female and female to male. They maintain an initiatory line back to the original coven.
- **Degrees:** Coveners can achieve three degrees (or levels) of initiation.
- **Ethics:** The coveners are oathbound to keep the traditions secrets.
- **Practice:** The tradition emphasizes individual freedom and creativity. With regard to Georgian practice, the founder is often reported to have said, "If it works, use it. If it doesn't, don't."

  Covens may or may not work skyclad.

Seax Wicca

Seax Wicca is a Saxon Wiccan tradition founded by Raymond Buckland. Raymond and Rosemary Buckland were initiates of Gardner's coven, and they brought Gardnerian Wicca to the United States in the mid-1960s.

Buckland describes the full Seax Wicca tradition in his book, *The Tree: The Complete Book of Saxon Witchcraft* (1974).

Buckland is very clear about the fact that he created all the material for the entire tradition. Seax Wicca is not a continuation or re-creation of the Saxon religion, and it's very similar to Gardnerian Wicca. Buckland discarded some

Gardnerian elements that were controversial, and his tradition allows self-initiation (Gardnerian Wicca doesn't).

The rituals of this tradition are open, published, and widely available. Openness and freedom abound in Seax Wicca. Leadership is democratic and not hierarchical.

Feri, Faery, Fairy

The Feri tradition is separate from Gardnerian-style Wicca. The early foundation of the tradition was developed in an Oregon coven in the 1920s. The Feri tradition developed parallel to Gardnerian Wicca and is different in many ways.

For much of his life, the founder spelled the name Feri, although today spelling varies, including Feri, Faery, Faerie, and Fairy.

Victor Anderson (1917–2001), the tradition's founder, was born in New Mexico in 1917. He lost most of his vision as a young child. After his family moved to Oregon, he experienced a mystical experience, which he felt was his initiation into the magical world. Early on, Anderson met and studied with people from diverse backgrounds, and his own tradition eventually incorporated American folk magic, as well as African (especially Dahomean-Haitian), African American, Appalachian, Celtic, Hawaiian Huna, and Tibetan beliefs and practices. These practices lie at the heart of the Feri tradition. During the 1920s and 1930s in Oregon, Anderson belonged to the Harpy Coven, where the early framework of the Feri tradition was in use. From that experience, as well as his impressive knowledge of spiritual traditions and practices, Anderson more fully developed the Feri tradition and began teaching it to others. By the 1940s, Victor and Cora Anderson were initiating people into the tradition.

In the early 1970s, Victor Anderson, his wife Cora, their friend Tom DeLong, known as Gwydion Pendderwen, and several others formed the Mahealani Coven, and the full Feri tradition was born.

Not for the faint of heart

This tradition is not for everyone. The Feri tradition involves an element of risk-taking. Practitioners are wilder, more spirited, and less inclined to operate within strict parameters than members of other traditions.

The tradition encourages a warrior ethic, balancing self-love and personal freedom with responsibility and respect for others. The Feri are urged not to coddle weakness or support others in their self-deceptions. A Feri does not submit his or her own lifeforce to anyone or anything. This fierce openness is called the *Black Heart of Innocence,* and is an ideal condition in which a person is free of guilt and shame. The Feri tradition demands rigorous self-honesty and a willingness to confront the most hidden parts of the self in order to transform fear and hate into self-healing, power, and love.

The intensity of the Feri tradition's rituals and practices may be overwhelming for some people.

Feri belief and practice

The following are some characteristics of the Feri tradition:

- **Deity and beliefs:** The primal Goddess is the center of Feri belief, but the tradition is polytheistic, and the individual Gods and Goddesses each exist and are worshipped. The male God springs from the primal creation Goddess. Each Goddess and God has both masculine and feminine aspects. Men and women are equal, and the tradition is open and welcoming to those of any sexual orientation.

  Followers of this tradition accept that much reality is unseen or has permeable boundaries. They recognize and use the power of the faeries.

  Beliefs include the doctrine of the Three Selves. The Self is divided into the unconscious mind, the conscious mind, and the God Self, which is the spirit that exists outside of time, space, and matter. The deepest level of wisdom is called the _Blue God,_ represented by two linked spirals or the infinity sign. (The explanation here is oversimplified. The well-known writer, Starhawk, includes a very good explanation of this idea and other Feri concepts in her books.)

- **Covens and solitaries:** Most Feri work is solitary or in very small groups. The coven experience is more tribal or clannish than in other traditions.

- **Leadership:** Covens usually don't have a High Priest or High Priestess, and the structure is loose. Many covens rotate leadership.

- **Degrees:** The tradition has no degree system, but training is emphasized prior to initiation and often is extensive. The tradition does have a wand system; every initiate holds a white wand, elders hold green wands, and grandmasters hold black wands signifying long-term achievement.

- **Ethics:** Candidates seeking initiation into a Feri coven usually must have the unanimous approval of all members of that coven. If someone receives initiation as a solitary, the person performing the initiation is responsible for his or her future conduct in the tradition.

- **Practice:** Most members celebrate the eight Sabbats and the Full Moons.

  Practice includes energy work using pentacles and visualizations. The Iron Pentacle is a meditative tool; the points of the pentagram represent sex, self, passion, pride, and power.

The evolution of the tradition has made its rituals and practices extraordinarily diverse, incorporating Celtic religion, Hawaiian Huna and other Shamanic practices, Tibetan meditation, and African beliefs and practices, especially Dahomean-Haitian.

Currently, several different lines descend from the original coven, and because of the tradition's diversity, the Feri groups vary widely in ritual and practice. Initiates can trace their lineage back to Victor or Cora Anderson, or Gwydion Pendderwen.

Reclaiming

Starhawk, the author and political activist, helped found this tradition and is its most high-profile member. Starhawk was initiated into the Feri (Faery) tradition, and Reclaiming is strongly influenced by it. Starhawk writes books of profound beauty, and her contribution to the modern Craft is immeasurable. I highly recommend all of her books, fiction and nonfiction.

The Reclaiming tradition began in the late 1970s as a collective in the San Francisco Bay area. They were a working group that published a newsletter, organized public rituals, and taught classes in Witchcraft and magic. Some of the classes were week-long workshops.

In the late 1990s, the collective dissolved itself, and was replaced by the Wheel of Reclaiming, remaining in the Bay area. The Wheel is made up of working cells or groups, which do projects, and an Advisory Council. The Wheel makes decisions by consensus and acts in the name of Reclaiming. Today, Reclaiming groups can be found in many places in the United States and abroad.

The work of Reclaiming involves organizing public rituals, publishing a quarterly magazine *(The Reclaiming Quarterly)*, and offering classes and workshops focusing on various aspects of modern feminist spirituality and traditional teachings. In the summer months, Reclaiming groups offer week-long intensive workshops (Witch Camps).

People do not become members of Reclaiming by filling out an application or paying dues; they participate in the work and activities of the cells. Reclaiming also includes those who only attend rituals or other events, or who practice the Reclaiming tradition in their own covens or circles, or as solitaries.

They maintain a good Web site (www.reclaiming.org), with information about Reclaiming as well as special projects (books, music, and so on). The Reclaiming Web site offers the tradition's Principles of Unity, a statement of core values in the Reclaiming Tradition. Fundamental value is placed on reverence for the Earth, the natural cycles of life and death, individual autonomy, nonviolence, feminism, and responsible activism.

The following are characteristics of the Reclaiming tradition:

✔ **Deity and beliefs:** Followers of the Reclaiming Tradition worship the immanent Goddess. They honor both the Goddess and the God. Members are not required to worship any specific Goddesses or Gods. Members believe that the Earth is alive, and all of life is sacred and interconnected. The Goddess is immanent and manifest in the Earth's cycles of birth, growth, death, decay, and regeneration. Followers of this tradition have a deep, spiritual commitment to the Earth, to healing, and to the linking of magic with political action. They assert that everyone can do transforming magic, the art of changing consciousness at will.

✔ **Covens and solitaries:** Reclaiming recognizes both solitaries and coveners. Entrance to a coven is through initiation, usually after a long training period. Initiation has no formal requirements, and when initiations are undertaken, they are customized to the individual.

✔ **Leadership:** Covens are nonhierarchical, and every initiate is a Priest or Priestess. They try to foster personal and collective empowerment. They make decisions by consensus. Everyone is encouraged to develop new ritual.

✔ **Degrees:** The Reclaiming tradition has no degree system.

✔ **Ethics:** Reclaiming values peace and practices nonviolence in keeping with the Wiccan Rede ("An' it harm none, do what ye will."). They call for service to the Earth and the community, and work for all forms of justice: environmental, social, political, racial, gender, and economic. Reclaiming welcomes all genders, races, ages, sexual orientations, and all differences of life situation, background, and ability. They believe that each person embodies the Divine.

✔ **Practice:** Reclaiming has no set liturgy (except in certain large, rehearsed or semi-rehearsed public Sabbat rituals), but they provide training in principles of magic and the structure of ritual.

Practice is more Shamanic than ceremonial. Goals are ecstasy, self-empowerment, self-discovery, and creativity.

Chanting and breathwork are used in rituals. Raising energy is intense, often using the spiral dance, a dance in which participants follow a spiral pattern.

Reclaiming uses the Pentacle of Iron (the points represent sex, self, passion, pride, and power) and the Pentacle of Pearl (the points represent love, wisdom, knowledge, law, and power).

Dianic

The term Dianic is a confusing one in Wicca. The meaning depends on the perspective of the person using the term.

Dianic has become an umbrella term for any person or group that emphasizes the Goddess and whose spirituality and practice are women-centered. These groups may have little else in common.

Some of the groups are women-only, some include men, and some encourage men to form their own groups. All these groups are Goddess-centered; some, but not all, recognize the God(s), and may or may not invoke Him during rituals.

More precisely, Dianic refers to the tradition, sometimes called *feminist Dianic*, founded by Zsuzsanna Budapest and other modern feminists in the 1970s. Also in the 1970s, Morgan McFarland and Mark Roberts founded a Dianic tradition that was unrelated to the previously mentioned.

Dianic Wiccan tradition: Zsuzsanna Budapest line

Zsuzsanna Budapest is a Hungarian immigrant and a hereditary Witch who came to the United States when the Soviet Union invaded Hungary. By the early 1970s, she had created a tradition of Wicca based on feminist principles and values; her mother's rituals, healing techniques, and folk magic practices; Gardnerian Wicca; and Charles Leland's book, *Aradia, Gospel of the Witches* (1899, reprinted 1974).

She called her tradition Dianic, after Diana, the Roman Goddess of the hunt and untamed nature. However, Dianics celebrate the Goddess in all her forms.

In the 1970s, Zsuzsanna Budapest founded The Susan B. Anthony Coven #1 of Los Angeles, which serves as a role model for many of the other Dianic covens all over the United States. Budapest's early work, *The Feminist Book of Lights and Shadows* (1976), and later work, *The Holy Book of Women's Mysteries* (1989), were used as sources of ritual. She has continued to write about Goddess worship and the feminist Craft, and her books are popular Dianic resources.

The following are some of the characteristics of feminist Dianism:

✔ **Deity and beliefs:** Dianics believe in the Goddess. (Some Dianics consider the Goddess as the Web of Life. All reality is the actual body of the Goddess.)

Some don't recognize the God, while some acknowledge Him only as coming from and contained within the Goddess (they do not invoke Him during Dianic ritual).

Dianics believe in feminist principles and values and that women's bodies are a manifestation of the Goddess.

They foster awareness that women's experience is authentic, and patriarchy does not accurately reflect that experience.

They strongly feel obligated to heal and protect the Earth, secure safety and human rights for women and children, and seek justice and liberation for all people.

✔ **Covens and solitaries:** Dianics can be solitaries or join circles or covens. All women are welcome, and many groups have a strong lesbian presence.

✔ **Leadership:** Power is shared, and coven leadership is nonhierarchical.

✔ **Degrees:** Many groups don't have degrees; some have two: dedicant and High Priestess.

✔ **Ethics:** Covens and ritual circles are women-only (except for male infants and toddlers). Feminist Dianics do not teach women's magic to men until patriarchy no longer exists.

Dianics accept the Wiccan Rede and the Threefold Law, and they celebrate the Sabbats common to Wiccans.

✔ **Practice:** The practice is free-form with limited structure. Dianics encourage artistic expression (songs, dance, poetry, and prose) instead of scripted rituals.

Dianism, Texas style

In the early 1970s, Morgan McFarland and her priest, Mark Roberts, founded a Dianic tradition in Texas. Both men and women could become initiates and all were equal within the circle; however, only women start covens, and they choose their priests.

The covens of this tradition worship the Goddess in her three aspects: Maiden-Creatrix, Mother, and Crone. In her Mother aspect, the Goddess takes a consort, so a place for the God exists in this tradition, but the Goddess as creator is the focus of worship and practice. Protecting the environment was a high priority for the original coven. The Moon is a strong theme in rituals.

Wicca and Shamanism

More and more Wiccans are investigating other spiritualities, philosophies, and methods and incorporating these ideas into their Wiccan practices.

Some Wiccans are harkening all the way back to Wicca's ancient roots, and they are merging Shamanic methods with their Craft practice, forming new blended traditions, often called Shamanic Wicca, Wiccan Shamanism, and Shamanic Craft. (See Chapter 5 for more information on Wicca's origins.)

The seers

Feminist Dianic Wicca has been and continues to be informed and energized by the works of numerous authors. The following writers are widely read and referenced in universities and other settings outside of Wicca and Witchcraft.

Anyone who wants a full understanding of feminism, as well as the Craft, is wise to spend a few rainy nights curled up on the couch with one of their books. (This list is far from comprehensive.)

- Ruth Barrett
- Carol P. Christ
- Mary Daly
- Riane Eisler
- Marija Gimbutas
- Susan Griffin
- Hallie Iglehart (Austen)
- Diane Mariechild
- Shekhinah Mountainwater
- Charlene Spretnak
- Starhawk
- Diane Stein
- Merlin Stone
- Barbara E. Walker

The Shaman's gift

The modern mind has evolved to perceive everything in reality as a fixed and separate object. However, life is really an interconnected web or grid of energy. Ancient humans may have been able to easily shift their awareness or consciousness and perceive this energy. However, the ability to effortlessly shift back and forth between ordinary reality and the nonphysical world of energy was lost over time.

Ancient Shamans were early people who remained adept at making this shift in consciousness. In this altered state of consciousness, they explored nonphysical reality and accessed useful information.

They used this knowledge to improve the lives of their people by preventing and healing illness, meeting practical needs, and solving problems. Today, the principles and methods that the ancient Shamans originated are called *Shamanism*.

Modern Shamans continue to keep and use this body of knowledge accumulated since ancient times. The rich cultural heritage of indigenous and tribal peoples around the globe often includes Shamanic systems of belief and practice.

A modern *Shaman* is any man or woman who can shift from ordinary consciousness to Shamanic consciousness at will, defined as follows:

- *Ordinary consciousness* is when someone is fully aware of physical surroundings and can go about everyday activities. The mind handles a continual stream of sights, sounds, smells, and sensations.

- *Shamanic consciousness* is the state in which people can perceive the nonphysical world of energy, where energy is less dense, and form is freer than in ordinary consciousness. It is a state of trance. *Trance* is the opposite of ordinary consciousness; it's a state of narrowed and heightened focus. In trance, your attention narrows until it's drawn to events happening inside your own mind. You're unaware of your physical surroundings; you may be unaware of your physical body or the passage of time. The brain checks out of ordinary time and space and goes inward, tapping into the unconscious mind. (See Chapter 18 for more information.)

Even today, all people have the ability to enter trance and perceive the energy of the nonphysical world, but most modern humans require training and practice to do it. The process of shifting consciousness and exploring non-ordinary reality often is called *journeying*. A spirit guide (or guardian spirit), often in the form of a power animal, aids and protects the Shaman on this journey (see Chapter 3 for more information on animal helpers).

By journeying in the nonphysical world, a person can gain knowledge, enhance personal power, and restore physical, mental, and emotional health and wellbeing. One can undertake this journey for the self or for other people.

More intuition, less ceremony

Wicca has many ideas in common with Shamanism:

- The physical world is not the only reality. There are other states of consciousness or spiritual planes that are just as real and accessible. In Shamanism, the nonphysical world is often called *non-ordinary reality* (a term made popular by author Carlos Castaneda). In Wicca, the nonphysical world is called the *Otherworld* or the astral plane(s).

- A person can enter an altered or ritual state of consciousness to tap into non-ordinary reality or the Otherworld.

- A guardian spirit may help the person enter and journey in the Otherworld. In Shamanism, the guardian spirit is often a *power animal,* a spiritual being that guides and protects the Shaman. In Wicca, an animal that offers magical, psychic, or spiritual help and support is called a *familiar.* (However, a power animal generally is a spirit animal; a familiar typically is a physical animal.)

✔ In the Otherworld or non-ordinary reality, a person can accomplish goals that may be impossible in the physical world, including: restoring physical, mental, and emotional health; gaining knowledge unavailable in an ordinary state of consciousness; and enhancing personal power. The person can undertake these efforts for the self or for someone else.

✔ The forces of nature can be used to aid in the quest for knowledge and empowerment.

✔ Herbs, roots, and berries can be used for healing or other magical purposes.

Many methods are available to help an individual create the shift in consciousness from ordinary to non-ordinary reality. Most Wiccans today use ritual to make the shift. When Wiccans incorporate Shamanism into their practice, they use Shamanic methods for altering consciousness and journeying to the nonphysical world. These methods include drumming, rattling, chanting, dance, and trance. Intuition replaces ceremony.

The ceremonial magic that has become so prevalent in many Wiccan traditions is beautiful, but also detailed and complex, requiring specific tools, scripted rituals, and precise timing. Shamanic practice enables simpler and quicker access to the Otherworld.

The controversy over Shamanism

Some Wiccans are critical of the use of Shamanic methods by non-indigenous peoples. The critics see the use of these techniques as a co-opting of native spirituality, a sort of cultural theft.

The counter-argument is that Westerners' efforts to recover their own early European Pagan, tribal roots and re-create their own traditions are valid and may ultimately help the planet by encouraging the preservation of nature. However, Wiccans who merge Wicca and Shamanism need to be careful not to disrespect, dishonor, or exploit native cultures, and to help ensure the survival of these cultures.

Michael Harner (a leading authority on global Shamanism) maintains that Shamanism is similar throughout much of the world. He suggests that the uniformity of these techniques developed globally and consistently because they work. The lack of modern medicine compelled people to "develop to the highest degree possible the ability of the human mind to cope with serious problems of health and survival." Trial and error showed them which methods were the most effective, and over time, Shamans settled on the same methods. See Harner's book *The Way of the Shaman,* (1990) for more information. Based on Harner's point of view, Shamanic methods are a common thread through all cultures and are available to everyone.

Selena Fox is a leading authority in the blending of Wicca and Shamanism. In 1974, she founded Circle Sanctuary, a nonprofit organization dedicated to networking, research, spiritual healing, community celebrations, and education. The Circle sponsors gatherings and encourages nature preservation with nature meditations and workshops celebrated at diverse locations, including the Circle Sanctuary Nature Preserve, a 200-acre site in southwestern Wisconsin.

Additionally, Circle Sanctuary provides many services to the Pagan community, including various publications. Visit the Web site at: www.circle sanctuary.org.

Clearing a New Path: Eclectic Wicca

Most Wiccans agree that eclectic Wicca is the most common form of Wicca in the United States today. Eclectic Wicca is not a tradition; it's the absence of one. Solitary Wiccans often are eclectic, and covens also may be eclectic. Some non-Wiccan practices incorporated into eclectic Wicca include Eastern meditation techniques, feng shui, I-Ching, and Reiki.

Bits of belief and pieces of practice

An *eclectic* is a Wiccan who follows no specific tradition. Eclectics craft their own paths, adopting beliefs and practices from various Wiccan traditions, or developing their own. They may also explore teachings and practices outside of Wicca. Each eclectic decides what works for him or her.

Many Wiccans like to use their own wisdom and intuition to develop rituals and to guide magical practice. Eclectics have the freedom to do the following:

- ✔ Worship in their own ways. They don't use rituals designed for a specific tradition. They can create rituals to meet their own needs. They can select the tools and other objects that feel right to them in a given situation. They also can choose their own style of ritual dress.

- ✔ Choose the time for their spiritual work. A tradition may specify the exact times that ritual should be performed. Eclectics can choose to move the time to the night before, or even wait until the weekend.

- ✔ Change rituals and magical practice to evolve with the individual, to accommodate advancing age, different circumstances, or new beliefs.

- ✔ Tailor study and training to individual needs, instead of using the program prescribed by the tradition.

The case against eclectic Wicca

Eclectic Wicca may sound like the best of all possible Wiccan worlds. However, it's not for everyone. Some people are more effective and feel more secure with the guidance and instruction of a tradition. They don't want to feel like they're just making it up as they go along.

There is another good reason to consider a tradition over eclectic practice. Traditions provide structure and a framework for practice, for example, the lay of the altar for a given ritual or the size of the circle to be cast. With these physical considerations already out of the way, many Wiccans find that they can concentrate more fully on the spiritual aspects of practice — especially in a coven setting, where coveners may burn up valuable time arguing over details.

Because of the freedom and individuality it allows, eclectic Wicca will no doubt continue to grow.

Part IV
Following the Sun and the Moon: How Wiccans Worship

The 5th Wave — By Rich Tennant

@RICHTENNANT.COM

"I don't suppose we could discuss this at a time when the moon is in a different phase?"

In this part . . .

The heart of Wicca is ritual. During ritual, Wiccans seek to understand, experience, and feel their connection to Deity. For many Wiccans, the Esbats and the Sabbats (the holy days or holidays) are the best times to perform ritual and seek attunement with the Divine.

Wicca is a nature religion, and the holy days are directly timed to natural occurrences, instead of human events. The Esbats celebrate the phases of the Moon, especially the Full Moon. The Sabbats mark the Earth's journey around the Sun, and the Wiccan path through life. The Sabbat celebrations reflect the Pagan past, the Wiccan present, and the timeless mythology of the Craft.

In this part, you can find out how Wiccans turn the wheel of the year and draw closer to the Divine.

Chapter 11

Setting Up an Altar and Choosing Tools

*M*any people see only the physical aspects of Wicca. They see the pentacles, the strange knives, the cauldrons, and the altars. Some folks are amused, some are frightened, and some just scratch their heads.

This chapter puts the objects and symbolism of Wicca into context. To understand Wicca, you need to see the connection between the inner process and the outer landscape. In this chapter, you can find out why people in the Craft invest care and creativity in establishing their altars and selecting their magical tools. Wiccans create their own sacred space, and the altar is a place of security and solace, insight and transformation.

Creating Sacred Space

Location, location, location. That's the motto for this section. Wiccans create sacred space, a place where they stand at the threshold of the physical world and the Spirit world. Here, they perform ritual and work magic, and they develop their relationship with Divinity.

To grasp this idea, you need to be clear about three words:

▶ **Ritual** is a ceremony that a person does for a specific purpose. The purpose of a *religious ritual* is to understand, experience, or feel the connection to Deity.

✔ *Magic* is the art of moving and directing energy to accomplish a specific goal.

✔ *Sacred space* is the area that Wiccans use for ritual and magic.

When Wiccans create sacred space, they cast a circle. The space within the circle is sacred; the circle defines the precise boundary. To *cast* a circle means to symbolically create the circle with the mind. Wiccans often use a tool to draw the circle in the air (see Chapter 12 to find out how to ritually cast a circle). Evidence shows that ancient Pagans used the circle for their rites.

Defining sacred space

A magical circle isn't really a circle, but a sphere. It's a sphere of energy. When a Wiccan casts a circle, he or she sends out personal power to build a sphere or globe of protective energy around himself or herself. The space inside that sphere transforms and is no longer part of the ordinary, physical world. It stands apart, between the everyday world and the world of the Spirit, which Wiccans often call the Otherworld.

The circle keeps all distracting or negative energy out and keeps personal power in the sacred space. The space inside the sphere is used to define the *Cone of Power.* Inside the circle, a Wiccan performs ritual and invokes Deity. Wiccans work magic in the sacred space, too, because they usually want to invite the presence or participation of Deity in their magical work.

Most Wiccans think of the sacred space within a circle as being outside of time, space, and matter — a place to meet the Deity.

The area within a magical circle is cleansed and consecrated (dedicated to Deity). It is holy ground. For Wiccans, it is as holy as a church, mosque, or temple is to people of other religions. Wiccans generally don't have permanent buildings, and they create sacred space anew each time they cast a circle. For Wiccans, Deity is everywhere, so they can cast a circle anywhere and anytime. The site for a circle may be temporary (used once) or permanent (used regularly), but it only becomes sacred space when the circle is actually cast.

A coven or any other group can cast a circle and make sacred space for ritual and magical work performed together. Some covens have a *covenstead,* a place where the coven regularly meets as a group. A covenstead usually has a permanent site for the circle.

An individual can also cast a circle and create sacred space to perform ritual or work magic alone. A Wiccan generally has a personal area where he or she regularly creates sacred space to work solo. This area often is in his or her home or apartment, although some people use a secluded spot outdoors.

Every Wiccan is considered to be a Priestess or Priest and has the right to create sacred space.

Designing sacred space

If you are a Wiccan, or are seriously exploring Wicca, you may want to designate a place outside or inside of your home for ritual or magical work. The size and location of the space depends on your circumstances and preferences.

Communing with Mother Nature

Most Wiccans prefer to work outdoors, but that is rarely practical these days. Most people don't live in a climate hospitable enough to perform ritual or magic outside throughout the year, and few can find a spot that guarantees privacy.

If you do work outside, make sure that you have a legal right be on the property. To avoid trouble with authorities, don't trespass or break any other laws.

Some natural places make beautiful sites for sacred space. These include hill-tops; the banks of lakes, rivers, natural springs, or streams; forest clearings; spots near large, old trees; and gardens.

If the site is sufficiently secluded, you may mark off a permanent circle by using small stones, sand, or other natural materials to show the boundary of the circle. However, to avoid unwanted attention from neighbors or police, many Wiccans choose to return outdoor sites to their natural state after every ritual. Many traditions require that members return the site of a circle casting to its original state, which means making it "as it was before."

Bringing ritual home

Most Wiccans must use a portion of their home or apartment for sacred space. Some people are lucky enough to have a spare bedroom, a basement, an attic, or other separate area that they can reserve for Wiccan activities, but that luxury isn't necessary. You can choose any area of your living space, for example, a corner of a bedroom or a walk-in closet.

You may want to consider the following practical issues when you designate your own sacred space:

✔ Try to make the space as private as possible, away from the flow of family traffic, sounds from the television, and so on. Having a door and a lock help. Use a Do Not Disturb Sign.

✔ Remove carpet or rugs. A dripping candle can make a mess of a rug or carpet, as can burning incense. Both can set carpet on fire.

✔ Make sure that candles are several feet away from draperies and other flammable items. Candles get very hot and can ignite fabric and other materials from surprising distances.

✔ Cover windows with draperies or blinds that provide full coverage. Rituals and magical work generally are more effective in darkness illuminated by candlelight. A neighbor's security light or the neon sign from the pizza joint next door can spoil the ambience.

Besides, you don't want a modern-day Mrs. Kravitz discussing your activities with anyone who'll listen. (For those of you who don't watch reruns, Mrs. Kravitz was the very nosy neighbor on *Bewitched*.)

✔ Get creative. The space doesn't have to be a design wonder from a TV decorating show. No one needs to spend the rent money on decor for this area. However, if you have a bit of money and a lot of creativity, this is one area of the home where the style can reflect your own heart. Personal artwork, including hand-painted murals on the walls, sculpture, or photos, are great for building attachment to the area. Consider decorating the room to resemble a forest glade or other mystical outdoor spot.

Having some storage space is nice — a chest, dresser, trunk, or bookshelves to hold supplies, altar tools, stones, tarot cards, magical books, and the like. If the space isn't permanent, a small chest on rollers can do the trick. Thrift stores sometimes offer nice, used furniture for only a few bucks.

Make sure that everything in the area has meaning to you, and doesn't produce negative feelings that may interfere with magical work. This area is where you will cast the circle for your ritual and magic.

Casting the circle may be easier if you physically mark the boundary of a circle. You may draw the line with chalk, unwind a length of cord, or even paint the circle on the floor. Many Wiccan traditions require that the circle be 9 feet in diameter; others specify a different size. An individual may make the circle any size that is appropriate for the setting and circumstances. The circle doesn't need to be perfectly round or even symmetrical. Any shape that works within your space is fine. Most Wiccans place an altar in the center of the circle.

Focusing on the Altar

The altar is the focal point of Wiccan ritual. It's a sanctuary. At the altar, Wiccans perceive the Otherworld and experience connection with Divinity. It's the place where Wiccans can manifest their greatest power and envision their greatest potential. Regular meditation, ritual, and magical practice imbue an altar with energy.

Choosing an altar style and material

The altar serves an important purpose, but the object itself can be very humble. An altar can be a simple cloth draped over a cardboard box. The only rule is that the altar has to be strong enough to support the items on its surface — especially burning candles and incense — and big enough to work comfortably with those items.

The ideal structure depends on whether you're a kneeler or a stander. If you want to kneel or sit, a very low altar is in order. But if your preferences or tradition dictate that you stand up, you may need a taller piece of furniture.

Many Wiccans believe that natural materials are preferable to synthetic ones for altars because synthetic substances don't conduct energy as well or in the same way as natural materials.

The following sections offer some possibilities for altars. Wiccans may cast a circle and create sacred space either outdoors or indoors, and altar materials vary depending on the setting. (See the preceding section for advice on designating sacred space outdoors and indoors.)

Outdoor altars

For outdoor work, a large, flat stone makes a nice altar, as does a big tree stump that is free of debris, mold, insects, and so on. A garden bench may serve as a lovely temporary altar. You also may choose to place a cloth directly on the ground, or use a portable altar. A portable outdoor altar may be a folding table, a picnic basket with a lid, a tray, or any other movable flat surface.

Indoor altars

Having an altar indoors rather than outdoors opens up more options for style and individuality. All the following are options for indoor altars:

- a cloth or scarf placed on the floor
- a box or crate covered with a cloth (make sure that it's strong enough to support burning candles)
- a large square cutting board or other piece of wood
- a slab of marble or other stone (my own altar is a polished slab of marble that I purchased for $5.00 at a stone center catering to landscapers)
- two stones topped by a third, flat stone
- a stone or wooden bench
- tiles or flagstones
- a dresser, chest, cabinet, or box (you can store altar tools, books, matches, and other supplies inside)

> ✔ a coffee table, side table, end table or round decorator table
>
> ✔ an altar made and decorated specifically for the purpose — purchased from a retailer specializing in religious goods or handmade by someone you contract to build it

Altars to go

Many Wiccans prefer portable altars. A port-a-altar can go out into nature, when weather permits, or stay at home in a closet or corner out of sight when not in use.

Many people live in apartment buildings where staff and maintenance people regularly enter residents' living spaces. Wiccans who are not "out" about their spirituality may feel more comfortable with an altar that they can store or hide easily and quickly.

A few years ago, two maintenance men entered my apartment to fix a window that wouldn't open. They became alarmed at the sight of my altar (the pentacle was visible), and I had to prove that the white stuff in the little bowl on the altar really was sea salt.

The following can serve well as a portable altar:

> ✔ steamer trunk
>
> ✔ hard suitcase
>
> ✔ picnic basket with a flat lid
>
> ✔ folding table
>
> ✔ rolling chest or cabinet
>
> ✔ fold-up desk

Placing the altar in sacred space

Many Wiccans place an altar in the center of the ritual circle; others place it at the edge of the circle. Some orient the altar so that it (and the person performing the ritual actions on the altar) is facing north; some face the altar east, toward the rising Sun. The requirements of different traditions vary. Follow your own gut instincts, and don't be afraid to base the placement of your altar on the layout of your room and your own inner preferences.

If your altar area is inside, try to keep it clean. Cleaning keeps the energy around the altar unblocked and positive. This is a general cleaning, not a ceremonial purification. If the altar is outdoors, remove trash from its area and wash off the altar if possible. Don't pour cleaning chemicals or salt on the ground outside. These substances kill plants and may hurt wildlife. If you want to do a more formal cleaning and purification, such work is traditionally performed on the night of a New Moon.

Many Wiccans cover their altars with an altar cloth. The advantage is such a cloth can be easily removed for cleaning. This cloth may be any color and may be embroidered or imprinted with an appealing design. Some people place a sheet of glass over the altar or the cloth, so candle wax or burned incense doesn't ruin the cloth or the altar surface. After situating your altar, you may arrange altar tools on the surface.

If you have children or animals, don't leave a decorated altar within their reach. Herbs/plants used for their magical properties or for decoration may be poisonous if ingested. Candles are not suitable playthings for children. Children must not have access to some Wiccan tools, such as the athame (a Wiccan dagger).

Surveying the Tools of the Craft

When a Wiccan performs ritual, his mind heightens his awareness of Deity. When a Wiccan works magic, her mind is moving and directing energy to accomplish a specific goal. In both cases, the mind is doing the work, but certain objects or methods may give the brain a boost by triggering areas of human consciousness or expanding the mind's power to act.

An example of an everyday object with symbolic meaning is the broom. In everyday life, a broom sweeps dirt off of the back porch. But a Wiccan may use a broom symbolically. She passes the broom back and forth over the floor, in the air, or across an altar with the intention of sweeping negativity and blocked energy out of her space and out of her life. The process occurs in the mind, or perhaps the soul, but the broom is the tool that sparks the potential.

Craft tools offer Wiccans a beginning, a way for people to access power for positive change.

A Wiccan may purchase his or her tools, make them, find them, or receive them as gifts. Some traditions require that a Wiccan's tools be new, and that they are never used for anything other than ritual use. Other Wiccans routinely use their tools for practical, mundane activities. For example, some will use a ritual blade for peeling potatoes. Each Wiccan decides for him or herself.

Unfortunately, money may be an issue for a Wiccan who is setting up a first altar and acquiring tools. Web sites and stores that specialize in Wiccan goods offer tools of breathtaking beauty. Unfortunately, the price may take your breath away, too. You don't have to bust your budget buying every tool known to the Craft. You can choose a few, inexpensive implements or even make your own.

The tools that Wiccans use today are based on everyday implements that Pagans have used throughout history. Many of these items can be acquired with minimal expense. In practice, a humble cup is just as effective as a gold-plated goblet. You don't need an ornate censer (incense holder) to burn incense; use any heat-proof container lined with sand to hold the sticks or cones. The quality of spiritual experience is far more important than the accumulation of goods.

The following sections describe the most basic Craft tools and their uses. These elemental tools are the ones that most people in the Craft like to keep handy. However, no one has to use all or any of these implements to effectively practice Wicca.

Athame

Traditionally, the athame is a knife or dagger with a straight, double-edged blade and a black handle (see Figure 11-1). The blade usually is metal, although some Wiccans prefer stone, especially flint. The handle is supposed to be a natural substance, generally wood, instead of plastic. The size is up to the user, but a blade of at least 4 inches is standard.

Figure 11-1:
The athame is a key tool in Wicca and is used to direct a Wiccan's personal energy.

Athame is pronounced *ath*-ah-may, *ath*-e-may, a-*tham*-ee, a-*thah*-may, ah-*thaw*-may, ath-*ay*-mee, or a-*thame*. Good luck trying to figure out which is actually correct. Wiccans can't agree about the pronunciation for this tool, and everyone thinks that his or her own pronunciation is the correct one. The difference is largely regional, so just try to use the pronunciation common to your area.

The athame is not a weapon. The knife generally isn't used for practical cutting, for example for cutting herbs. It's used only for ritual purposes. If you're a klutz, like me, you may want to consider a dull blade.

Some consider the athame to be the most important tool of Wicca because it is so intimately tied to the energy of its owner. Its action is symbolic. The athame serves as a conductor of the energy of the wielder. The athame directs this energy outward from the user like a beam of light. Wiccans use the athame to direct energy, or some say to control energy. It draws and takes down the circle that defines sacred space, and it also traces pentagrams.

Some Wiccans decorate the hilt and the blade; others do not. Many feel that if an athame ever draws blood, even accidentally, it is no longer an acceptable sacred tool.

If you use an athame, make sure that you don't accidentally cut someone when you wield the blade during ritual or when you transport it (keep it in a sheath). Be aware that laws vary on the possession of blades. Make sure that your athame is legal, and that you are old enough to carry it.

Never touch the blade of any athame with your fingers. The oil and residue from your fingers cause the blade to rust (if the metal is not very carefully cleaned after each use).

Candles

Candles serve several important functions:

- ✔ Many Wiccans place two candles in the middle of the altar to symbolize the Goddess and the God.

- ✔ A candle is placed in each of the four quarters (North, East, South, and West) of a ritual circle in order to mark the boundary of sacred space.

- ✔ Most Wiccans place additional candles on the altar (usually in the closest portion of the altar), as well as around the ritual space.

- ✔ Candles provide the light by which Wiccans perform ritual or work magic.

✔ Candles are available in many colors and serve as a way to introduce different colors during spellwork and other magic.

✔ Candles appeal to the primal Self, and trigger changes in consciousness.

Many Wiccans wear robes, especially with bell sleeves, during ritual. Take care not to touch your robe to the candle flames. Make sure that your altar candles aren't too close to draperies or other fabric; also ensure that candles are in sturdy holders that won't tip over and ignite carpet or other materials.

Candles purchased for use in ritual are generally not used for any other purpose. Select candles that appeal to you or have symbolic associations with their purpose. For example, many people associate a particular color with each of the directions and use a candle of that color for that direction. Consider buying pillar candles in glass containers. They are safer to use because the glass protects the flame.

Censer, brazier, or thurible and incense

A censer, also known as a brazier or a thurible, is an incense burner. The incense burner may be as simple as a can of sand to hold incense sticks or cones, or it may be a more expensive decorative holder (see Figure 11-2) with a lid and handle or chains for carrying it. Incense comes in many different forms (sticks, cones, and powdered or ground herbal incense).

Which form of incense you use is a matter of personal preference. Self-igniting incense is more convenient but gives you less control over how much you burn at one time; incense that is not self-igniting requires charcoal blocks for burning.

Incense is usually stored in an air-tight container and can last for an extended period. Most people use scents that they enjoy, although many Wiccans select incense based on the magical properties of the ingredients (see Appendix B for the magical properties of various herbs).

Never use barbecue charcoal inside a house or other building. It's dangerous. Some Pagan stores or religious supply stores sell special charcoal for burning incense. As with candles, make sure that the incense is in a sturdy holder and that it is away from draperies or other flammable materials. Stick incense is easier and safer to use.

For Wiccans, fire is cleansing because it can change something from one form to another. The smoke from incense has been purified by the fire; the smoke purifies sacred space by forcing out other energy.

Figure 11-2:
The censer,
also called a
brazier or
thurible,
holds the
incense on
the altar.

Chalice, cup, or goblet

The chalice can be anything from a humble, simple cup to an elaborate stemmed goblet, handpainted with symbols (see Figure 11-3).

The chalice holds sacred water, wine, or juice for any ritual purpose. The chalice may hold the water that seals a ritual circle. Some Wiccans see the chalice as a miniature cauldron, representing the womb of the Goddess and associated with regeneration. Like all your tools, select a chalice that you find attractive and feel is right for the purpose. What makes the chalice a magical tool is that it is set aside for ritual (sacrificed from day-to-day use).

Many Wiccan traditions perform the Great Rite. During this rite, words, such as "as the cup is the female and the athame is the male, together they are one" are spoken. The athame is then thrust into the chalice to consecrate its contents. The Great Rite symbolizes sexual intercourse and reflects Wicca's history as a fertility religion.

Figure 11-3:
The chalice
holds
sacred
water, wine,
or juice.

Deity images and symbols

As the focus of the altar, many Wiccans place a symbol or an image of the Goddess and/or the God. Some people use two candles, one for the Goddess and one for the God. Images of the Deity include statues, drawings, paintings, flowers, shells, seeds, or anything else that draws you to Divinity (see Figure 11-4).

Wiccans place symbols of the Deity on the altar to remind them of the Divine presence. Such an image or symbol helps the mind to open to a fuller awareness of the ongoing deep connection with Deity. However, the image or symbol itself is not the Goddess or the God.

Pentagram and pentacle

A pentagram is a five-pointed interlaced star. It is the primary symbol of the Craft. The five points represent the four elements: Earth, Air, Fire, and Water, plus Spirit (the top point). The pentagram is also a symbol for humanity, and to some it means self-improvement. Historically, a drawing of a person often is superimposed on the pentagram. The head is at the top, the middle points are outstretched arms, and the bottom two points are legs.

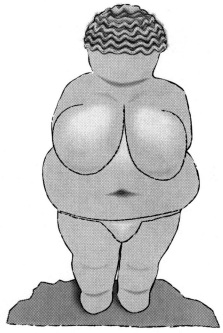

Figure 11-4:
An image at
the center
of the altar
as a
represen-
tation of
Deity and as
a focus for
the altar.

A pentacle is a disk with a pentagram inscribed on it. When setting a ritual altar, a pentacle is an altar plate with a pentagram on it (see Figure 11-5). Purchasing a pentacle requires access to a store that specializes in Craft tools, so many people make their own by modifying an existing plate or disk. In fact, creating a set of tools for your own use is a requirement for initiation in some traditions.

Inside a ritual circle, pentagrams are drawn in the air in order to invoke or banish energy or unseen forces. When drawing a pentagram, a Wiccan may start at several different points, depending on the goal he or she wants to accomplish or the requirements of the tradition (see Figure 11-6).

On the altar, a pentacle serves as the gateway to the Otherworld. It is the symbolic threshold between the physical world and the Spirit world (the astral planes). Sacred cakes may be served from it. Wiccans use pentagrams in many ways during ritual and magic. Pentagrams can be used to cleanse an item of negative energy, to bless an item or individual, and to seal a magical working.

Figure 11-5:
The pentacle is used as a ritual tool with meanings associated with providing a framework and serving as a threshold.

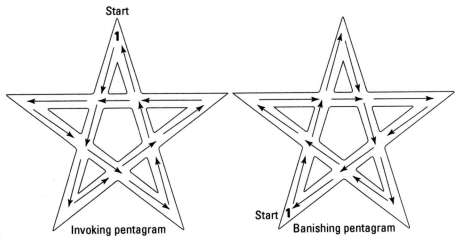

Figure 11-6:
The invoking pentagram invites or summons energy. The banishing pentagram sends unwanted energy away.

Invoking pentagram

Banishing pentagram

Salt

Wiccans use salt for cleansing and purifying. Salt is always used in the consecration of objects, places, or people. (See the section, "Carrying Out the Three Cs: Cleansing, Charging, and Consecrating Tools," later in this chapter.) Some Wiccans use salt for protection. Almost all altars present a bowl of salt.

Some Wiccans believe that sea salt must be used for ritual, instead of table salt. To prepare salt for magical uses, hold a tablespoon of salt in the palm of your dominant hand and call upon Deity to bless it.

Wand

A wand may be any short stick. Some Wiccans prefer to use natural tree branches. Others purchase elaborate wands made of wood, glass, crystal, precious metal, stones, and so on (see Figure 11-7). To make a wand of the correct size, some people cut the wood to match the length from the crook of the elbow to the tip of the forefinger.

My own wand is a dropped branch from an apple tree that is special to me. For many years, a lone cougar periodically visited the tree. In the heat of late summer, she stretched out under the tree's low branches. She gave a lazy warning growl if anyone wandered too close.

The wand conducts, directs, or invokes energy. Wiccans may use the wand to direct the Cone of Power within a ritual circle and to invoke the Goddess and the God. Generally, the wand is a tool used to manifest personal will power.

Some Wiccans believe that the wand and the athame are interchangeable (see the preceding section "Athame"). If you don't like blades and don't want to use an athame, the wand is an alternative. While most Wiccans have only one athame, they may have several different wands, each for a specific purpose.

Water

Many believe that water for ritual use must be purified, blessed, or consecrated. Wiccans differ markedly about how to go about doing this. One way is to leave a large bottle of water outside during a Full Moon. Under the Moon, ask that the water be returned to purity. Next, hold a tablespoon of salt in the palm of your dominant hand and call upon Deity to bless it. Add the salt to the water. You can store the water in any container.

Some believe that natural elements require no additional preparation (although most would agree that water from a stream or well is better than tap water for this purpose).

Wiccans use water in a variety of ways during ritual. Water is for cleansing and purifying. It is always used in the consecration of objects, places, or people. See the section, "Carrying Out the Three Cs: Cleansing, Charging, and Consecrating Tools," later in this chapter.

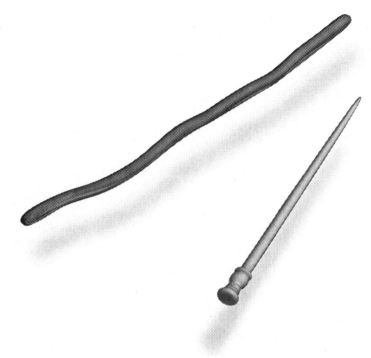

Figure 11-7:
The wand
directs
energy and
manifests
the
Wiccan's
will.

Other tools

In addition to the basic tools discussed in previous sections, many Wiccans use the following:

- ✔ **Bell:** A bell alters the vibrations of a ritual area. It can activate the auditory sense during the working of magic. Some use a bell to invoke the Goddess, to evoke positive energy, to halt storms, or to protect the living space. A bell may play a role in casting, cleansing, or closing a circle.

- ✔ **Boline or boleen or bolline:** This knife usually has a white handle and a curved blade; some of them look like a hand sickle. Traditionally, a boline was used for cutting herbs. It also can accomplish practical tasks at the altar, such as cutting cord or carving symbols into candles. The athame cuts energy; the boline cuts physical objects.

- ✔ **Broom or besom:** A broom sweeps an area clean of negative energy before ritual. The bristles usually don't touch the ground. The sweeping is symbolic, and the one doing the sweeping visualizes the negative or distracting energy leaving the scene. During handfasting ceremonies, a couple may jump the broom to show that they are jumping into a new life together. Many cultures have Goddesses who are associated with brooms.

✔ **Cauldron:** Traditionally, the cauldron is black metal and has three legs and a handle. It can do both ordinary or magical cooking. Placing candles inside creates the illusion of a fire. It represents the womb of the Goddess and is associated with creation and regeneration. I found an inexpensive, traditional-looking cauldron in a store specializing in camping goods, so think creatively before you spend a fortune on a cauldron.

✔ **Cord or cingulum:** Cords play a role in various forms of magic and ritual. Generally, cords made of natural material are preferred. A cord can be knotted to store magical energy for later release. Some traditions use different colored cords to denote specific degrees of advancement in the Craft, and in some cases the initiate is expected to spin his or her own cord.

✔ **Herbs:** Wiccans use herbs for their magical properties and also for healing.

✔ **Mortar and pestle:** You can grind herbs and other substances with a mortar and pestle.

✔ **Staff:** A staff sometimes substitutes for a wand, particularly in large public rituals. Like swords, staffs may be very dangerous in crowded settings.

✔ **Stones, crystals, gems:** These natural materials have varying magical properties. Wiccans use them as tools. Although Wiccans revere nature, they don't worship crystals or other objects.

✔ **Sword:** A sword often substitutes for an athame. The sword is a ceremonial weapon to protect against unwanted energies. In Wicca, it's never used as an actual weapon to threaten or hurt living beings. Swords may be very dangerous in crowded settings.

In addition to the tools in this section, many Wiccans consider the following to be tools that they use during ritual:

✔ chanting

✔ dance

✔ gestures

✔ music (especially drumming)

✔ visualization

You may wish to leave room on the altar for an open Book of Shadows, your own personal journal and sourcebook of Wiccan life. It includes the details of ritual and magical work.

Carrying Out the Three Cs: Cleansing, Charging, and Consecrating Tools

You can't just take a new tool out of the sack and begin to use it in the same way that a plumber pulls out a wrench to tighten a fitting. Before you use any tool for ritual or magic, you must cleanse, charge, and consecrate it, according to most Wiccans. These terms sort of overlap because Wiccans hold different views of these actions. The following are some working definitions:

- *Cleanse:* to remove any and all energy or vibrations that are attached to an object; to make an object pure; to purify

- *Charge:* to imbue an object with energy; to transmit power into an object

- *Consecrate:* to dedicate an object to the service of Deity or to the Craft

Sometimes Wiccans use the word *consecrate* to encompass all three of these processes. The three Cs can be done to objects, places, or people. Wiccan tools may be charged and consecrated within a group ritual (often during an initiation) or by an individual alone during ritual. See Chapter 12 for a ritual to consecrate tools. Some Wiccans employ elaborate rituals for consecrating tools, but a simple one can be elegant and effective.

Don't swipe a sigil

A sigil is a sacred or magical symbol or design. A sigil may be a rune symbol, a letter from a magical alphabet, an animal symbol, or an original design that you create. Many books are available that list Pagan, occult, Wiccan, and other symbols. You also can find potential sigils on the Web.

If you decide to use a sigil on your tools or for other practices in the Craft, make sure that you do research first. Know what the symbol means and what type of energies you may be inviting into your environment. Decide whether it's a symbol or design that you will continue to be happy with in the future.

In addition, some sigils are associated with specific groups. In some traditions, a person may use a certain sigil only after he or she has attained the required degree or level. Followers of a specific aspect of the Goddess or the God sometimes use a common sigil.

No copyright police will hunt you down if you co-opt the use of one of these sigils, but you may get some dirty looks if you take a well-known sigil that everyone else in the Craft assumes is the property of a specific group.

Before you begin the consecration ritual, make sure that you physically clean the object by washing, polishing, or doing whatever is appropriate. You can inscribe the tool with your Craft name, a personal motto, or a sigil (a magical design or symbol). You can make the inscription permanent, by carving into the object, or make it temporary by using pen and ink.

The consecration ritual usually involves claiming the object, cleansing the object with the four elements (Earth, Air, Fire, and Water), and dedicating it to the service of Deity.

Most Wiccans believe that cleansing, charging, and consecrating only needs to be done once, prior to first use of the tool. Some Wiccans believe that tools must be cleansed and/or charged and/or consecrated once a year or before every ritual. At some point, this process becomes obsessive, but each person must decide where to draw the line.

Arranging Tools on the Altar

After tools are cleansed, charged, and consecrated, most Wiccans keep their tools on their altars. A ritual case or bag is also an option for storing them until time to use them.

Wiccans differ about the purpose of specific tools and the way to arrange individual tools on an altar. However, the next section outlines a general framework that many Wiccans accept.

Quartering the sacred circle

Wiccans generally place the altar at the center of sacred space inside a ritual circle. Four candles sit at the outer edges of the circle to mark the boundary. Wiccans place one candle at each of the four directions: North, East, South, and West. The sacred circle divided into quarters is a very important concept in Wicca, and is common to many other religions.

For Wiccans the four quarters and the center of the circle correspond to parts of the Self and the elements of nature. The following list shows a set of *correspondences* used by many traditions:

- ✔ North corresponds to Earth and to the human body.
- ✔ East corresponds to Air and to the human mind.
- ✔ South corresponds to Fire and to human energy.
- ✔ West corresponds to Water and to human emotions.
- ✔ The center of the circle corresponds to Spirit.

So when a person casts a circle, all aspects of the Self and nature are activated and unified.

A Wiccan may adjust the correspondences so that they make sense to him or her. For example, in some areas of the world, the West may not be associated with Water. Perhaps the ocean lies to the East. An active volcano may lie to the North, so the North becomes associated with Fire.

Some Wiccans invoke the four directions (North, East, South, and West) because they believe doing so brings actual energy forms into the circle. These forms are the spirits of the physical elements — Earth, Wind, Fire, and Water — called the *Guardians of the Watchtowers*. These spirits guard the boundary of the circle and heighten awareness of the Deity.

Many Wiccans believe that specific tools symbolize — or represent the forces of — the directions, the elements, and the aspects of Self. The tools are arranged on the altar according to their corresponding directions and elements, so the altar reflects the quarters of the sacred circle:

- Earth tools in the North
- Air tools in the East
- Fire tools in the South
- Water tools in the West

You can place your tools in a circle, according to their corresponding positions. For example, a chalice or cup symbolizes water, and is placed on the west side of the altar. Incense is an air tool and appears on the eastern part of the altar.

Table 11-1 shows the correspondences and placement of the most common tools. These correspondences vary, according to the tradition the Wiccan follows and also personal preference.

Wiccans differ about the way that certain tools are characterized. For example, some people believe that the athame is an air tool, others associate it with fire. The same argument pertains to the wand.

Candles may be a fire tool to be placed on the southern portion of the altar. However, many people place two candles, representing the Goddess and the God, in the center of the altar. In this case, the candles represent Spirit, and not fire.

Table 11-1		Arranging Tools on the Altar	
Tool	*Element*	*Direction*	*Altar Placement*
Athame	Air Fire	East South	Eastern Southern
Candles	Spirit Fire	Center South	Central Southern
Censer, brazier, or thurible (incense and burner)	Air	East	Eastern
Chalice, cup, or goblet	Water	West	Western
Deity images and symbols	Spirit	Center	Central
Pentacle and pentagram	Earth	North	Northern
Salt	Earth	North	Northern
Wand	Fire Air	South East	Southern Eastern
Water	Water	West	Western

Table 11-1 is a simplified version of the correspondences. Each of the directions/elements is linked to specific animals and plants, seasons, times of day, senses, colors, and aspects of the Goddess and the God. For example South/Fire corresponds with lions and dragons, summer, the noon hour, sight, the colors red and orange, and the Goddess Pele, to name just a few.

Instead of dividing tools by element and direction, some Wiccans use an entirely different plan. They dedicate the right side of the altar to the God and the left side to the Goddess (if they perceive Deity as God and Goddess). This arrangement means that the masculine symbols (athame, sword, wand, and censor) appear to the right on the altar, and the feminine symbols (chalice, broom, bells, cauldron, and so on) appear on the left of the altar.

Following tool etiquette

Wiccans disagree about who may touch tools that are displayed on an altar. Some in the Craft believe that after a tool has been consecrated to Deity and its owner, anyone can safely touch it. However, most Wiccans think that tools are suffused with the owner's own energy. The touch of someone else may disturb or disperse that power.

Never touch someone else's magical and ritual tools without permission.

Another common custom is that Wiccans don't haggle over price when they purchase any spiritual or magical tool to add to their collection. During the haggling, the seller may unwillingly be forced to drop his or her price. This may constitute harm done to the seller, and is a violation of the Wiccan Rede (which says, "An ye harm none, do what ye will.").

Most people feel that tools should be kept free of any type of negative energy. If a tool is exposed to a situation where negative energy can be picked up by association, the tool then needs to be cleansed of that energy.

If you have a permanent altar area, you may benefit from visiting it every day, even if only to sit and meditate. Such visits can be a daily time to seek grounding, comfort, reassurance, and peace.

Chapter 12

Designing and Performing Rituals: The Heart of Wicca

* *

In This Chapter

▶ Figuring out what ritual really is

▶ Designing and conducting ritual

▶ Looking at a sample ritual

* *

Ritual is the essence of Wicca. When a person performs a ritual, he or she has access to both information and revelation. A ritual is a link to the Divine energy within and without.

Rituals can be ecstatic and dramatic, powerful and joyous. Spiritual rituals nourish the mind, the heart, and the soul.

This chapter explains how to design and conduct a Wiccan ritual. Some Wiccans believe that ritual is more effective and more fulfilling if a person creates his or her own words and format, instead of following prepared rituals outlined in books or on the Web. Other Wiccans follow and hold respect for the rituals of their chosen traditions, but occasionally create their own. Either way, knowing the basic components of ritual is part of a solid understanding of Wicca. This chapter shows how to easily develop rituals based on your own needs, desires, and beliefs.

Understanding What a Ritual Is

A *ritual* or *rite* is a ceremony that a person performs for a specific purpose. The purpose of a *religious* or *spiritual ritual* or *rite* is to experience, understand, communicate with, honor, worship, or celebrate Deity.

This chapter on ritual focuses on Deity, but keep in mind that I'm using the word Deity very loosely. Wiccans have many different ways of perceiving and describing the Divine. Deity may be the Goddess and the God, the primal Great Goddess, a specific Goddess or God, the Gods, the Higher Self, or a symbol emerging from a person's own unconscious mind. (See Chapter 2 for more information on Wiccan ideas about the Divine.)

During ritual, Wiccans invoke, evoke, or welcome Deity, according to their traditions and beliefs. Wiccans may perform ritual for the sole purpose of developing relationship with the Divine, or they may conduct ritual for two additional reasons: to work magic and/or to celebrate (especially the Wiccan holidays and life passages).

Wiccans work magic and celebrate during ritual because they want to invite the presence or participation of Deity in their activities. Also, the ritual setting provides power and security for celebrations and magical work.

Rituals are performed by covens, by other groups, and by individuals who practice alone (solitaries). This chapter focuses more on the solitary, and the information is general. Most covens honor specific traditions, and they have their own ritual structure and format, which the group's Book of Shadows spells out for members.

Creating and Performing a Ritual

In some Wiccan traditions, the structure and liturgy of the rituals are elaborate and formal, and people follow them closely. Other traditions adopt a very loose format for rituals; these Wiccans allow rituals to evolve naturally as participants follow their own hearts and spirits or welcome the involvement of Deity. Many people incorporate both traditional liturgy and their own creative words and actions. Of course, solitary practitioners (people who practice alone, instead of in a coven) are free to shape their rituals any way that they see fit.

Designing a ritual

This section lists the basic parts of a Wiccan ritual. Although these are common throughout Wicca, not every Wiccan incorporates every one of these activities into every ritual, and not everyone follows the steps in this order. I present the ritual structure in simple steps so that everyone can adapt it to his or her own needs and beliefs.

The following are the most basic steps for conducting a Wiccan ritual:

1. **Decide why you want to conduct a ritual. Make sure that your intention is clear.**

2. **Decide how you want to perform your ritual; write the words that you want to use during the invocation and the other steps.**

3. Decide when to do the ritual; for example, you may want to time your ritual to a specific phase of the Moon or to a Wiccan holiday.

4. Decide where to do the ritual, set up an altar, and assemble the tools and other necessary objects.

5. Purify the space.

6. Purify yourself.

7. Cast a circle to create sacred space.

8. Invoke, evoke, or welcome Deity, according to your beliefs.

9. Conduct a ritual observance (for example, celebrate a Sabbat or an Esbat), if you desire.

10. Raise power and work magic, if you have a good reason.

11. Earth the power.

12. Thank (or dismiss) Deity.

13. Take down the circle.

Deciding why, how, when, and where to perform ritual

Wiccan spirituality revolves around ritual. Rituals require an investment in time and effort, and they reap big spiritual rewards. Because rituals are so important, most Wiccans take some time to think through their plans and the goal for each ritual they perform. That doesn't mean that you can't have a purely spontaneous ritual if the Spirit moves you.

Why to conduct ritual

A fulfilling ritual begins with positive and specific intentions. If you are going to conduct a ritual, know why. Is your ritual for worship alone, or also for celebration and/or magic? What do you want to accomplish with the ritual?

The following are some examples of ritual intentions. The list is just a small sample of the limitless possibilities:

✔ **Rituals for worshipping, honoring, or petitioning Deity:**

 • To seek guidance. You may want to ask the Divine for help in making career or relationship decisions. You may need help in meeting your basic physical and emotional needs. Some people ask Deity for help in determining their personal mission or reason for being alive in this time.

- To seek comfort or solace. Many Wiccans turn to the Divine for help releasing grief, dealing with crisis, coping with emotional pain, or working through other powerful emotions. Some people ask for Divine help in handling guilt or anger.

✔ **Rituals for celebration:**

- Most Wiccans celebrate the Sabbats and the Esbats, the Wiccan holy days (holidays). The next two chapters discuss these celebrations in more detail.

- Wiccans also ritually celebrate times of personal significance. Rites that commemorate life passages are a combination of celebration and petition for the blessings of Deity. These may include:

  the personal dedication and/or initiation into Wicca

  legal marriage and/or handfasting

  the naming, or Wiccaning, of a child

  puberty rites for an adolescent

  Croning or Eldering (for older Wiccans)

  Wiccan funerals or passing ceremonies

  Chapter 9 explains dedication and initiation into Wicca, and Chapter 6 describes life-passage rites.

✔ **Rituals for magic:**

- Healing for physical and emotional illness. Many Wiccans work magic within a ritual setting so they can ask for Divine help in healing themselves or others.

- Self-development. Wiccans often work magic for personal growth. They may work magic during ritual in order to break addictions, face fears, promote productive traits (will power or compassion, for example) or banish unproductive thoughts and behaviors (such as materialistic thinking).

- Divination. Many Wiccans want Divine participation in tarot readings, scrying, or other divination attempts to gain insight into the present and possible future(s). See Chapter 19 for more information about divination.

How to conduct ritual

After you are clear about why you are conducting a ritual, you can figure out the most appropriate format for the ritual. Decide which of the ritual steps you want to incorporate into your ritual. Don't be afraid to alter the steps to meet your own needs.

You may want to write the words that you intend to use for the ritual, including words to invoke Deity (see the later section "Invoking, evoking, or welcoming Deity") and the words for any spells that you want to cast.

Even if you are a solitary (a Wiccan who doesn't belong to a coven), you have the option of inviting other people to conduct ritual with you. It's usually best to invite people who understand the basic principles of Wicca and who have a positive intention for participating. Inviting someone to a ritual for reasons rooted in ego (for example, in order to show off knowledge or magic) is ethically unsound.

When to conduct ritual

Figure out when you want to perform your ritual. Most Wiccans time their rituals to the Sabbats (Wiccan holidays) or the Esbats (the Full Moon or other phases). The following two chapters describe the Wiccan holy days and can help you pick an appropriate time for your ritual.

Where to conduct ritual

After you know how and when you want to conduct your ritual, you can consider suitable locations. Chapter 11 provides detailed information on choosing an appropriate ritual site, establishing an altar, and assembling ritual tools.

Most Wiccans prefer to perform ritual outdoors. Hilltops, river and creek banks, forest clearings, gardens, and areas near natural springs or old trees are all great places for ritual. However, outdoor ritual isn't practical for many people, and they use a room or a corner of a residence for ritual. A good location is physically safe and offers freedom from unwanted distractions.

Many Wiccans place an altar in the center of the ritual space, facing north. Some face the altar east, toward the rising Sun. The requirements of different traditions vary. Your arrangement depends on your own setting and circumstances.

Sacred space is the area that Wiccans designate for ritual.

The preceding chapter explains all the logistics of sacred space. Turn to that chapter to choose a site (indoors versus outdoors, for example), select the style and placement of the altar, pick out Wiccan tools, and assemble the tools on the altar. If you intend to include magic in your ritual, gather any stones, herbs, candles, poppets, or other symbolic objects that you may need for working magic (see Chapter 17).

Purifying the space

Clean up all that old, messy energy! Most Wiccans prepare for ritual by physically and psychically cleansing the ritual space and the body. The idea of purification is not only to clean but to remove any energy that is counterproductive to the purpose of the ritual. Negative, chaotic, or distracting energy gathers around people and places. During ritual, most Wiccans dedicate the sacred space to Deity.

To purify an indoor space and ready it for ritual, begin by vacuuming or mopping the floor to remove dirt and germs. Make sure that the altar and tools are clean. Open a window or turn on an air cleaner to bring fresh air into the space.

Purify the space psychically by any one or more of the following methods:

- ✔ Sweep away negative or distracting energy by using a broom. Any broom is fine. Most Wiccans use a broom that is reserved for ritual use. The bristles don't need to touch the ground, because the sweeping is symbolic. Visualize the unwanted energy leaving the scene.

- ✔ Sprinkle salt (or salt water) from your altar throughout the area. You may want to mix the salt with a traditional purifying herb (such as anise, bloodroot, broom, chamomile, cinnamon, eucalyptus, fennel, hyssop, lavender, lemon, myrrh, pine, rosemary, saffron, sandalwood, or verbena).

- ✔ Burn a purifying incense throughout the area. If you own one, you may use a censor (also called a brazier or thurible) to disperse the smoke. Stick incense also works. Don't drop burning ashes on the floor or other surfaces. You may want to use incense of one of the purifying herbs in the preceding bullet.

- ✔ Beat a drum, shake a rattle, ring a bell, or play another instrument in each of the four directions. The vibrations clean out the old and unwanted energy.

To purify an outdoor space and ready it for ritual, pick up any garbage in the vicinity. Generally, outdoor spaces don't accumulate negative or chaotic energy like indoor areas do. However, you may use a ritual broom to sweep away any negative energy or use any of the other previously mentioned methods. However, don't throw salt onto the ground because salt kills the plant life.

Many Wiccans reverse this step and the next one. They purify themselves, and then they purify the space before performing the ritual. I prefer to clean my space and then take a purifying bath to remove negative energy from myself and settle down. After I have relaxed in a bath, I can smoothly transition into grounding and centering before I conduct the ritual. Read about these activities in the next section and then decide on the best sequence for yourself.

Purifying yourself

It's bath time! Wiccans usually purify themselves in some way prior to per-forming ritual, usually by ritual bathing. The purification bath removes physi-cal perspiration and soil from the day's activities, but it also prepares the mind for the coming ritual. During a ritual bath, the mind relaxes and shifts from everyday activities and stress to a more spiritual mind-set. Humans have always cleansed themselves in ponds, lakes, rivers, and oceans. Water is an ancient symbol that engages the unconscious mind and prepares it for ritual work.

You may want to add plain salt or herbal salts or oils to the bath. Purchase products made for bathing and labeled as safe. If you make your own herbal products, consult a reputable source (person, book, or Web site) for informa-tion about the use and handling of the specific herb. Burn candles and incense during the bath, if you want to. Showering, instead of bathing, is cer-tainly acceptable, although not customary. You can rub the herbs on your body during a shower.

After bathing, some Wiccans rub anointing oils onto their bodies. Anointing oils are made by steeping herbs in oil. Traditionally, mint was crushed and steeped in olive oil. Today, many Wiccans steep herbs in almond oil, which smells wonderful. Make sure you use herbs and oil that are safe for this pur-pose. Rub the oil on your forehead, on your chest over the heart, or all over your body, as you see fit.

Instead of an indoor ritual bath, some Wiccans use other, creative ways to purify the body. These include standing or sitting:

- under a Full Moon
- in a strong wind
- in an ocean, river, or lake
- in a place where you can feel the rain and electrical energy of a thunder-storm (of course, stay in a place where lightning can't strike you!)

The last is my personal favorite. I always feel renewed by a lightning storm.

After purification, dress (or undress) for the ritual (see the sidebar, "Dressing for ritual success"). Many Wiccans further prepare their minds for ritual by relaxing, grounding, centering, and/or meditating.

Dressing for ritual success

People of many religions, including Wiccans, sometimes place a great deal of emphasis on ritual garb and jewelry, but I'm not convinced that Deity cares very much about what people are wearing. Here is a basic truth: You can wear any type of garment — or no garment at all — to perform a Wiccan ritual. My advice is to wear comfortable clothing, so that you can focus on the ritual and be open to Divine revelation and the full ritual experience.

If certain styles, fabrics, colors, or jewelry help to trigger your unconscious mind and make your ritual more effective and fulfilling, then wear them. Otherwise, don't feel compelled to spend big money on a variety of clothing and decoration. Having a certain robe or outfit that you wear strictly for rituals and not for everyday activities can be beneficial because putting on the same clothing helps prepare your mind for the ritual.

Many Wiccans wear ritual garb, such as a cotton robe. Some Wiccans have robes of different colors for various kinds of rituals. (Appendix B provides suggestions for pairing colors with magical goals, and Chapter 14 recommends colors appropriate for different Wiccan holidays.)

Robes may be tied with a cord. A *cord* is a belt that is a single twisted strand or is braided from three strands of string, rope, or fabric. In some Wiccan traditions, people wear cords to denote their degree (level of advancement) in their specific tradition of Wicca. In traditions with several degrees (or levels), distinct cord colors may represent each degree. Some traditions require that a sacred circle be a standard size, and the length of the members' cords is the radius of their circles. (Some Wiccans use cords as symbolic objects to aid in the working of magic. They imbue the cord with their magical goal as they braid it.)

Some Wiccans wear jewelry that has spiritual meaning for them, including: silver or gold wrist or arm bands adorned with symbols; crowns with silver crescent moons or horns made of flowers, vines, leaves, or other natural materials; amulets; talismans; pentacles; or pendants made of stones chosen for their specific properties. Some Wiccan traditions also prescribe certain jewelry. For example, many High Priestesses wear amber and/or jet jewelry or wear ritual garters just above the knee (the garter decoration sometimes signifies the number of covens that have spun off, or *hived off,* from the High Priestess's original coven).

Okay, brace yourself. Some Wiccans do, indeed, perform ritual nude, or *skyclad.* This choice is more common in solitary practice (when someone performs ritual alone). Some covens (closely knit, small groups of Wiccans) perform ritual skyclad. The ritual nudity is not sexual, however. Individual Wiccans cite a variety of reasons, including any or all of the following:

✔ When participants in a ritual are nude, clothing can't be used as a sign of social class or status. Nudity is thought to reflect the equality of all people. Every person embodies Deity, and all people are equal before the Goddess and the God. Economic wealth is not readily apparent when people are free of clothing and the rest of society's entrapments.

 Nudity is a way for all participants in a ritual to gather as equals. Many Wiccans believe that this tradition has continued from feudal times or earlier, when peasants resisted the values of class division.

✔ Ritual nudity is a way for Wiccans to reject current societal values. Wiccans celebrate the human body as a beautiful and miraculous manifestation of Deity. They reject the notion that the nude body is sinful, shameful, or vulgar.

✔ Nudity is sometimes incorporated into specific rituals to signify rebirth.

✔ Some Wiccans believe that clothing interferes with the flow of energy between people.

✔ Some Wiccan traditions, covens, and other groups prescribe ritual nudity. Some perform only certain rituals skyclad, but others always practice this way. Some even require that members practice skyclad (in other words, members may not be allowed to remain clothed while others are nude). However, no one will force you to join one of these groups that work skyclad. You are free to join a group that always works clothed, or practice as a solitary (alone) and make your own decision. Before you become involved in a group and/or a tradition, make sure that your views on ritual nudity are in keeping with its practice.

Ritual nudity is a matter of personal choice, and the individual's choice must be respected. Many Wiccans don't practice skyclad, and no one should feel pressure to experience Deity this way.

Relaxing

Stress diminishes the quality of ritual or magic and negatively affects the outcome. For Wiccans, relaxation is nearly always a part of the preparation for ritual and magic. Relaxation aids focus and concentration.

A common exercise is to breathe deeply and focus on and relax each of the muscle groups in the body, one at a time (the hands, and then the arms, and then the shoulders, and so on). You may choose to do this exercise during the purification bath.

Grounding power or Earthing power before ritual

Grounding power, or *Earthing power,* means to connect personal energy with the Earth. Many Wiccans Earth power after a ritual, but some also ground themselves before ritual in order to allow energy to flow unobstructed through them during the ritual.

Grounding releases excess, negative, or nervous energy from yourself into the Earth. If you are depleted and need energy, grounding enables you to draw energy up from the Earth, offering a wellspring of power that can flow through you without exhausting your own resources.

To ground yourself, begin by taking three deep breaths. Sit or kneel down and flatten the palms of your hands on the ground or floor, or lie down and place your body flat on the ground. To release energy, visualize the energy flowing through your hands or your body and into the Earth. An alternative method is to imagine the excess energy flowing down your spine and deep into the Earth. If you need energy, reverse the image and picture the energy flowing up from the Earth.

Some people picture themselves as a tree with roots sinking into the Earth. The roots carry the energy.

Centering

Before you begin the ritual, you may want to center your own energy or power. Your *physical center* is your center of gravity, your place of balance, where your weight is equally distributed. It is usually somewhere between the breastbone and the navel, although it may be lower. You also have an *energy center,* the source of all your personal energy. It's probably in the same area as your physical center.

If you don't know where your center is, try picturing something that you truly love (your dog or cat, a piece of music, and so on). When you bring up that loving, self-satisfied, serene, warm feeling, try to pinpoint its source in your body. That's your center. To *center* yourself, bring your mental, emotional, and physical awareness at that spot.

Meditating

Meditation is a technique to turn off the chatter of the mind and achieve contemplation or deep relaxation. Meditation is a way to clear the mind and prepare for ritual.

The following is a simple type of meditation:

1. Sit or lie in a comfortable position with your eyes closed.

2. Focus on the sensation of each breath as it moves in and out of your body. An alternative is to focus your attention on the repetition of a word, sound, phrase, or prayer, doing this silently or whispering.

3. Every time your attention wanders (which occurs naturally), gently redirect it back, without judging yourself.

When you are fully relaxed and ready, begin the ritual by casting a sacred circle.

Casting a circle

Evidence suggests that Pagans have conducted rituals in circles for thousands of years. Stone circles exist in many locations from many different times and cultures. Stonehenge is a circular grouping of giant megaliths that were probably erected during the Neolithic period (8,000 to 3,500 BCE). The awe-inspiring power of Stonehenge and similar structures still draw pilgrims and tourists today.

Most Wiccans conduct ritual in sacred space, and to create sacred space, they cast a circle. To *cast a circle* means to symbolically create the circle with the mind. A Wiccan ritual circle is made of energy, not matter. The power of the mind shapes the energy that forms the circle.

Actually, I lied! A ritual circle isn't really a circle at all; it's a sphere. When someone casts a circle, he or she sends out personal power in all directions to build a sphere or globe of protective energy around himself or herself. The sphere is sometimes called the *Cone of Power.* The sphere keeps in the personal power and keeps out unwanted energy.

The sphere is a safe, consecrated place for a Wiccan to engage the unconscious mind and escape the bounds of time and space. The area inside the sphere transforms and is no longer part of the physical world. It stands apart, between the world of matter and the world of the Spirit (sometimes called the *Otherworld* or the *astral planes*).

The area within a cast circle is sacred. The sacred space within a cast circle is outside of time and three-dimensional space.

Declaring holy ground

The area within a sacred circle is *consecrated,* or dedicated to Deity. It is holy ground. Many Wiccans refer to the sacred space within a cast circle as a *temple.* This term may sound pretentious to the non-Wiccan, but for Wiccans, this space is as holy as a church, mosque, or synagogue is to the people of other religions.

Knowing whether to cast a circle

Of course, you don't have to cast a circle in order to experience the Divine presence. A Wiccan can sit under a tree and feel connection to the Goddess and the God. Wiccans believe that Deity manifests throughout creation and exists everywhere, all the time. If a ritual is for the sole purpose of honoring, petitioning, or celebrating Deity, a circle may not be necessary. Likewise, it's possible to work magic without a sacred circle, although Wiccans do cast a circle for most types of magic.

Here are some of the benefits of casting a ritual circle:

✔ The circle keeps in the personal power for the ritual. This is the reason that Wiccans usually cast a circle for a ritual to work magic. To work magic, a person focuses mental power. He or she uses the power to move and direct energy toward a desired change or outcome. The ritual circle serves an important purpose: The circle keeps the power in and lets it accumulate and become strong and focused, and then the power can move and project energy with intensity toward the goal.

✔ The circle keeps out distracting, negative, or unwanted energy. The Wiccan can safely and effectively concentrate on the goal of the ritual.

✔ The circle casting helps prepare a person psychologically for a spiritual experience.

✔ The circle is a safe, consecrated place to enter a light trance state and engage the unconscious mind (see Chapter 18 for more information). The circle is a portal through which to explore outside of time and space, but it also serves as an anchor to the physical world.

A circle can be cast anywhere and anytime because Deity is present anywhere and anytime. For this reason Wiccans don't need — and some practitioners don't even want — permanent buildings of worship. A Wiccan creates sacred space anew each time he or she casts a circle. The site for a circle may be permanent or temporary.

Every Wiccan is clergy, a Priestess or a Priest, and has the right to cast a circle and create sacred space, alone or with a group, at any time and in any place.

Defining the circle

Casting a circle is easier if you physically mark the boundary. Try one of these methods:

- Place stones, crystals, shells, salt, vines, or other natural materials in a circle.
- Draw the circle with chalk.
- Trace the circle in the dirt with a sword, a wand, or a broomstick.
- Unwind a length of cord into a circle.
- Stick down colored tape in a circle.
- Paint the circle on the floor.

The minimum size for a fully functional circle is probably 6 feet in diameter. Many Wiccan traditions require that a cast circle be 9 feet in diameter. *Diameter* is the length of a line passing through the center of a circle or sphere. The circle needs to be large enough to accommodate any activities you plan for the ritual, for example, dancing. You're going to have a hard time dancing ecstatically in a space the size of a linen closet.

Also, consider the size and placement of your altar. Don't forget that you need room to move around the altar. Wiccans often place the altar at the center of sacred space inside a ritual circle and face it North or East.

The measurements of your circle may be limited by your setting and circumstances. That's fine. The people of the Craft have always adapted their practices to their surroundings.

The physical circle that you draw doesn't have to be perfectly round or even symmetrical. You may draw around large furniture or make other accommodations. Any shape that works within your space is fine. However, please understand that a Wiccan circle is made of energy, not matter. When someone casts a circle, he or she sends out personal power to build a sphere or globe of protective energy. During the mental process of moving and shaping the energy, you may want to picture in your mind an actual sphere forming around you, not an uneven shape that you drew on the floor.

Beginning the ritual, making the circle

Get ready! This is the official beginning of the ritual.

A circle may be cast in dozens of ways. Most people combine physical and mental action to cast a circle.

Some circle-casting techniques rely more heavily on physical movement (acting out the casting of the circle). Other methods emphasize mental imagery, or visualization. *Visualization* means to picture an event in your mind, in this case, the forming of the circle. Most people experiment until they find the most effective balance of physical and mental activity.

After you have relaxed, grounded, centered, and/or meditated, officially begin the ritual by casting the circle.

Begin by feeling your personal power building up within you. Everyone experiences this power differently. It may feel like a build up of static electricity, a beam of sunshine, or the emotional feeling of a warm embrace. My heart always thumps, my skin tingles, and I get a rush of adrenaline!

You may want to listen to drumming or use one of the other techniques for raising power and inducing a light trance. (See the later section, "Raising power and working magic.") Wiccans raise power for working magic, but they also raise power to cast a circle and for other ritual purposes.

When you feel your own power, try doing the following steps simultaneously. I have separated them into mind and body methods because you may find that doing them separately or only doing one of them works better for you.

- **Body:** Choose a direction from which to begin. Most Wiccans begin to cast a circle from the North or the East. Stand on the edge of the circle, facing the direction that you have chosen. Turn and walk clockwise (known as *deosil* in Wicca) around the edges of the circle. (If you are in the Southern Hemisphere, walk counterclockwise; see the paragraph at the end of this section for an explanation.)

  You may want to extend your arm and use your hand to draw the boundaries of the circle in the air. You also may use an athame (a ritual knife) or a wand to trace the boundaries of the circle in the air. Follow along the outline that you created to define the circle. When the circle is complete pull your hand, athame, or wand back to your body.

- **Mind:** In your mind, picture the spark of personal power within you. See your power build up inside of you and then push out of you, flowing through your hand, athame, or wand and moving out into the room or space. The power attracts and moves patterns or spirals of energy. See the energy begin to gather around the outline of your circle.

Some people see this energy as a vibrating string of brilliant blue or white light. In your mind, shape the energy so that it extends and connects to form a full circle. When the circle is strong, stretch the energy into a sphere (a globe or an egg shape) to extend above you and below you. See yourself standing at the center of a powerful, vibrating sphere of protective energy. Some people see the sphere as a web or an electrified grid. It is sometimes called the Cone of Power.

To attract or bring in energy, Wiccans in the Northern Hemisphere move clockwise (or *deosil*), the direction that the sun appears to move in the sky. To banish, remove, or disperse energy, they move counterclockwise (or *widdershins*). However, for people in the Southern Hemisphere, the sun appears to travel in the opposite direction. So many of the Wiccans in the Southern Hemisphere move in reverse during ritual, traveling counterclockwise to bring in (invoke) energy and clockwise to remove or disperse (banish) energy.

Quartering the circle

Wiccans divide the sacred circle into four quarters, a concept that is common to many other faiths. Wiccans place one candle at each of the four directions to mark the boundaries of the circle. You may use the traditional colors for the quarter candles: green for the North, yellow for the East, red for the South, and blue for the West.

The four quarters and the center of the circle correspond to parts of the Self and the elements of nature. The most common associations are:

✔ North corresponds to Earth and to the human body.

✔ East corresponds to Air and to the human mind.

✔ South corresponds to Fire and to human energy.

✔ West corresponds to Water and to human emotions.

✔ The center of the circle corresponds to Spirit.

A Wiccan may adjust the correspondences so that they make sense to him or her. For example, in some areas of the world, the West may not be associated with water because the ocean lies to the East. An active volcano may lie to the North, so the North is associated with Fire, and so on.

The casting of the circle engages and unifies all aspects of the Self and of nature.

After the circle is cast, many Wiccans *call the quarters*. This means to call the four directions (North, East, South, and West), and some people link these to the basic elements (Earth, Wind, Fire, and Water). Beliefs about this custom differ throughout Wicca.

Some people believe that they are calling basic, archetypal forms of energy for use during the ritual.

Other people believe that they are calling actual beings, spirits, or other energy forms that guard or watch the four directions. Some people refer to these beings as the *Guardians of the Watchtowers.* Some Wiccans see them as the *Mighty Ones,* guardians who hold enormous power. Some people think that they may be evolved humans who have progressed during multiple rein-carnations and now dwell with Deity. Some Wiccans call them only for impor-tant rituals, such as initiations, rites of passage, or healing of serious illness.

Some Wiccans believe that these Guardians provide protection during ritual and guard the boundary of the circle, as well as prepare for or heighten awareness of Deity.

The following explains how to quarter the circle and call the Guardians of the Watchtowers. If you don't want to call the Guardians, just eliminate the call step. Simply walk the circle, draw the pentagrams, and/or light the candles.

Follow these steps to quarter the circle and call the Guardians of the Watchtowers.

1. **Stand at the North, East, South, or West point of your circle.**

   You may begin at any point you choose. For this example, the beginning is the East.

2. **Use your athame, wand, or hand to draw an invoking pentagram in the air.**

   Draw the pentagram with five smooth strokes. Figure 11-6 details the pattern.

   Say something like:

   > I welcome you, Guardian of the Watchtower of the East, Being of Air.

   > I ask that you guard and protect this sacred circle and me within it.

3. **Concentrate on the power of Air and of the human mind. Light the East candle.**

4. **Travel clockwise (deosil) around the circle, and stop at the South.**

5. **Use your athame, wand, or hand to draw an invoking pentagram in the air.**

   Say something like:

   > I welcome you, Guardian of the Watchtower of the South, Being of Fire.

   > I ask that you guard and protect this sacred circle and me within it.

6. **Concentrate on the power of Fire and of human energy. Light the South candle.**

7. **Travel clockwise (deosil) around the circle, and stop at the West.**

8. **Use your athame, wand, or hand to draw an invoking pentagram in the air.**

   Say something like:

   > I welcome you, Guardian of the Watchtower of the West, Being of Water.

   > I ask that you guard and protect this sacred circle and me within it.

9. **Concentrate on the power of Water and of human emotions. Light the West candle.**

10. **Travel clockwise (deosil around the circle), and stop at the North.**

11. **Use your athame, wand, or hand to draw an invoking pentagram in the air.**

    Say something like:

    > I welcome you, Guardian of the Watchtower of the North, Being of Earth.

    > I ask that you guard and protect this sacred circle and me within it.

12. **Concentrate on the power of Earth and of the human body. Light the North candle.**

In addition to the Guardians, some Wiccans evoke other forms of energy to be part of the circle. These may include ancestors, elementals, winds, fairies, and so on (see Chapter 3). Some traditions teach that energy forms must sit at the four directional points (North, South, East, and West) just outside of the protective circle, because to invite them into the circle is dangerous. Others believe that they need to be inside the circle in order to offer their energy to the proceedings.

Keep in mind that you may choose to call only Deity during a ritual. You don't need to call, summon, stir, invite, or welcome anything or anybody else. None of these practices are required or necessary. Feel free to explore these Wiccan ideas, for example, calling the Guardians of the Watchtowers. However, I suggest that people study and get a solid understanding of what they are calling up before they issue any invitations to beings and entities of any type.

Cutting a doorway

After a circle is cast, no one should pass through it during ritual; it disperses the energy and collapses the circle. Children or animals wandering in and out weaken the circle, although some people maintain that cats do not.

If you need to leave a sacred circle, Wiccan tradition advises that you cut a doorway. When you leave, you open a door, walk through it, and seal the door. If you return, you open the same door, walk through it, and seal the door. Follow these steps:

1. **Stand at the edge of the circle.**

2. **Begin down low and use your athame (or wand) to pierce the energy of the sphere and trace an archway tall enough to provide access to the outside.**

    Cut clockwise along the archways. The athame (or wand) holds the circle's energy cut from the hole.

3. **Use the athame or wand to close the door behind you when you leave.**

    Draw a line where the door meets the circle, resealing the circle.

4. **To re-enter the circle, again cut the archway with your athame (or wand).**

5. **Close the door behind you by again drawing a line to reconnect the door and the circle.**

    Some Wiccans draw an invoking pentagram in the air to further seal the hole where the doorway was cut.

Invoking, evoking, or welcoming Deity

This is it! This is the key part of a Wiccan ritual, and this is the only activity that is necessary in order to label a ritual activity "Wiccan." As Wiccans begin a ritual, they call to Deity to be present or to participate inside the sacred circle. This call may be in the form of a simply worded appeal, a prayer, a poem, a chant, a song, a gesture, a dance, and so on. Traditionally, many Wiccans make the invocation rhyme. Poetic, rhyming language helps to activate the unconscious mind and the deepest Self.

This call is not only a welcome but a celebration of interconnection, of the Divine energy within the soul and the Divinity that infuses all of existence.

When most Wiccans describe this appeal, they say that they are *invoking* the Divine, and this portion of the ritual usually is called the *invocation*.

Invoking versus evoking

You also may hear Wiccans use the words *evoke* and *evocation* when they talk about ritual. Unfortunately, the meanings of the words invoke and evoke aren't consistent throughout Wicca.

The pentagram problem

A pentagram is a five-pointed interlaced star. It is an ancient symbol used in many religions, in magic, and in mathematics and geometry. It's the primary symbol of the Craft. For most Wiccans, the five points represent the elements: Earth, Air, Fire, and Water, plus Spirit (the top point). Spirit is on top because it rules the other elements and the parts of the human Self that are associated with them (body, mind, energy, and emotions).

The problem is that the Wiccan traditions don't agree on which points of the pentagram represent which elements. Nearly everyone agrees that the top is Spirit and the Center, but after that the consensus unravels.

One common way of looking at the pentagram is this:

✔ The top point is Spirit.

✔ The bottom two points represent Earth (the bottom-left point) and Fire (the bottom-right point). These elements are on the bottom because they are bound in one place and can't go anywhere else.

✔ The middle two points represent Air (the middle-left point) and Water (the middle-right point). They are in the middle because they are free-flowing elements and are not bound.

However, some Wiccans arrange the elements very differently.

In addition to the point labels, Wiccans disagree about the drawing of the pentagrams for invoking (bringing in energy) and banishing (removing energy).

The invoking and banishing pentagrams in this chapter are used commonly throughout Wicca (see Figure 11-6). When the two pentagrams are drawn this way, the invoking pentagram brings Spirit down through the elements, and the banishing pentagram releases Spirit back up.

However, some Wiccan traditions reverse these (so that the invoking pentagram's drawn clockwise, and the banishing pentagram's drawn counterclockwise).

Now, here's where the whole issue gets really confusing. If you're getting a headache, feel free to stop reading right here and go eat chocolate.

The elements are associated with the directions of the compass (Earth = North, Air = East, Fire = South, and Water = West). Some Wiccan traditions have separate invoking and banishing pentagrams for each of the elements and their corresponding directions. That's five invoking and five banishing pentagrams!

As a person calls each of the quarters of a sacred circle, he or she draws a separate pentagram, and each one begins at a different point. The point of beginning and the direction that the drawing follows depends on whether the person wants to invoke or to banish the energy of that particular element (Earth, Air, Fire, and Water).

Wiccans don't agree on the beginning points or the directions for drawing these five invoking and five banishing pentagrams. However, everyone usually is convinced that his or her way is the right one. In general, a good strategy is to start out with the pair shown here and then experiment to find what works best for you.

The following are common explanations for these words:

- **Invoke/invocation:**

  - **Definition 1.** *To call to.* A call or prayer to Deity or other higher power to be present inside the sacred circle.

  - **Definition 2:** *To call into.* An invitation to Deity to come from outside and enter into a person. For example, during the Drawing Down the Moon ritual, the Goddess is drawn into the High Priestess and speaks directly through her.

- **Evoke/evocation:**

  - **Definition 1:** *To call out.* Calling a Deity, a spirit, a being, or other energy from inside of a person.

  - **Definition 2:** *To invite, summon, stir, or request* a spirit, being, or other energy (that is not inside the person) to be present or appear, usually in a designated area just outside of the sacred circle, but not within the actual protective circle.

For many Wiccans, invoking Deity simply means to acknowledge the ongoing presence of the Divine. They believe that Deity is always present, and an invocation simply heightens or enhances a person's experience of the Divine. They don't see the invocation as a call for Deity to travel from some other place and drop in. I agree with this perspective.

I confess that I'm confused by the use of the words *invoke* and *evoke.* I believe that Deity is immanent (present everywhere, all the time). The light of the Divine energy burns *within* me but also flows throughout existence *outside* of me. For me, the distinction between calling Deity from within or from without is very blurry. I'm never sure about the conflicting definitions of *evoke* and *invoke,* and which is actually correct.

Invocation language

For invocations, you can use the language that you are comfortable with and that flows naturally. When I perform ritual, I use a prayerful, respectful tone and wording, and I simply *welcome* Deity into my circle. Some people chant the words Goddess or God, Lord or Lady. Some people say or chant a specific name for Deity.

Wiccans often use poetic, lyrical, and even flowery language in their invocations. For example: "Oh, Great Goddess of the silver moon and the gentle tides" or "Oh, Great God of the deep forests and the wild animals."

The traditional prose poem, the *Charge of the Goddess* offers some beautiful language describing the Goddess. (See the sidebar, "Wiccan literature and liturgy.")

Wiccan literature and liturgy

A body of Wiccan poetry and prose is available for use in rituals. Wiccans are not required to use any specific text in their rituals, but much Wiccan literature has been created since the Wiccan revival in the 1950s. Wiccans use these texts to add meaning and beauty to their rites.

The most popular is probably the *Charge of the Goddess*. It is a beautiful piece of poetic prose that is the traditional address of the Goddess to her followers, and it has been incorporated into many Wiccan rituals. Many versions of the *Charge of the Goddess* have been written over the years. The original version may have been the one that appears in the book *Aradia: Gospel of the Witches* (originally published in 1890) by Charles G. Leland.

A version of the Charge appeared in Gerald Gardner's system of Wicca (Gardner sparked the Wiccan revival of the 1950s). Doreen Valiente, a Gardner High Priestess, produced a rewritten and very popular version of the *Charge of the Goddess,* and her text serves as the basis for most of the versions published since the Wiccan revival. It has been re-published in the book, *Charge of the Goddess* by Doreen Valiente (revised edition published 2000), available from various sources in the United States and abroad.

My personal favorite is the version of the *Charge* written by Starhawk and included in her book, *The Spiral Dance* (1979, 2nd revised edition 1989, 3rd revised edition 1999).

Many other Charges have been written from various perspectives, including numerous versions of the *Charge of the God.* All these texts are modeled after the original versions of the *Charge of the Goddess.*

Conducting a ritual observance

The *ritual observance* (after the invocation) is the time to carry out the reason for the ritual and to develop relationship with Deity. Wiccans may seek guidance and direction, solace and comfort, or forgiveness and closure. They may ask for help with physical or emotional needs or healing.

During ritual, many Wiccans enrich their lives by taking stock of their blessings and expressing gratitude and thanksgiving to Deity. Some Wiccans offer thanks during the *Cakes and Wine ceremony,* which is sort of a ritual within a ritual (see the sidebar, "The Cakes and Wine ritual," later in this chapter).

A Wiccan may conduct ritual whenever he or she is moved to do so. However, many Wiccans perform ritual on the Wiccan holy days, or holidays, which are timed to the seasons and to the natural cycles of Earth. The people of the Craft celebrate Earth's journey around the Sun, and the Moon's passage around the Earth.

The solar, or Sun, holy days are called *Sabbats.* These eight main Wiccan holidays are the solstices and the equinoxes, as well as the four halfway points between each solstice and equinox. The lunar, or Moon, holy days are called *Esbats.* Most Wiccans celebrate an Esbat on the Full Moon, on the New Moon, or on both.

Wiccans have traditional types of rituals for each Sabbat and Esbat, although no one is required to design and conduct ritual in keeping with custom and tradition. In the following two chapters, you can find detailed information about the traditional Esbat and Sabbat celebrations.

Sometimes Wiccans choose to raise power and work magic after the ritual observance. Working magic is an optional part of ritual. Some Wiccans always work magic; some never do. Most incorporate magic into some rituals, but not others.

Raising power and working magic

Most Wiccans raise power to work magic during a ritual. To work magic, a person visualizes a desired change or outcome, and then focuses mental power to move and direct energy to bring about that result. A Wiccan raises the power until it is at its most intense, then releases the power while visualizing the desired outcome. The power moves energy to accomplish the goal. The energy affects conditions in the world.

Wiccans may raise power by chanting, speaking, or singing a spell, a word, a phrase, or a prayer; listening to repetitive drumming or shaking a rattle, focusing on breathing, dancing, or staring at a candle flame, a bowl of water, a crystal ball, or another reflective surface. Any activity that grows in intensity (stronger, deeper, louder, or faster) may be used to raise power.

Raising power induces a light trance state, engaging the unconscious mind and creating alpha brain waves. Chapter 18 explores the trance state and its value in ritual. Other chapters in this book cover working magic in detail. (Chapter 3 explains the theory of magic, and Chapters 15, 16, and 17 provide instructions.) In this chapter, you only need to understand that this is the time in a ritual when Wiccans raise power to work magic.

The ritual setting invites the presence or participation of Deity in the magic, and the sacred circle concentrates the power in one area, making the magic more effective.

Activities to raise power, such as drumming, can be used throughout the ritual process, not only for magic. Some people use them to raise power to cast the circle, for example. All these activities empower the person performing the ritual, making the experience more effective and fulfilling. These techniques can be incorporated into any type of ritual, including those for worship and celebration, as well as magic.

Grounding power or Earthing power after ritual

Wiccans ground power after ritual so that the power raised dissolves or dissipates naturally. All rituals are powerful, and lingering energy that isn't grounded may turn into tension or anxiety, and perhaps result in a headache or another physical ailment. Even if Wiccans don't make a special effort to raise power for working magic, they usually Earth the power from the ritual itself.

To Earth the power, take three deep breaths. Sit on the ground or kneel and flatten the palms of your hands on the ground or floor, or lie down, placing your body flat on the ground. Visualize the energy flowing through your hands or your body and into the Earth. An alternative method is to imagine the excess energy flowing down your spine and deep into the Earth. Some people picture themselves as a tree with roots sinking into the Earth.

Other simple activities may help you Earth the power, including the following:

- ✔ Say your own name or have someone call your name.

- ✔ Pat your body all over.

- ✔ Wash your face and hands with a damp, cool cloth.

- ✔ Hold a favorite stone or crystal.

- ✔ Think about something from your everyday life (such as a favorite TV show or restaurant).

- ✔ Visualize the energy and imagine it being drawn into your athame, a candle, a stone, and so on.

- ✔ Eat food and/or drink something. You may want to engage in the traditional Wiccan Cakes and Wine ritual (see the sidebar, "The Cakes and Wine ritual").

The Cakes and Wine ritual

After conducting the ritual observance or after the working of magic, many Wiccans perform a ritual within a ritual called *Cakes and Wine* or *Cakes and Ale*.

I don't like these traditional titles and the implication that alcohol is necessary for spiritual practice. If you or someone in your ritual group struggles with alcoholism, don't put the person at risk by serving wine, ale, or beer. Today, many Wiccans now serve juice or cider or some other alternative to alcohol during ritual.

For that matter, many Wiccans interpret the word *cakes* loosely. Other Pagans sometimes, rather disdainfully, call this ceremony "Wiccan cookies and milk" and, indeed, some people serve cookies and milk for this rite. Cakes may also be crackers, fruit, or any other food. Some Wiccans serve a full meal.

Traditionally, Wiccans have served grain-based (oat-, wheat- or barley-flour are common) cakes that are cut and baked in crescent moon or other shapes. (I use a rich oatmeal cookie recipe and use traditional Irish oatmeal.)

The food and drink are kept on the altar or beside it. Sometimes the cakes are served from a pentacle plate. The solitary practitioner (or a Priest or Priestess of a coven) lifts a plate of the food and a chalice or cup and then speaks a blessing, which is usually a prayer dedicated to Deity (use your own term to refer to the Divine). For example:

Great Goddess

Thank you for the boons and blessings in my life.

You are my constant Source of wisdom, solace, and sustenance.

May this food give me strength in my service to you and your Earth.

To peace and to justice.

Blessed be.

Use the chalice or cup to toast Deity. If the ritual is being conducted by a group, the members pass the chalice or cup around and share words of gratitude to the Divine. During group rituals, people socialize and have fun while they feast.

Some people leave a small portion of food and/or drink for Deity in an offering bowl on the altar. Some people pour the offering into a fire or a cauldron. After the ritual, some people take the offering into the woods and place it at the base of an old tree or some other place of significance.

Some Wiccan traditions perform the symbolic Great Rite prior to the Cakes and Wine ceremony or to consecrate the wine itself. The person conducting the ritual says something like, "as the cup is the female and the wand (or athame) is the male, together they join in perfect balance", or the person then thrusts the wand (or athame) into the cup or chalice filled with drink.

The Great Rite is symbolic sex. For many Wiccans, it represents the balance of nature. The idea is that energy flows in two opposite directions in nature, which creates the familiar cycles of the natural world, for example: life and death, light and dark, summer and winter, and male and female. Many Wiccans see the Goddess and the God in the same way, and the Great Rite reflects this polarity. For some Wiccans, the Cakes and Wine ceremony reflects Wicca's history as a fertility religion. This ritual represents the wild, creative, and transformative energy of sexual intercourse. The symbolism of the union of a man and a woman emphasizes fertility, rather than or in addition to polarity. In addition to procreation, fertility encompasses the birth of ideas (creativity, art, and self-development).

Not all Wiccans practice the Great Rite. Some Wiccans consider this symbolism to be heterosexist, and some believe that it is an outdated way of looking at sex and gender.

Some couples may engage in the actual Great Rite — sexual intercourse within a ritual setting — as a private act done at home. However, Wiccans do not engage in public or group sex as part of their religious or spiritual experience.

Some people enjoy the Cakes and Wine ceremony *before* working magic, as a break in the ritual. Many wait until *after* the magic. For them, Cakes and Wine is a traditional way to help Earth the power after magical work and bring the ritual to a close. You may decide on the best sequence for you.

Whether a ritual includes magic or not, the Cakes and Wine ceremony is typically done at some time before thanking or dismissing Deity and taking down the circle. Wicca has no doctrine, so you are not required to perform this ceremony if you don't find it meaningful, but Cakes and Wine is a fairly standard part of Wiccan practice.

Thanking or dismissing Deity

Before ending the ritual, thank the Divine for Her/His/Its/Their presence and participation, as well as any other spirits, beings, or energies whose attendance you welcomed. Express your gratitude aloud and with feeling.

Some people believe in *dismissing* or *releasing* Deity and other energies. These terms mean that you let them know that the ritual is over, and that they can and should now depart. Some Wiccans dismiss everyone. Some people *thank* Deity but *dismiss* any other energies. I believe that the Divine remains within me, so I don't use the dismissal language in reference to Deity. (Besides, who am I to dismiss the Goddess!?!) You can make up your own mind about which language is appropriate.

Taking down the circle

Even though a sacred circle is made of energy, not matter, most Wiccans take it down when a ritual is complete. Some Wiccans believe that to take down a circle, you need to reverse the thoughts and actions that you used to cast the circle. The following paragraphs describe the idea.

Go to each quarter in the circle, draw a banishing pentagram (see Figure 11-6), and snuff out the candle. Thank the Guardians of the Watchtowers for their help and protection, if you called them.

Because a Wiccan walks clockwise (deosil) to cast a circle, some Wiccans walk counterclockwise (widdershins) to take down a circle. However, other Wiccans get all fearful and shivery when someone suggests that they walk counterclockwise (widdershins) during a ritual.

Some Wiccans believe that clockwise (deosil) movement is for invoking, and counterclockwise (widdershins) movement is for banishing. Others believe that moving clockwise (deosil) is for working positive magic, and moving counterclockwise (widdershins) is for working negative, nasty magic. So some Wiccans can come a little undone when someone suggests that they move counterclockwise (widdershins) because they associate that movement with evil.

After you take care of the quarters, you can undue your circle casting. As with casting a circle, perform the following body and mind recommendations concurrently:

- ✔ **Body:** Walk around the circle. Because you walked clockwise to cast the circle, walk counterclockwise to disperse the circle, or you can just re-walk the circle clockwise. Extend your hand, athame, or wand and draw back in the energy that you sent out to cast the circle.

- ✔ **Mind:** Visualize the energy that you shaped into the circle. See the sphere that you were standing in, the Cone of Power, collapsing. In your mind, picture the energy returning to its original patterns or spirals. Re-absorb the personal power that you used to shape the energy.

Many Wiccans believe that you don't need all the effort above to take down a circle. These folks simply snuff out the candles, announce that the ritual is over, and break the circle. They may perform some final act, such as holding a hand, athame, or wand up to the sky and touching it to the ground. Then they thrust it into the circle at the Northern or Eastern point, breaking up the energy.

They may make a final declaration, saying something like:

The circle dissolves, but love remains.

I [we] go in power; I [we] go in peace.

Blessed be.

If you are performing ritual with a group, you may substitute *I* for *we. Blessed be* is a traditional phrase of blessing to all and is a common way to complete a ritual. Some people finish a ritual with the phrase "Merry meet, and merry part, and merry meet again." This phrase purportedly harkens back to the days of the vast Witch hunts (see Chapter 5), when Witches wanted to celebrate a safe gathering and wish each other security and a happy reunion in the future. The phrase also reflects the belief that Wiccans remain connected to each other and to Deity, in this life and beyond.

Getting Inspiration: A Sample Ritual

In general, ritual is more successful and fulfilling when a person writes his or her own. The following is a sample ritual for cleansing, charging, and consecrating an altar tool or other object to prepare it for use in ritual.

The ritual here is very simple. Many Wiccans write exquisitely worded rituals with elegant poetic prose. Rituals may be dramatic, be full of movement, and make lavish use of altar tools and other objects. Some people find these elaborate rituals inspiring and beautiful; others find them contrived and awkward. To each his or her own. Make your rituals comfortable for you.

For the sake of a clear sample ritual, suppose that you want to consecrate a small iron cauldron for use in ritual work. The following steps show how you adapt this goal to the basic ritual design that this chapters details.

1. **Decide why you want to conduct a ritual. Make sure that your intention is clear.**

   This ritual is for cleansing, charging, and consecrating a small iron cauldron for later ritual work. Here is what you intend to do to the cauldron:

   - *Cleanse:* to remove any and all energy or vibrations that are attached to it, and to purify it

   - *Charge:* to imbue it with energy and to transmit personal power into it

   - *Consecrate:* to dedicate it to the service of Deity

2. **Decide how you want to perform your ritual; write the words that you want to use during the invocation and the other steps.**

   This is a simple ritual, using these basic steps. This type of consecration ritual usually involves cleansing and charging the object with the energy of the four elements (Earth, Air, Fire, and Water) and your own energy. Then you dedicate the object to the service of Deity.

3. **Decide when to do the ritual; for example, you may want to time the ritual to a specific phase of the moon or to a Wiccan holiday.**

   Traditionally, tools are blessed on the Imbolc (Candlemas) Sabbat of February 2. Any Esbat (Full Moon or New Moon) is an appropriate alternative.

4. **Decide where to do the ritual, set up an altar, and assemble the tools and other necessary objects.**

   For this ritual, you need salt, water, a candle, and incense.

5. **Purify the space.**

   Follow the standard procedure for purifying space (see the earlier section, "Purifying the space").

6. **Purify yourself.**

   Follow the standard procedure for purifying Self (see the earlier section, "Purifying yourself").

7. **Cast a circle to create sacred space.**

   Follow the standard procedure for casting a circle (see the earlier section, "Casting a circle").

8. **Invoke, evoke, or welcome Deity, according to your beliefs.**

   Say something like, "Goddess and God, I welcome your presence to pre-pare this cauldron for service to you and your Earth."

   Light a candle in the center of the altar to represent Deity.

9. **Conduct a ritual observance (for example, celebrate a Sabbat or an Esbat), if you desire.**

   In this case, the ritual observance is consecration of the cauldron. Here are the steps.

   1. Wash, polish, or use some other means to physically clean the cauldron. Say:

      May you be cleansed and purified.

   2. Visualize all energy that is negative, chaotic, or unwanted (for example, linked to someone else) leaving the cauldron.

   3. Pour or sprinkle some water that has been purified and blessed over the cauldron; see Chapter 11 for more information on water. Dampen the entire surface. Say:

      May you be charged with the power of Water.

   4. Light some incense. You can place the incense in a censor (also called a thurible or brazier), if you have one. Pass the cauldron through the smoke of the incense. Say:

      May you be charged with the power of Air.

   5. Pass the cauldron through a candle flame if the material is inflam-mable and won't be damaged. (If a tool is flammable, the incense smoke can serve as both the fire and the air elements, or you can touch the object to a fire tool, such as a wand.) Say:

      May you be charged with the power of Fire.

   6. Sprinkle salt over the cauldron. Say:

      May you be charged with the power of Earth.

   7. Paint or carve a personal name, initial, or symbol on the bottom or sides of the cauldron. Touch the cauldron with your own saliva or menstrual blood. The idea is to charge the object with your own energy and connect it to you. Say:

      By the powers of Earth, Fire, Wind, and Water,

      By Self and Soul

      I charge you to work with me in the service of Deity.

   8. Touch the cauldron to your heart, your lips, and your forehead. Say:

      Goddess and God,

      the Source of all that is

bless this cauldron and its work.

9. Raise the cauldron to the sky and touch it to the ground.

10. **Raise power and work magic, if you have a reason for a magical working.**

   The cauldron consecration ritual doesn't involve magic, although nothing stops you from working any magic within the circle you erected for this ritual.

11. **Earth the power.**

   Follow the standard procedure for Earthing the power of the ritual (see the earlier section, "Grounding power or Earthing power before ritual").

12. **Thank (or dismiss) Deity.**

   Follow the standard procedure for thanking Deity (see the earlier section, "Casting a circle").

13. **Take down the circle.**

   Follow the standard procedure for taking down the circle (see the earlier section, "Taking down the circle").

Getting the Idea: A Ritual for Self-Dedication

The preceding section offers a ritual for charging and consecrating tools. This section also provides a sample ritual, but this one is for people!

Some people feel drawn to Wicca and decide to commit themselves to a serious exploration of the Wiccan spiritual path. This promise of devoted study and reflection is entirely voluntary and is called a *dedication,* or in the case of a solitary practitioner, a *self-dedication.* The person making the commitment is called a *dedicant* or *dedicate.* (Chapters 8 and 9 provide additional explanation about beginning and following the Wiccan path.)

Declaring intention to study

Self-dedication does not make one a Wiccan; it is merely a personal vow to engage in a diligent exploration of Wicca. The dedicant's goals during the dedication period are to establish relationship with Deity; successfully perform ritual; and gain understanding of the principles, practices, and ethics of Wicca. Dedication is not a binding oath or a life-long commitment. The time period often is clearly defined; the period of a year and a day is common.

The format for a self-dedication is a personal choice. It may be as simple as the dedicant saying, "I dedicate myself to the Goddess and the God." Or the dedicant may choose to perform a full self-dedication ritual. The ritual can be simple or elaborate. The following is an example of a very simple Wiccan ritual for self-dedication. This ritual demonstrates the basic steps introduced earlier in this chapter. This is only a general template. Wiccan traditions have specific prescribed rituals or portions of rituals for the purpose of dedication. In addition, traditions differ on the customs for dedication and initiation (see the next section "Dedicating versus initiating").

1. **Decide why you want to conduct a ritual. Make sure that your intention is clear.**

   A self-dedication ritual is for dedicating oneself to the exploration of Wiccan belief and practice. The purpose of the ritual is to declare out loud your intention to learn all you can about Wicca. Performing the ritual indicates a willingness to engage in sincere study of Wicca for a specific length of time.

2. **Decide how you want to perform your ritual**

   Write the words that you want to use during the invocation and the other steps.

   This is a simple ritual, using the basic steps and text that I outline here. Feel free to incorporate additional steps or write additional words of self-dedication, as feels appropriate to you.

3. **Decide when to do the ritual.**

   You may want to time this ritual to a specific phase of the moon or to a Wiccan holiday (a Sabbat or an Esbat) or a specific time of day such as dawn. See Chapters 13 and 14 for an explanation of these holy days.

4. **Decide where to do the ritual, set up an altar (if desired), and assemble the tools and other necessary objects.**

   Consider performing this ritual outdoors, in private, in the wild. Choose a place where you feel safe and at peace. An appropriate spot may be a forest clearing, a garden, an orchard, a natural spring, the bank of a creek or river, a beach, the base of an old tree, or the top of a hill.

   For this ritual, you don't need to assemble an altar, unless you want to do so. You may want to bring water, salt, and a white candle (and matches) to the ritual site. Dissolve the salt in the water before beginning the ritual. Chapter 11 provides information about preparing salt and water for use during ritual.

5. **Purify the space.**

   Follow the standard procedure for purifying space (see the earlier section, "Purifying the space").

6. **Purify yourself.**

   Taking a ritual bath prior to the dedication ritual is customary. If you are going to conduct the ritual outdoors, in the wild, consider bathing in a lake, river, creek, pond, or natural spring at the site of the ritual. You also may bathe in the rain. Follow the standard procedure for purifying the Self (see the earlier section, "Purifying yourself" for more information).

7. **Cast a circle to create sacred space.**

   Follow the standard procedure for casting a circle (see the section, "Casting a circle"), if you want to do so.

8. **Invoke, evoke, or welcome Deity, according to your beliefs.**

   Say, "Goddess and God, I welcome your presence," or similar words. Use your own chosen term for Deity.

   Light a white candle to represent the Divine presence. Concentrate on the candle flame.

9. **Conduct a ritual observance (for example, celebrate a Sabbat or an Esbat) if you desire.**

   In this case, the ritual observance is the self-dedication. This is the time in the ritual when you declare out loud your intention to learn the ways of Wicca.

   Relax, ground, center, and/or meditate. If you are outdoors, fully experience your physical surroundings. Take time to notice details: a bee flying in and out of a flower bloom, the lonesome call of a mourning dove in the distance, or the smell of moss on a tree. Focus on any repetitive sound, for example, water trickling. Make sure that your own mind and body are attuned. When you are fully relaxed but alert, say something like:

   > "I promise to devote myself to the study of the Wiccan Way.
   >
   > For a year and a day, I will live and learn, love and grow in the ways of Wicca.
   >
   > I dedicate myself to the Goddess and to the God and pledge my service to the Divine community.
   >
   > I acknowledge my kinship to all of nature and my place in the web of life."

   Speak from your heart and soul. Use your own term for Deity. Sprinkle the salt water over your body, perhaps anointing your forehead, chest, belly, and feet.

   Breathe deeply. Feel at one with the natural world around you. Pay attention to the birds and other wildlife that grace your presence at this time. Note any change in the weather or other conditions. Sit quietly until you feel ready to leave.

10. **Raise power and work magic, if you have a good reason.**

    Working magic during a self-dedication isn't customary, although technically, it isn't prohibited.

11. **Earth the power.**

    Follow the standard procedure for Earthing the power of the ritual (see the section, "Grounding power or Earthing power before ritual").

12. **Thank (or dismiss) Deity.**

    Follow the standard procedure for thanking Deity (see the section, "Casting the circle").

13. **Take down the circle.**

    Follow the standard procedure for taking down the circle (see the section, "Taking down the circle").

I recommend that you record your dedication experience in a Book of Shadows (see Chapter 20 for more explanation).

After the dedication period (usually a year and a day) is complete, the dedicant may decide to abandon Wicca and, perhaps, move on to another spiritual path. Or he or she may decide to seek initiation into Wicca. A Wiccan *initiation* or *self-initiation* is a spiritual rebirth into Wicca, and is a complete commitment and oath.

Dedicating versus initiating

Keep in mind that Wiccan ideas about dedication and initiation differ dramatically. Some Wiccans consider dedication and initiation to be the same thing, rather than a two-step process that happens over time. In other words, they combine dedication and initiation into one ritual.

Some Wiccans believe that a person can *dedicate* himself or herself to Wicca but cannot *initiate* himself or herself. To these Wiccans, a coven is necessary in order to conduct an initiation ritual, so initiation is reserved for someone who is joining a coven and is not for people who want to practice the Craft alone.

You, of course, are free to make up your own mind about what is appropriate for you.

Chapter 13

Waxing and Waning with the Moon: The Esbats

*E*very culture throughout history has created mythology about the Moon. All over the world, stories, statues, and structures honor the lunar presence. The landing on the Moon was one of the most profound moments in human history.

The people of the Craft have always revered the Moon. Wiccans perform ritual and work magic according to the phases of the Moon. In this chapter, you can find out why and how. The chapter also includes a few Moon facts, so you can truly understand the Wiccan practices and appreciate the world-wide fascination with all things lunar.

Celebrating the Moon

Wicca is a religion or spirituality based on nature. The Wiccan holy days, or holidays, are directly timed to the seasons and to the natural cycles of the Earth. The people of the Craft celebrate the Earth's journey around the Sun, as well as the Moon's passage around the Earth.

The solar, or Sun, holy days are called *Sabbats*. These key days in the solar cycle are the eight main Wiccan holidays during the year: the winter solstice, the spring equinox, the summer solstice, and the autumn equinox, as well as the four halfway points between each solstice and equinox. All the Wiccan Sabbats are based on festivals of ancient Pagan Europe. You can find out more about the Sabbats and their observance in the next chapter.

The lunar, or Moon, holy days are called *Esbats*. Wiccans differ in their usage of the word Esbat. Some Wiccans celebrate an Esbat only on the Full Moon, on the New Moon, or on both. Some people also celebrate the Quarter Moons. Some use the word Esbat to describe any Wiccan gathering (especially if ritual or magical work takes place) that doesn't occur on a Sabbat.

For many Wiccans, the Sabbats are the primary holy days or holidays. The Esbats offer a chance to consistently set aside some time to step away from the mundane world and devote oneself to spiritual reflection or magical work — sort of parallel to a regular church service for people of other religions.

Many Wiccans reserve the Sabbats for performing intense or formal ritual (perhaps from their own specific tradition) and developing the relationship with Deity. On the Esbats, they work magic (including divination) or perform rituals of a more practical nature, for example, focusing on self-improvement, problem-solving, or building personal strength and confidence. Sabbats and Esbats are celebrated by individuals alone and by covens or other groups, as shown in Figure 13-1. Wiccans who belong to covens may choose to celebrate privately or with the group.

Figure 13-1:
A wood cut of a Moon Dance, celebrating the Full Moon.

© Bettmann/CORBIS

This approach to the holy days is not universal, however. The Esbats, especially the Full Moon, are often considered more Goddess-oriented. Some groups have specific rituals for each phase of the Moon, and some groups even have different rituals for each of the Full Moons during the year.

Enlightening Lunar Lore

I'm often amazed at the number of Wiccans and Witches who celebrate the Esbats and time their magic to the phases of the Moon, but don't know what a Moon phase really is. In order to effectively work in sync with the Moon, people need to know how the Moon actually behaves.

The Moon is Earth's only natural satellite, and it's about 238,857 miles (384,403 kilometers) away.

Cool cosmic coincidence

Here is one of the coolest science facts that you'll ever hear:

- ✔ The Moon *rotates* (spins around on its own axis) every 27.3 days.
- ✔ The Moon *revolves* (travels around the Earth) every 27.3 days.

That's right: It's the exact same amount of time! I love coincidences like this one, because they make me see the balance and beauty in the universe.

Anyway, this dandy moon fact is the reason that the same side of the Moon's surface is always facing the Earth. Earthlings never get to see the other side of the Moon.

A far side of the Moon, the portion that people on Earth never see, does exist. However, the Sun shines on all sides of the Moon in turn, so there is no "dark side of the Moon." (Well, that was the name of a classic album by Pink Floyd, but you may be too young to know that.)

The Moonlight myth

The Moon does not emit any light. That's right, Moonlight is a myth. The light of the Moon is actually Sunlight reflected from the Moon's surface. The appearance of the Moon changes, depending on the position of the Sun and the way its light is reflecting off the Moon's surface. At different times of the month, the Moon appears as a full circle, a half circle, or a crescent. These are called the phases of the Moon, as Figure 13-2 shows. In other words, the actual shape of the Moon doesn't change, it just appears different (a quarter or full, for example), depending on the angle that Sunlight is bouncing off it.

The following list describes the different Moon phases and the way that they appear to Earthlings. Note the use of the words *waxing* and *waning;* those concepts are important in the working of magic (see the next section):

- ✔ **The New Moon or Dark Moon:** When the Moon is between the Earth and the Sun, it appears dark or invisible, a New Moon. The Moon is between the Sun and the Earth so that no light is reflected; the Moon's unilluminated side is facing the Earth.

- ✔ **Waxing Crescent Moon:** In between the New Moon and the Full Moon, the Moon's illuminated surface appears to increase, or *wax,* to full. The Moon appears to be partly but less than one-half illuminated by direct Sunlight.

- ✔ **First Quarter Moon:** One-half of the Moon appears to be illuminated by direct Sunlight. The fraction of the Moon that is lit is increasing.

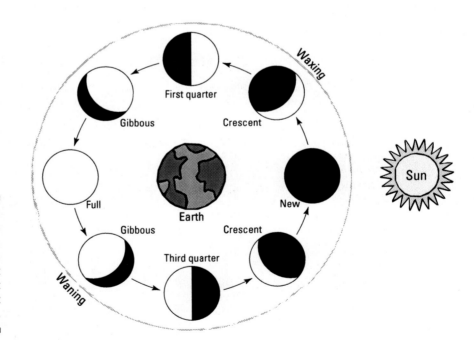

Figure 13-2:
The phases of the Moon showing the amount of light reflected at each phase.

- ✔ **Waxing Gibbous Moon:** The Moon appears to be more than one-half but not fully illuminated by direct Sunlight. The fraction of the Moon's disk that is lit is increasing.

- ✔ **The Full Moon:** When the Sun and the Moon are on opposite sides of the Earth, the Moon appears full or whole, a Full Moon. The Moon's illuminated side is facing the Earth. The Moon appears to be completely lit by direct Sunlight. Some years have 13 Full Moons. When two Full Moons occur in a single month, the second one is called a *Blue Moon*.

- ✔ **Waning Gibbous Moon:** The Moon appears to be more than one-half but not fully illuminated by direct Sunlight. The fraction of the Moon's disk that is lit appears to decrease, or *wane*.

- ✔ **Last Quarter Moon:** One-half of the Moon appears to be illuminated by direct Sunlight. The fraction of the Moon's disk that is lit is decreasing.

- ✔ **The Waning Crescent Moon:** In between the Full Moon and the New Moon, the Moon's illuminated surface appears to be partly but less than one-half illuminated by direct Sunlight. The fraction of the Moon's disk that is lit is decreasing.

The *lunar month* is the 29.5 days it takes to go from one New Moon to the next New Moon or one Full Moon to the next Full Moon.

In the preceding section, I say that the Moon travels around the Earth in 27.3 days, and now I tell you that the lunar month is 29.5 days. What's up? Well, the 27.3 is the actual time it takes for the Moon to revolve around the Earth. Simple math! But the lunar month depends on the Sun, too, so the math gets a little more complicated.

The positions of the Earth and the Sun determine what Moon phase Earthlings see. Remember that the Moon doesn't change its actual shape, it just appears in a different phase (a quarter or full, for example), depending on the angle that sunlight is reflecting off it, as viewed from Earth. So the length of the lunar month has to take into account the ever-changing position of the Earth in its orbit around the Sun. As the Moon revolves, it takes 29.5 days to return to the same point in its relationship to the Sun, so the Moon phase appears the same on Earth.

Working with the Moon: A Labor of Love

Throughout history, people of the Craft have claimed that working magic in sync with the phases of the Moon and the natural rhythms of the Earth makes the effort easier and more successful. Celebrating the Esbats also is a way of revering nature and honoring the Divine.

This section shows the split between science and Wicca regarding the effects of the Moon and offers some advice on Moon magic.

Going from Luna to lunacy

Luna was the Roman Moon Goddess. From this grand Goddess, modern culture has created the words *lunacy* and *lunatic*.

The Full Moon's bad press

The Full Moon has been blamed for increased rates of addiction, aggression, births, crime, emergency room admissions, epilepsy, fertility, gambling wins, natural disasters (especially earthquakes), sleep walking, suicide, traffic accidents, violence, as well as general insanity — oh, and attacks by both vampires and werewolves.

That's a long rap sheet for the Moon. Studies have been conducted for decades on the effects of the Full Moon, but the evidence is slim that the Moon plays a measurable role in any of these phenomena, according to most researchers. In fact, many modern scientists declare that the Moon doesn't have a significant effect on the human body or even human psychology.

Scientists do know that the Moon is the primary cause of the ocean tides on Earth. The Moon's gravity pulls on the oceans. However, even though the human body is made mostly of water, scientists say that the Moon's effect on that fluid is negligible.

The Full Moon is very bright, and that may affect human behavior, at least from a practical standpoint. Certainly, humans can engage in more activities at night when the Moon is full, for example, harvesting crops. Many animals have reproductive cycles that depend on the lunar phases.

The length of time for the Moon's rotation and revolution (27.32 days) as well as the length of the lunar month (29.53 days) are all remarkably similar to the menstruation cycles of women, a fact that has been noted and celebrated globally throughout history. Probably for this reason, the Moon has been closely associated with the Goddess. Today, Dianic, woman-centered, and/or feminist Wiccan traditions often place equal or greater importance on celebrating the Esbats, as opposed to the Sabbats, the solar holidays. Traditionally, Full Moons have been the traditional monthly meeting time for Wiccans and other Witches.

Science and Wicca agree to disagree

I did my scientific duty and admitted that researchers find little evidence that the Full Moon has more than a negligible effect on people. But now I also have to tell you that most Wiccans and other Witches are just as convinced that the phases of the Moon create shifts in energy — energy that people can harness during ritual and magic. The types of workings done for each phase is coordinated with that energy.

I know that I *feel* different during the Full Moon, and the effect the Full Moon has on me is distinct from that of the New Moon, to which I also have a strong reaction. I usually want to contemplate the future or begin something new on the New Moon. I never have much patience with old projects at this time. At Full Moon, I'm more motivated to finish what I've started, and my emotions are more engaged with my mundane, as well as spiritual, efforts. I see the big picture better at the time of the Full Moon.

Maybe that's enough; the shift that occurs in my mind is what boosts my magical and ritual workings. You can decide for yourself.

Working Moon magic

The following sections describe the basic principles of working magic in tune with the Moon. See Chapters 15 through 17 for more detailed information about working magic and taking advantage of its potential in your life.

The New Moon

The New Moon or Dark Moon is the first phase. The time of the New Moon is appropriate for working magic associated with decrease. This phase is the best time for *banishing* (sending away or removing an undesired energy or thing).

During the New Moon, Wiccans often honor secrets and solitude. It's also the threshold for change and new beginnings. Rituals for the purpose of letting go of old habits or for help in starting new projects are most appropriate in this phase. This Moon phase symbolizes the time between death and rebirth.

Most Wiccans view the New Moon as a powerful time for working magic, second only to the Full Moon.

The Waxing Moon

The Waxing Moon, from the time of the New Moon to the time of the Full Moon, is the time for *invoking* (bringing a desired energy or thing to you). The area of the Moon that is lit is increasing when the Moon is waxing, and power also increases as the Moon waxes.

This time is best for magic involving gain, increase, accumulation, expansion, growth, and productivity.

The Full Moon

During the Full Moon, the entire visible disk of the Moon is fully illuminated. This is also the time of the highest energy and the greatest power for magical work. It's the best time for invoking.

Full Moon magic is for achievement, completion, conclusion, fruition, fulfillment, or love. The Full Moon time also is appropriate for healing.

The Waning Moon

The Moon is waning at any time after the Full Moon and before the New Moon. The Moon's illuminated area is decreasing, and power decreases as the Moon wanes. The Waning Moon is associated with banishing.

The Waning Moon phase is best for magic involving endings of projects, ideas, or relationships. This also is a time for secrets and self-reflection.

Celebrating an Esbat: The Ritual of the Moon Trees

This section includes a sample Esbat ritual based on the mystery of the Moon Trees.

Did you know that trees from the Moon are growing on Earth? They have been found in big cities and small towns all across the United States. Only a few have been located, and hundreds may be growing. NASA would like to find the rest. It's true. Really.

Apollo 14 launched on January 31, 1971, for a trip to the surface of the Moon. After a five-day journey, Alan Shepard and Edgar Mitchell walked on the Moon. Stuart Roosa, a former U.S. Forest Service smoke jumper, remained in the command module. Packed in Roosa's personal kit were 400 to 500 tree seeds. He brought the seeds from the Earth to the Moon as part of a joint experiment for NASA and the United States Forest Service.

After Apollo 14 returned to Earth, the seed canisters burst during decontamination. Everyone thought the seeds were ruined, but the Forest Service germinated them anyway. The seedlings sprouted and were planted all over America. Unfortunately, nobody kept records indicating where all the trees were sent. The known trees are flourishing, and NASA calls them Moon Trees. For more information, see `http://nssdc.gsfc.nasa.gov/planetary/lunar/moon_tree.html`. NASA maintains a list of believed locations for the Moon Trees at that site and asks that you send NASA an e-mail if you know of one that hasn't been recorded.

I developed the following ritual after reading the Moon Tree story. You may use the basic ritual design, or you may create your own. Turn to Chapter 12 for detailed explanations for these steps.

The ritual is written as a solitary meditation designed to provide cleansing and renewal of your energy and is best performed at the Full Moon (although you can easily adapt it for any Moon phase). If you do ritual work with others, you may want to divide up the ritual activities (gathering the materials, casting the circle, reading the meditation, and so on).

1. **Decide why you want to conduct a ritual. Make sure that your intention is clear.**

2. **Decide how you want to perform your ritual; write the words that you want to use during the invocation and the other steps.**

3. **Decide when to do the ritual, for example, you may want to time it to a specific phase of the moon or to a Wiccan holiday.**

   Many Wiccans believe that an Esbat ritual must be conducted on the exact day of the Full Moon or the New Moon, for example. Others perform ritual at the best time for them personally, as long as the date is within three days or so of the astronomically true day. This Moon Tree ritual is ideal for the Full Moon.

4. **Decide where to do the ritual, set up an altar, and assemble the tools and other necessary objects.**

   If at all possible, perform an Esbat ritual outdoors, especially if you are celebrating the Full Moon.

   Full moon rituals done in the dark of the night are certainly more dramatic, but be practical in your timing. Setting up your altar is much easier when you can actually see the tools. If you have to work the next morning, doing your ritual in the evening rather than waiting for nightfall may be a better option.

   Arrange the tools on the altar and add any special materials you will need. For example, place your Book of Shadows or specific candles, stones, or herbs on the altar.

   For the Moon Tree Ritual, you may want to gather the following: a CD of drumming or other repetitive music (to help your mind reach a state of deep relaxation and begin generating alpha waves), a silver or white candle, and a small branch from a tree. (Don't use your magic wand.) A white branch is ideal but not necessary. In the Midwest, where I live, we have wonderful white sycamore trees which work well for this ritual. A willow or olive branch also is especially appropriate.

   Decorate the branch with Moon images, for example:

   • Draw or carve the phases of the Moon, or glue pictures of the Moon.

   • Wrap the branch in night-blooming flowers, such as jasmine or lily.

   • Anoint the branch with spring water, if you have easy access.

   • Affix a picture of an owl, a luna moth, or a bat.

- Affix a moonstone to the branch, if you have an inexpensive stone, or use any found stone that reminds you of the Moon.

5. **Purify the space.**

See Chapter 12 for information on purification.

6. **Purify yourself.**

7. **Cast a circle and create sacred space.**

See Chapter 12 for a detailed explanation of circle casting.

8. **Invoke, evoke, or welcome Deity, according to your beliefs.**

See Chapter 12 for information on invocation.

Invoke the Goddess and the God, or any Deity you wish. For the Moon Tree Ritual, you may want to name a Deity specifically associated with the Moon or simply use a more general phrase, such as "Goddess of the Moon."

Speak any words you want to communicate to Deity. Honor the presence of the Divine. Express your gratitude for any boons and blessings in your life. Ask for any pressing needs to be met.

9. **Conduct a ritual observance.**

This is the point in the ritual to engage in activities that are specific to the Esbat.

Relax at your altar. If desired, play your drumming or other relaxation music.

Light the silver or white candle.

Watch the flame of the candle. In your mind, picture yourself walking in a garden glade or a light woods. You stop at a natural spring for a drink of water. Next to the spring is a magnificent tree. You know it is a Moon Tree, grown strong from the seeds that went to the Moon on Apollo 14.

Pick up your decorated branch from your altar. Rest it in both hands. Feel the texture of the wood. In your mind, picture yourself touching the Moon Tree.

Your feet can feel the roots of the tree. You feel safe, grounded in Mother Earth.

You look up into the swaying branches. The Full Moon is radiant in the night sky.

The branches seem to sweep the surface of the Moon. Your hands rest lightly on the tree's trunk. You begin to feel the energy of the Moon running down through the tree.

The Moonlight seeps into you like sap. You feel the light dancing in your veins. Brilliant rays of silver and white play in your mind.

Draw in the Moon's energy. The Moonlight rushes through your body. Healing is swift and complete. Strength radiates from the marrow of your bones. Your mind is renewed, all the pathways polished like silver. You are luminous, and the path before you is clear.

Say: Great Mother Moon, shine through me. Let me be radiant in your service.

Bring your mind back to your altar. If you received clear guidance or direction, write it down in your Book of Shadows.

Enjoy cakes and wine, if you desire (see Chapter 12).

10. **Raise power and work magic, if you have a good reason.**

   See Chapter 15 for information on working magic during a ritual. Many Wiccans work magic on the Esbats, especially on the Full Moon, and they reserve the solar holidays, the Sabbats, for ritual to honor or seek attunement with the Divine. Divination, such as scrying or tarot card readings are popular activities on the Esbats. See Chapter 19 for more information about practicing divination.

11. **Earth the power.**

   See Chapter 12 for a detailed explanation of Earthing or grounding.

12. **Thank (or dismiss) Deity.** Thank the Moon Goddess for Her light and insight.

13. **Unseal the circle.**

   See Chapter 12 for instructions for taking down a circle.

Drawing Down the Moon

Drawing Down the Moon is a ritual that has been passed down through the Craft. The ritual of Drawing Down the Moon is performed during the Full Moon Esbat. According to tradition, a coven participates in the ritual or, at minimum, two people. It's possible for a solitary (someone who practices alone) to draw the Goddess into himself or herself, but not customary. A solitary may have difficulty remembering what the Goddess says through him or her. Also, Drawing Down the Moon can be a disorienting experience, and someone else should be present to help ease the transition back to mundane reality.

During this ceremony, the High Priest invokes, or *draws down,* the Goddess into the High Priestess.

Not all covens draw down the Moon, and Wiccans debate about the process and the meaning. Some Wiccans believe that the Goddess is *evoked* from within the High Priestess herself, instead of being drawn into her from some outside source. Some Wiccans believe that the Goddess can be drawn into a man or a woman; most see this as exclusively the role of the High Priestess. Some traditions also *Draw Down the Sun,* invoking the God into the High Priest.

During the ceremony, the High Priestess *becomes* the Goddess incarnate. Wiccans believe that the Goddess is actually present within Her High Priestess at this time. The High Priestess may deliver prophecy, Divine guidance, or a formal speech, but at this time and within the sacred circle, she is speaking as the Goddess Herself. The High Priestess usually has some prepared words, in the event that the Goddess doesn't manifest.

I do not offer a Drawing Down the Moon ritual in this book because this ceremony usually is performed within established covens, and each tradition has its own version of this rite. In addition, events during this particular ritual are sometimes unpredictable and unexpected, and may be unsettling for new seekers who have not had prior training or study — especially if a new solitary practitioner were to perform the ritual alone. Drawing Down the Moon is advanced Wicca. I strongly recommend that people engage in study and training, and evolve from the beginner level before participating in this ritual in a group and, especially, as a solitary.

Chapter 14

Turning the Wheel of the Year: The Sabbats

*T*he root of the word holiday is *holy day*. The Sabbats, the Wiccan holy days, are timed to the seasons and the natural rhythms of the Earth. For most Wiccans, ritual is central to the Sabbat celebrations. Gift giving and other activities are peripheral, though that focus may change as Wicca grows and spreads through families and communities.

For now, the Sabbats are a celebration of the Earth's journey around the Sun, and the Wiccan spiritual path through life.

This chapter describes the timing, the lore, and the ritual of Wicca's holidays.

Celebrating the Sun

Wicca is a nature-based spirituality, and the Wiccan holidays, called *Sabbats,* are based on the Earth's path around the Sun, sometimes represented as the *Wheel of the Year.* Wiccans often refer to celebrating the Sabbats as *Turning the Wheel.* The main Wiccan holidays are directly timed to natural occurrences, instead of human events, unlike the holy days of many other calendars.

Timing of the Sabbats

Most Wiccans celebrate eight Sabbats during the year: the winter solstice, the spring equinox, the summer solstice, and the autumn equinox, as well as the four halfway points between each solstice and equinox. The eight Wiccan holidays are spaced evenly throughout the year, approximately a month and a half apart.

Solstices occur two times per year (winter and summer), when the sun is at its greatest distance from the celestial equator. In Earth's Northern Hemisphere, the summer solstice occurs when the sun is farthest north. This is the longest day and the shortest night of the year. The winter solstice occurs when the sun is farthest south. This is the shortest day and the longest night of the year. (The opposite is true in the Southern Hemisphere.)

Equinoxes occur two times per year (spring and fall), when the sun crosses the plane of the earth's equator. On an equinox, day and night are of equal length.

Most ancient peoples around the world celebrated the solstices and equinoxes of each year, and most cultures had festivals of the changing seasons and of the planting and the harvest.

All Wiccan Sabbats are based on festivals of ancient Pagan Europe. The four Sabbats that occur halfway between each of the solstices and equinoxes are Celtic in origin. These mid-point holy days are *Samhain, Brigid/Imbolc, Beltane,* and *Lughnasad.* Some Wiccans consider these to be the *Greater* or *Major Sabbats.* The solstices and equinoxes are the *Lesser* or *Minor Sabbats.* The winter solstice is *Yule,* and the summer solstice often is called *Litha.* The autumn equinox is *Mabon,* and the spring equinox often is called *Eostar or Ostara.* In the next section, you can find information about the individual Wiccan Sabbats, or holy days.

Figuring out the Sabbat cycles

The Sabbats reflect the Pagan past, present-day Wicca, and the timeless mythology of Wicca. The Sabbats represent three different cycles:

- ✔ The Sabbats mark the changing of the seasons and the accompanying personal changes for modern Wiccans.

- ✔ The Sabbats are based on the early European Pagan's agricultural cycles, including the planting and harvesting cycle and the life cycles of livestock.

- ✔ The Sabbats' lore includes the Wiccan mythology about the Goddess and the God, and their perpetual cycle of interaction. This mythology is rooted in early Pagan explanations of the seasons.

Dictionary drivel

The word *Sabbat* comes from the Hebrew word, *Shabbath,* which means rest.

If you look up the word Sabbat in dictionaries and encyclopedias, you can find some thoroughly goofy definitions. Many dictionaries define a Sabbat as a midnight meeting of Witches, held to reaffirm Witches' loyalties to Satan and involving orgies with all manner of demons. Many of the longer explanations are quite lurid.

The language in the dictionary definitions is drawn from the Witch trials of medieval and Renaissance times. This view of the Sabbats prevailed at that time in history. During the Witch trials, people accused of Witchcraft were mercilessly tortured. The victims often said anything to stop the pain of torture and frequently confessed to whatever bizarre and obscene scenarios that the Inquisitors suggested, including descriptions of violent and vulgar sex acts with Satan's minions. This definition of Sabbat comes directly from the perverse minds of those who carried out the Witch hunts. (See Chapter 5 for more information on the Great European Witch Hunt.)

Modern-day dictionaries continue to offer this biased and archaic language, and they usually don't include the contemporary definition of Sabbat, or, for that matter, other words related to Wicca.

In many (but not all) Wiccan traditions, the Sun symbolizes the God, and the Earth represents the Goddess. As the Earth travels around the Sun and the seasons change, the Deities also change and so does the relationship between them.

- ✔ **The Goddess** shifts in Her aspects from Maiden to Mother to Crone, and back to Maiden. The *Maiden* represents independence and youth. The *Mother,* of course, represents giving birth (not only to children, but to ideas, insight, and projects), and also nurturing, sensuality, and creativity. The *Crone* symbolizes age, maturity, wisdom, and the command for respect.

- ✔ **The God** progresses through a full life cycle. He is born, grows to manhood, marries and impregnates the Goddess, and dies. He is then reborn as the child of the Goddess. He once again grows from the Divine Child to the Sun God, and begins the entire cycle again.

Some Wiccan traditions focus on the Goddess during the dark, cold months and the God during the warm, light months.

The following sections dedicated to the specific Sabbats outline this Deity mythology. However, many Wiccans find this lore to be heterosexist as well as provincial and narrow-minded. Some are altering the language to be more inclusive and to reflect a more sophisticated understanding of polarity.

Observing the Sabbats during Ritual

Ritual is a ceremony that a person does for a specific purpose. The purpose of a *religious ritual* is to understand, experience, or feel the connection to Deity. For many Wiccans, the Sabbats are the best times to perform intense or formal ritual and to seek attunement with the Divine.

Working Sabbat observance into basic ritual

The following sections offer some ideas for observing the Sabbats. You may use the basic ritual design from this book and include a Sabbat observance after you invoke, evoke, or welcome Deity.

The following is the basic ritual design (turn to Chapter 12 for explanations of these steps.):

1. **Decide why you want to conduct a ritual. Make sure that your intention is clear.**

2. **Decide how you want to perform your ritual; write the words that you want to use during the invocation and the other steps.**

3. **Decide when to do the ritual, for example, you may want to time it to a specific phase of the moon or to a Wiccan holiday.**

   Many Wiccans believe that a Sabbat ritual must be conducted on the exact day, for example, the actual day of the winter solstice. Others perform ritual at the best time for them personally. Some people wait for the weekend, when they are more rested and less distracted, regardless of the real date of the Sabbat.

4. **Decide where to do the ritual, set up an altar, and assemble the tools and other necessary objects.**

   Arrange the tools on the altar and add any special materials you will need. For example, place your Book of Shadows or specific candles, stones, herbs.

5. **Purify the space.**

   See Chapter 12 for information on purification.

6. **Purify yourself.**

   See Chapter 12 for information on purification.

7. **Cast a circle to create sacred space.**

   See Chapter 12 for a detailed explanation of circle casting.

8. **Invoke, evoke, or welcome Deity, according to your beliefs.**

   See Chapter 12 for information on invocation and evocation.

9. **Conduct a ritual observance.**

   This is the point in the ritual to engage in activities that are specific to a Sabbat (Yule, Brigid, Eostar, Beltane, Litha, Lughnasad, Mabon, or Samhain). See the following sections for ways to observe the Sabbats.

10. **Raise power and work magic, if you have a good reason.**

    See Chapter 15 for information on working magic during a ritual. Magical work may be performed during any of the Sabbat rituals. Many Wiccans work magic at Samhain (especially divination) and at Litha, the summer solstice.

11. **Earth the power.**

    See Chapter 12 for a detailed explanation of Earthing or grounding.

12. **Thank (or dismiss) Deity.**

    See Chapter 12 for further explanation.

13. **Take down the circle.**

    See Chapter 12 for instructions for taking down a circle.

Understanding how to celebrate the Sabbats

The Sabbat names, explanations, and forms of celebration differ widely among Wiccans. You may see information that varies markedly from the general descriptions later in this section. Each Wiccan decides for himself or herself which aspects of the Sabbat to celebrate and what specific ritual elements carry the most meaning.

The section for each Sabbat is divided into three parts:

 ✔ **The basic explanation of the Sabbat, including the lore and symbolism for the holy day.**

   The explanation includes the perpetual pattern of interaction between the Goddess and the God (the Deity myth), as well as common beliefs about the planting and harvesting cycle of the early Pagans, and the changing of the seasons for modern Wiccans.

✔ **Tips for decorating an altar for each of the Sabbat observances.**

Don't worry; the folks from the Home and Garden TV network aren't going to burst into your sacred space and judge your altar for style and creativity. People decorate altars because seasonal decorations help them stay attuned to the natural world and the seasons.

Also, and this aspect is important, the items from nature trigger the unconscious mind and may make the Sabbat ritual more powerful and fulfilling. The vivid colors and natural textures awaken the personal unconscious mind. The natural goods also arouse the collective unconscious. Humans have deep, primal memories of nature's bounty (including berries, grains, herbs, nuts, pinecones, seashells, seeds, stones, and especially fire). We share our common experience of these items with our ancient ancestors, and these natural things excite the inherited, instinctive part of the brain.

The decorations don't have to be Martha Stewart perfect; they just need to provide vivid images and stimulate the senses.

If you have children or animals, don't leave a decorated altar within their reach. Herbs/plants used for their magical properties or for decoration may be poisonous if ingested. Candles are not suitable playthings for children. Children must not have access to some Wiccan tools, such as the athame (a Wiccan dagger).

✔ **Ideas for observing the Sabbat.**

The information in the following sections is geared toward the Northern Hemisphere. The Sabbats for the Southern Hemisphere are reversed. For example, winter solstice in the Northern Hemisphere is summer solstice in the Southern Hemisphere.

In addition, the seasons vary widely all over the world, depending on the location. For some people, spring equinox (Eostar) is truly the beginning of spring. The forests and fields turn green, the weather warms, and new life bursts forth. For people in other areas, the fields are still brown and barren at Eostar, and spring is still just a promise. For these folks, spring isn't in full swing until Beltane. Gear your ritual to your own surroundings, instead of following an arbitrary calendar.

Exploring the Individual Sabbats

One of the central commitments of Wicca and Witchcraft is to live attuned to nature. If you celebrate the Sabbats, adapt them to your life in your own area and environment. Perform the Sabbat rituals in the way that is meaningful for you and your own location. Ritual is much more satisfying and productive if it is personal. Begin with the basic ritual design and the general information in this chapter, but use the wisdom, words, and ways that spring from your own heart and apply to your own life.

Yule, winter solstice

Wiccans celebrate Yule (pronounced *yool*) on the actual date of the winter solstice. This date differs from year to year, and falls around December 21.

Yule occurs when the Sun is at 0 degrees Capricorn.

Yule lore and symbolism

The Goddess is worshipped in Her Mother aspect.

Deity myth

The Goddess labors throughout the longest night of the year. At dawn, the Goddess once again gives birth to the Sun God, in the form of the Divine Child. Wiccans celebrate the birth and the return of the Sun.

For traditions that consider the dark or cold half of the year to be dedicated to the Goddess, this day marking the return of the Sun is the one God day in the middle of the traditional time of the Goddess.

Common beliefs

Yule is the longest night and the shortest day of the year. Some Wiccans consider Yule to be either the year's beginning or the end. Starting with the day of Yule, the days begin to get longer, and the light increases. This is the time to celebrate the return of the light.

Yule is the solar turning of the tides, and the newborn Sun offers a fresh start and, literally, a new day. It is a time of renewal and hope.

Altar tools and decorations

Altar cloth color: red or green

Candles: white, red and green; the ritual candles and the lights on the Yule tree are symbols for the growing light in the darkness of winter.

Herbs and plants (for magical work or decoration, not for eating): cinnamon sticks, cloves, evergreen boughs, holly, ivy, mistletoe, nutmeg, sunflowers, wintergreen

Stones: clear quartz, ruby, garnet, and green tourmaline

Other tools and decorations: owl feather (a feather dropped naturally, not as a result of bird being harmed); pinecones; stars, sun, and moon decorations

A small white candle in a cauldron on the altar. The cauldron symbolizes the womb of the Goddess. The light from the candle represents the rebirth of the Sun in the winter darkness.

Ideas for ritual observances

Yule ritual: Because Yule marks the return of the light and signifies rebirth and renewal, it is the time to plant a seed in your consciousness. Do you have a big dream? Do you have a goal or desire that you don't dare even consider? Do you want to write a book, get involved in a political cause, study a new subject, or make a commitment to more closely align your life with your Wiccan beliefs? At Yule, allow the first rays of the newborn sun to create a spark in your soul. Give yourself permission to harbor hope and nurture the seed of possibility that you can accomplish this important goal. (Make sure that your goal harms no one.)

During the Yule ritual, light the white candle in the cauldron and clearly state your intention to pursue your goal or desire. Ask for strength and guidance from Deity. Trust that your power to act and overcome obstacles will gain momentum as the sunlight grows in duration and intensity every day. Be sure to thank the Divine for the blessing and continued guidance.

Yule activities: A traditional practice is to decorate a Yule tree. This old Pagan custom was incorporated into the modern Christmas tradition. You may cut an evergreen tree or use a potted one. If you cut down a tree, get it from a farm that plants trees for this purpose; don't remove a tree from the woods or countryside.

I love to buy a large potted rosemary plant and decorate it at Yule. At this time of year, you can buy them shaped like small evergreen trees. The smell is wonderful. However, they are finicky plants and can be difficult to keep alive indoors after the holiday. The soil must be light and have very good drainage. The plant requires full sun. Rosemary doesn't usually survive cold northern winters, if planted outside. It must winter indoors.

Many Wiccans exchange Yule gifts. The gift exchange may happen at any time, starting at Yule and continuing through Twelfth Night on January 6.

Many Wiccans burn a Yule log on the winter solstice. The Yule log is traditionally a part of the Maypole from the previous Beltane or a log of sacred wood specially cut and decorated for this purpose. Of course, make sure that you have a working fireplace, wood stove, or a safe place outdoors to have a fire. At sunset, they light the Yule log, and then tend it all night, keeping it burning until dawn. At the first rays of morning, they welcome back the sun, thanking the Deity for the return of the light and the promise of spring.

Brigid, Imbolc

Wiccans celebrate Brigid, also called Imbolc (*im*-bolk or *im*-bolg), on February 1 or 2. Other names for this Sabbat include Candlemas, Oimelc, Imbolg, and Brigit's or Brigid's Day.

Brigid occurs when the Sun is at 15 degrees Aquarius.

Brigid lore and symbolism

This Sabbat celebrates the awakening Maiden aspect of the Goddess.

Deity myth

The Sun God, the Divine child born of the Mother Goddess, is growing strong and thriving.

Common beliefs

Brigid, or Imbolc, is a preparation for spring. For many people, this Sabbat falls at the end of winter, when the weather is coldest, and the land is still covered with snow or barren of new growth. The days are lengthening, and the early Pagans had visible hope that the time of long, dark nights, deprivation, and the winter struggle for survival was almost over. (Brigid also is a time of hardship for many modern people. Now is a good time to take unneeded clothes or extra food to shelters for the homeless and impoverished.)

Brigid is the Celtic Triple Goddess (Maiden, Mother, and Crone) of fire and inspiration. She is associated with poetry, smithcraft, and healing. Some see Her as a protector and preserver of knowledge. The Sabbat is identified with fire and light, and is sometimes called the Festival of Lights or the Feast of Torches. At Brigid, the sun is growing in intensity and holds the promise of the approaching spring. Fire chases away the last of the bitter winter cold, and is cleansing and purifying.

This is the time to begin spring cleaning, both physically and mentally. At Brigid, Wiccans clean and organize their living environments, as well as their minds and hearts, in preparation for the upcoming season of growth. It's a time to shake off the doldrums of late winter and light the fires of creativity and inspiration.

Special altar tools and decorations

Altar cloth color: white

Candles: white and yellow

Herbs and plants (for magical work or decoration, not for eating): cedar, chamomile, evergreen branches, rose hips, sage, sunflowers, white flowers (if you can comfortably afford them)

Stones: amber, amazonite (feldspar) carnelian, clear quartz, citrine, and rose quartz

Other tools and decorations: a small bowl of seeds (flower or vegetable) on the altar, along with a small pot filled with potting soil

Ideas for ritual observances

Brigid ritual: Brigid is the Goddess of poetry. The theme of this Sabbat is inspiration and creativity. Write a short essay, poem, song, or other creative work that reflects who you want to become or what you want to accomplish. Focus on the important goal or desire that you voiced during your Yule Sabbat (if you did so). Be very specific about the change you want to initiate. Make sure that it harms no one. If you aren't much of a writer, choose to paint, sculpt, or use other art techniques to demonstrate your intention.

During ritual at Brigid, read the words that you've written (or unveil the artwork). From the bowl on your altar, pour the seeds into your hand. Concentrate on sending your personal energy into them. Plant the seeds in the small pot. Say, "As these seedlings grow, I will grow in strength, in wisdom, and in commitment to my goal" (or "to my true self") or similar words. Ask Deity to bless and guide your growth. Be sure to thank the Divine.

Brigid activities: At sunset, many Wiccans follow the old Pagan custom of illuminating every room in the house to celebrate the Sun's rebirth. They turn on all lamps or light a candle in every room. (This is a symbolic display that lasts for only a few minutes; don't leave the lamps, and especially the candles, burning all night.)

Many Wiccans read avidly at this time of the year. You may want to choose a book that you know inspires you and sparks your creativity. Keep the book on or near your altar to charge it with energy.

Eostar, spring equinox

Wiccans celebrate Eostar (*O-star*) on the actual date of the spring equinox. This date differs from year to year, and falls around March 21. Other names for this Sabbat include Ostara and Oestarra.

Eostar occurs when the Sun is at 0 degrees Aries.

Eostar lore and symbolism

The Goddess is making Her transformation from Crone into the Maiden aspect.

Deity myth

The Divine child, the Sun God, is growing up. The Goddess is transforming into a Maiden, who will develop parallel with the Sun God.

Some Wiccan traditions celebrate the change from the dark part of the year, associated with the Goddess, to the light part of the year, associated with the God.

Common beliefs

Winter is now over. Light is increasing. The day and night are equal in length at the equinox. Spring has arrived or is coming soon.

The modern symbols of bunnies and colored eggs were taken from the old Pagan spring festivals. These symbols were connected with the Goddess, fertility, and birth. Eostar is the time of fertility, birth, and renewal. The ice is thawing, and the growing season for plants and animals begins. Growth is the theme of the day.

The early Pagan Goddess, Eostar (or Ostara, Ostera, Eostre, Estara, or Eostra), was a Goddess of spring, as was the Welsh Goddess, Blodeuwedd. In mythology, Blodeuwedd is changed into an owl and is a symbol of wisdom.

Special altar tools and decorations

Altar cloth color: light green or other pastel cloth

Candles: white, pastel green or yellow

Herbs and plants (for magical work or decoration, not for eating): bulb flowers (for example, crocuses, daffodils, irises, tulips, or lilies), jonquils, lilacs, lily of the valley, marjoram, thyme, willow

Stones: clear quartz crystal, pink or green tourmaline, rose quartz

Other tools and decorations: colored eggs, flowery incense, potted plant (use the plant that you began at Brigid, if you did so). Place water and plant food near the altar.

Ideas for ritual observances

Eostar ritual: Now is the time to act on the seed of change that you first planted in your consciousness at Yule. Dare to bring your big dream or your goal to fruition.

During ritual at Eostar, water the potted plant on your altar and give it some plant food. Ask Deity to bless the plant and your life. Sit comfortably before the altar. Relax deeply; you may want to listen to some drumming in order to induce a light trance state.

Visualize yourself walking just after dawn along a path through a dense forest (or perhaps down a country lane surrounded by food crops or orchards). Take in the abundance of energy from the lush plant life as it absorbs the morning sun. In your mind, use all your senses. Hear the bees buzzing as they pollinate the plants. Feel the rays of the spring sun on your skin and the moisture of the morning dew. Smell the different plants and the rich soil. Taste a berry or a mushroom. Allow yourself to be energized by the pulsating plant energy around you.

Make a vow aloud to use this energy wisely, as fuel for your actions as you pursue your goal. Thank Deity for being present and for blessing your progress. Think of your visualization any time you're tired, your resolve wanes, or you're filled with doubt.

Eostar activities: Many Wiccans, especially those with children, color eggs and hold egg hunts. Many of the Goddesses of old Paganism were thought to shapeshift into hares. Today, bunny-related events are common at Eostar. Sometimes people dress up as Eostar bunnies to hand out candy eggs. Giving stuffed bunny toys may be appropriate. (Please don't give real rabbits.)

Beltane, May Eve

Wiccans celebrate Beltane (pronounced _bel_-tayn or _bell_-tain) on April 30 or May 1. Other names for this Sabbat include Beltaine, Bealtaine, and May Day.

Beltane occurs when the Sun is at 15 degrees Taurus.

Beltane lore and symbolism

The Goddess begins the transition from the Maiden aspect to the Mother.

Deity myth

The Goddess and the God reach puberty and adulthood. At Beltane, Wiccans celebrate this sacred marriage and sexual union.

In the Celtic traditions, Beltane represents the major change from the dark part of the year, associated with the Goddess, to the light part of the year, associated with the God. (Beltane and Samhain are the major turning points of the Celtic year.)

Common beliefs

Beltane is the time of the marriage and union of the Goddess as Mother Earth and the God of the Greenwood. It is an ancient fertility festival marking the beginning of the planting cycle. The festival was to ensure a good growing season and a bountiful harvest. In the old Pagan cultures, people sometimes made love in the fields. This act was thought to boost the growth of the crops and the fertility of the livestock.

Beltane is most likely named after the Celtic Sun God Bel (or Belos, Balar, Balor, or Belenus), known as the Bright One. Beltane is the opposite of Samhain on the Wiccan calendar and is also opposite in spirit. Samhain is solemn and intense; Beltane is light-hearted and joyful.

Traditionally, at the Beltane festivals of the old Pagan cultures, great balefires were lit. In some places, fire festivals are still common today at this time of the year.

Often two balefires were built from nine different woods representing various sacred trees, and cattle and other livestock were driven between the fires for protection and blessing before they went to the summer pastures. Couples joined hands and jumped the fires for good luck and fertility.

Special altar tools and decorations

Altar cloth color: green

Candles: white, green, yellow

Herbs and plants (for magical work or decoration, not for eating): blessed thistle, broom, flaxseed, mint, mushroom, nettle, rosemary, rue, yarrow. All spring flowers are appropriate (especially wildflowers gathered in the woods or countryside).

Stones: clear quartz, emerald, jade, malachite, moonstone, opal, and peridot

Other tools and decorations: a large candle or a can of the fuel used in warming trays in a cauldron to symbolize the giant balefires of old Paganism. Assemble foods, flowers, and useful items to fill a May basket. Keep the basket and the contents beside your altar.

Ideas for ritual observances

Beltane ritual: Wiccans traditionally assemble and exchange *May baskets* at Beltane. Buy a basket or, if you are crafty, weave one yourself from branches, vines, or other natural materials. The baskets are filled with small gifts for the receiver.

During ritual, fill a basket with foods and useful items; top the contents with some of the wildflowers that you've gathered. Concentrate on sending your own positive energy into the basket as you pack it. Say to Deity, "I am creating this basket with positive intent, and I ask for the best possible outcome." Thank the Goddess and the God for their presence and attention.

After you release your ritual circle, take the basket to someone who is suffering hardship (for example, poverty or severe illness). Leave the basket anonymously or give the basket without fanfare. Don't violate the person's dignity by making a big deal of your efforts or expecting a show of gratitude.

In addition to the spiritual significance of Beltane, May Day traditionally is a time to focus on economic and social justice. If you are lucky enough to live in abundance, or even luxury, ask the Divine how you can effectively work to see that everyone shares your comfortable standard of living. Every human being is a manifestation of Deity, and every person embodies Deity. All the children of the Goddess are equal, and all have the same rights to resources and opportunities.

Beltane activities: Some Wiccan groups (covens and others) erect a Maypole (a phallic symbol), which represents sexuality, fertility, birth, and creativity. A *Maypole* is a tall pole stuck into the ground. Streamers or ribbons are attached at the top and flow down far enough to be comfortably grasped. Participants each clutch a streamer. Women dance in one direction; men dance in the other. Dancers weave in and out, braiding their streamers around the Maypole. The Wiccan community dances joyously around the pole. If you are a solitary, meaning that you practice Wicca alone, you also may want to dance and sing at Beltane.

Many Wiccans follow the old Pagan tradition of lighting balefires at Beltane. The fires are an emotionally moving sight. Please be sure that you pick a safe area, and that you have permission to be use the land for the purpose.

Litha, summer solstice

Wiccans celebrate Litha (pronounced *lith*-ah) on the actual date of the summer solstice. This date differs from year to year, and falls around June 21. Litha is also called Midsummer.

Litha occurs when the Sun is at 0 degrees Cancer.

Litha lore and symbolism

The Goddess is in Her Mother aspect.

Deity myth

The Goddess is pregnant by the Sun God.

This is the Goddess day in the middle of the traditional time of the God.

Common beliefs

Litha is the longest day and the shortest night of the year. Light triumphs, but will now begin to fade into darkness as autumn approaches. The crops are planted and growing. The woods and forests have reached their peak fullness. This is the time of abundance for wildlife — including people.

Litha shares much of the character of Beltane. The ancient festivals were wild and passionate. The time is joyous. Today, handfastings (sort of a Wiccan wedding) often are performed during Litha. Because of the thunderstorms and lightning that occur in many places at this time of the year, fire is an important element at Litha. As at Beltane, balefires were traditionally lit. Herds of livestock were driven between the fires for blessing and protection.

Fresh summer flowers play a big role in the Litha rituals.

Special altar tools and decorations

Altar cloth color: gold

Candles: white, red, and gold

Herbs and plants (for magical work or decoration, not for eating): basil, fern, feverfew, honeysuckle, lavender, mint, rosemary, vervain. If you're lucky enough to find wild roses (or similar flowers) while out walking, spread the petals on the altar. Many herbs are said to have the strongest magical properties at this time of the year. (See Appendix B for some information about the magical properties of specific herbs.)

Stones: amber, black tourmaline, bloodstone, cat's eye, clear quartz crystal, garnet, and ruby

Other tools and decorations: Fill a cauldron full of flowers and, perhaps, some summer fruit. Arrange mirrors on the altar to reflect the light of the sun. Lavender incense is nice for this time of year. (Some clinical trials suggest that the aroma of lavender may help lift mild depression. Check with your physician before using any type of aromatherapy.)

Ideas for ritual observances

Litha ritual: During the ritual at Litha, many Wiccans raise power and work magic. Magic is strong now because it works with the powers of nature, which is at its zenith at midsummer. Herbs gathered at Litha are the strongest of the year. This is the time for spellcasting and other magical workings. See Chapters 15–17 for detailed instructions for working effective, personal magic.

Litha activity: Take a long summer hike through the forest or countryside. Gather a wide variety of wildflowers for your altar and the rest of your home. I like to gather the wild lilies and violets at my family's woodland home.

Lughnasad, Lammas

Wiccans celebrate Lughnasad (pronounced loo-*nuh*-sa or loo-*nah*-sah or *loo*-nah-sah) on August 1. Other names for this Sabbat include Lughnasadh, Lugnassadh, Lughnassad, Lughnasa, Lunasa, Lunasda, Lunasdal, and Lammas.

Lughnasad occurs when the Sun is at 15 degrees Leo.

Lughnasad lore and symbolism

The Goddess is fully in Her Mother aspect.

Deity myth

The Goddess is heavy with the Sun God's child.

The Sun God is at full maturity. He displays the full scope of His wisdom and prowess. This is His last hoorah before death.

In Wiccan mythology, the Sun God dies when the first grain is ready for harvesting. For some locations and traditions, His death occurs at Lughnasad, because it is the first harvest. For many locations, the grain isn't ready for reaping until Mabon, the next Sabbat. Wiccans commemorate the death of the Sun God either at Lughnasad or at Mabon, depending on the timing of the great harvest.

For much of the bread-basket area of the central United States, Lughnasad is a bit early for the major harvests of wheat, corn, and other grains. For Europe, the timing depends on the latitude (how far north the location is). Of course, for the Southern Hemisphere, all the seasons and the corresponding Sabbats are reversed.

Common beliefs

The grain harvest has been critically important — and has been ritualized — in nearly every culture on Earth. Lughnasad is the European celebration of the first harvest and of thanksgiving. For the northern Pagans of old, this was the main harvest. For Pagans further south, it was the first harvest, to be followed by the main harvest at Mabon. Lughnasad is the Festival of Lugh, the Celtic Sun God.

For the ancient Pagans, Lughnasad was a time of both hope and fear. They held hope for a bountiful harvest and abundant food, but they feared that the harvest wouldn't be large enough and that the cold months would be filled with struggle and deprivation. The shorter days and diminishing light kept them ever mindful of the creeping approach of winter's cold and darkness.

At Lughnasad, the God is in His full mature splendor, demonstrating His profound abilities.

Traditionally, the early Pagans were very healthy at Lughnasad from the fresh produce of the summer, and they held games and contests at Lughnasad. Like their Sun God, they wanted to show off their own skills, strength, and cunning.

This is the time when modern Wiccans also face their fears, concentrate on developing their own abilities, and take steps to protect themselves and their homes.

Altar decorations

Altar cloth color: gold or white

Candles: white, yellow, orange, and brown

Herbs and plants (for magical work or decoration, not for eating): carnations, clover, goldenrod, ivy, marigold, myrtle, poppies, roses, sunflowers

Stones: black tourmaline, cat's eye, citrine, clear quartz, lodestone, turquoise

Other tools and decorations: early grains (sheaves of early wheat, barley, oats, ears of corn), small loaves of bread, summer fruits (apples, berries, pears, peaches, tomatoes), vegetables (especially orange, red, or green peppers)

Ideas for ritual observances

Lughnasad ritual: Carl Sagan said, "Our lives, our past and our future are tied to the sun, the moon and the stars. . . . And we, we who embody the local eyes and ears and thoughts and feelings of the cosmos, we have begun at least to wonder about our origins — star stuff contemplating the stars" (*Cosmos*, 1980). As Sagan said, we truly are made of "star stuff." Life arose, and humans evolved from the elements created by the stars.

During the warmth of the night at Lughnasad, try to perform your ritual outdoors, or at least, near a window so that you can see the sky. Lughnasad (and all the Sabbats) are solar rituals; they are tied to Earth's Sun, a star. We are "star stuff," born from the stars, and they are our oldest ancestors.

Lughnasad is the time to face fears and anxieties. Like the Pagans of old who faced the long, dark winter trusting that the harvest would sustain them, Wiccans today also seek the confidence and strength to face what lies ahead.

For ritual, invoke Deity and then relax deeply, look into the sky, and concentrate on the stars. Allow yourself to gaze unhurried at the summer sky. Know your link to the cosmos. Open up to the star energy; let the power fill you up. All your fears and worries fall away as you take your place in the vastness of the universe, at one with the stars.

Ask the great Star Goddess to help you to remember this moment, so that you can maintain your perspective about everyday concerns. You can be responsible: Pay your bills, do your taxes, find a new job, and so on, without allowing anxiety or fear to overcome you. You are a child of the stars. Thank Deity for the opportunity to appreciate the glory of the cosmos and the limitless web of life.

Lughnasad activities: The Perseid meteor shower begins to appear around July 17. The meteors continue through Lughnasad until as late as August 24 or so. A meteor is a small, solid body traveling through space.

During the Perseids, you may see a few meteors an hour, or many meteors may grace the sky for short bursts. In July and August, at least ten other minor meteor displays are active at various times. They don't compare to the Perseids, but they offer some sky excitement. Watching the meteors is one way to maintain connection with the cosmos and to reinforce the power of the Lughnasad star ritual previously described.

Mabon, fall equinox

Wiccans celebrate Mabon (pronounced *may*-bun or *mah*-bon or *may*-bon) on the actual date of the fall equinox. The date differs from year to year, and falls around September 22. Harvest Home is another name for this Sabbat.

Mabon occurs when the Sun is at 0 degrees Libra.

Mabon lore and symbolism

The Goddess is settling into Her Crone aspect.

Deity myth

The God is dead. The Earth receives His body and the great harvest. The God willingly sacrifices His life for the people, and He crosses over into the Summerland. He will rest and wait to be reborn to the Goddess at Yule, when the Sun returns.

Some Wiccan traditions celebrate the change from the light part of the year, associated with the God, to the dark part of the year, associated with the Goddess.

Common beliefs

At Mabon, the day and the night are equal in length, in sublime balance. For many locations, Mabon coincides with the final harvest of grain, fruits, and vegetables.

Mabon, also called Harvest Home, is the time of thanksgiving. Many modern Wiccans hold feasts at Mabon. The early Pagans gratefully stored food for the winter months. The beauty and bounty of summer give way to the desolation of winter, and the darkness overtakes the light.

Special altar tools and decorations

Altar cloth color: gold, orange, red, or copper

Candles: white, brown, and red

Herbs and plants (for magical work or decoration, not for eating): acorns, brilliantly colored leaves, poppies, seed pods, walnut leaves and husks, yarrow

Stones: amber, cat's eye, clear quartz, peridot, yellow topaz

Other tools and decorations: fall fruits (apples, berries, persimmons, pumpkins), gourds, grains (sheaves of early wheat, barley, oats, ears of corn), small loaves of bread, vegetables

Many Wiccans place a corn dolly on the altar as a symbol of the Goddess or the God. *Corn dollies* are cornstalks or sheaves of wheat woven together, tied, and decorated to look human.

Ideas for ritual observances

Mabon ritual: Mabon is the traditional time of thanksgiving for Wiccans, and it is the last Sabbat before the end of the year and Samhain, the Witches' New Year. In the spirit of gratitude and the upcoming new year, take some time to think about your progress. Consider the past year and make a list of achieved goals, moments of insight, fulfilling events, and times when you were genuinely happy. Write the list in your Book of Shadows (see Chapter 20 for more information on these spiritual journals).

During ritual, after invoking Deity, read your list aloud. In your own heartfelt words, express your gratitude to the Divine for your life.

Did you have difficulty compiling a list? If you are struggling to meet your basic needs, are seriously ill, are clinically depressed, or are suffering from loss, then ask the Divine to provide guidance or show you the way through your situation so that you can meet the new year more empowered, with a definite plan of action. Ask for a clear message and accurate understanding. Assertively seek help from others if possible. All people embody Deity, and all people deserve a satisfactory quality of life. Wicca is not a religion that glorifies suffering.

Mabon activities: Many Wiccans enjoy a feast at Mabon. The feast may be eaten in sacred space, as part of the Mabon ritual. However, it's easier to simply bless the food or sample a small amount during ritual, release the circle, and then enjoy the feast.

If possible, at Mabon walk through a field, woods, park, or orchard and gather items for food, decoration, and magic. Every year at Mabon, I begin my search for the best native persimmons. My ancestors have made persimmon pudding from the wild fruit for generations. They are beautiful on the altar.

This is also the time when the walnuts are ripening in many areas. Walnuts are very difficult to remove from their husks for drying, and it's a very messy process. The husks leave walnut stains on everything they touch. I always know when the walnuts are ripe because the squirrels all have dark stains around their mouths — and sometimes all over their little faces.

Mabon is one of the times during the year when the animals are most active. Many are in rut (mating). Others are eating all they can and preparing for hibernation. As you walk through nature, watch the animals carefully. Ask Deity to guide you to animals that can give you a valuable lesson or message. Watching animals is truly a form of divination, and I have received some of my most valuable lessons from them.

Samhain, Witches' New Year

Wiccans celebrate Samhain (pronounced *sow*-in, rhymes with "*cow*-in") on October 31, although some Wiccans consider the actual holiday to be November 1. Other names for Samhain include: All Hallow's Eve, Hallowmas, Feast of the Dead, and Ancestor Night.

Samhain occurs when the Sun is at 15 degrees Scorpio.

Samhain lore and symbolism
The Goddess is honored in Her Crone aspect.

Deity myth
The Goddess mourns Her slain consort, the Sun God. He sacrificed His own life, sending His energy into the Earth, so that the community could enjoy the harvest of the grain. This Sabbat commemorates the death of the God as He journeys to the Land of Shadow. The Goddess is already preparing Herself for the birth of the Sun God's child.

Common beliefs
Many Wiccans consider this Sabbat to be the beginning of the new year, and October 31 to be the equivalent of New Year's Eve. They deem Samhain to be the most important Sabbat of the year. However, other Wiccans consider the winter solstice (Yule) to be the start of the new year, brought about by the rebirth of the Sun after the longest night.

Wiccans generally agree on three aspects of Samhain:

- ✔ **It's the time to remember those who have passed on before — the ancestors.**

   The terms *ancestors* is not restricted to family and also can include friends or admired people. Samhain often is the most solemn of the Sabbats.

   Some Wiccans honor the dead with a *dumb supper,* a dinner held in total silence. Attendees use this time to remember those who have gone before. Typically, one plate of food is set aside as an offering for the ancestors. Some Wiccans leave the food on this plate outdoors for the woodland creatures.

During Samhain, some Wiccans try to contact the spirits of the dead ancestors. This holy day is considered to be the time when the various parts of the Otherworld are easiest to access. However, whether a Wiccan tries to communicate with the dead depends on his or her view of the afterlife. Wiccans may not engage in this practice, depending how and when they believe that the dead reincarnate and return to physical existence on Earth. Some Wiccans try to reach only the souls of people who are recently departed (usually within one year). These Wiccans believe that people who are long-deceased may have reincarnated, leaving no portion of the soul or essence available for communication. Other Wiccans may attempt to communicate with those who have passed on at any time, recently or otherwise.

✔ **It's the time when the veil between the worlds is thinnest.**

Many Wiccans feel a profound shift of energy at Samhain. They note the increase in their own psychic energy, and they feel close to the Otherworld, astral planes, the Summerland, or other non-physical realities.

I personally think that the expectation that the veil is thinner may cause a shift in the collective unconscious, the inherited, deep part of the mind that that is linked with all other humans, and probably animals. This shift could put people in closer touch with the energies of other planes.

I think that, for reasons scientists don't yet understand, certain times of the year, like Samhain, may put humans in closer touch with other dimensions and fields of energy.

Regardless of the explanation, for most Wiccans, the Samhain ritual is the time to engage in some form of divination; tarot card readings are most common.

✔ **It's the time to celebrate the harvest and all that has been accomplished during the year.**

Samhain was the time when the early Pagans gathered the root vegetables and culled the herds of animals. *Culling* means that they thinned the herds, slaughtering animals and storing meat. This practice cut down on the numbers of animals that had to be fed over the long winter. Sometimes, people call Samhain the Blood Harvest for this reason (this term is *not* a reference to human sacrifice). In hunting cultures, this was the time of the great hunts.

Based on this theme of eliminating and simplifying, many Wiccans examine their lives on Samhain. They may use this time to break negative habits, kick addictions (such as smoking), write off unfinished projects, or concentrate on curing physical illnesses or conditions. It's a time for organizing life and disposing of papers and expendable junk collected over the year. It's also a time for focusing on what is important, for setting goals, and clarifying priorities.

Special altar tools and decorations

Altar cloth color: gold, shades of orange-red, copper, deep browns

Candles: white, black, orange, gold

Herbs and plants (for magical work or decoration, not for eating): acorns, brilliantly colored leaves, poppies, seed pods, walnut leaves and husks, yarrow

Stones: amber, cat's eye, clear quartz, peridot, yellow topaz

Other tools and decorations: crow or raven feather (a feather dropped naturally, not as a result of bird being harmed), fall fruits (apples, berries, peaches, persimmons), gourds, nuts, pomegranates

You may want to include some type of divination tool on the altar (for example, a deck of tarot cards or a crystal ball).

Place pictures and remembrances of ancestors or people who have recently passed on.

Ideas for ritual observances

Samhain ritual: Traditionally, Samhain is the time to use divination. See Chapter 19 for information on the types of divination and how to use them.

Samhain activities: For many Wiccans, Samhain observances are for honoring those who have died, particularly in the past year. Look at photographs of your ancestors or concentrate on other items of remembrance. Voice your feelings, for example, by expressing your respect for specific people.

If you have unresolved issues, find a way to let them go. If you need to grieve, allow yourself to experience the full onslaught of your wild grief within the safety of the circle and the presence of the Goddess and the God. Cry. Ask for or give forgiveness. Make peace.

Part V
Practicing the Craft: What Wiccans Do

The 5th Wave   By Rich Tennant

ALWAYS KEEP YOUR TAROT DECK IN A SAFE PLACE AWAY FROM CHILDREN

"What does it mean when Pikachu appears between two sphinxes?"

In this part . . .

Well, all aboard for the magical, mystery tour! This part is the how-to of magical practice. You can find out how to work magic and how to boost your efforts with candles, herbs, and stones.

This part also offers an introduction to dream and trance work, as well as divination (from scrying to tarot cards).

In the last chapter, you can find out how to record your spiritual trip in your own Book of Shadows, a personal journal of ritual and magical work.

Chapter 15

Making Magic Happen

*W*hen a person visualizes an event (sees it as a detailed picture in the mind), he or she moves and directs mental energy. The energy of the mind isn't separate from the energy of the world. By focusing enough mental power and causing enough energy to shift, a person's mind can affect events or conditions in the physical world. The process is called *magic*. Magic is that simple.

Popular culture portrays magic as illusions, tricks, special effects, and fantasy. Some people dismiss magic with amusement, snide cynicism, or outright ridicule. Others accept the possibility of magic but discuss it in lofty and obscure terms. The truth is that magic is a natural force, and Pagans throughout history have recognized it as such. Magic follows the laws of modern physics. It is a tool, like mathematics.

Magic offers a means for people to improve their lives and the world. In order to use magic effectively, safely, and ethically, people need information. This chapter gets down to the nitty-gritty, practical details of magical work. Who can use magic? When is the best time to try magic? Where do Wiccans do magic? Read on for answers to the basic questions — the who, what, when, where, and why of working magic.

Who Can Work Magic?

Anyone can work magic. To *work magic* means to perform or conduct it, to make it happen. Everyone has the natural ability, and a person doesn't need to understand how magic works in order to do it. However, Wiccans generally agree that training and study are necessary before anyone attempts to perform magic. Knowledge increases the likelihood that a magical working:

✔ Is effective

✔ Results in the best possible outcome

✔ Is ethical and doesn't harm or have a negative effect on anyone, including the person doing it

Part I of this book outlines the beliefs, principles, and ethics that underlie the use of magic. Chapter 3, in particular, explains what magic is and how it works. I recommend that you read those chapters, and then engage in more advanced study before trying magic.

Some Wiccans don't work magic. First and foremost, the goal of Wicca is to develop relationship with Deity. Although many Wiccans do magical work, magic isn't technically part of Wicca. Don't feel pressured to explore magic if you aren't drawn to it, or you don't feel that it's right for you.

What Are the Principles of Magical Work?

Magic is not a part of Wiccan spirituality, however, it is a part of many Wiccans' lives. This section offers a look at the practice of magic, Wiccan-style.

What is magic? The short answer is that magic is a natural force. The following is a slightly longer explanation.

The conscious mind perceives the physical world as a bunch of fixed and stable objects. In truth, all of reality is an unbroken circle of vibrating energy. If you break matter up into molecules and then atoms and then even smaller particles, eventually you have pure energy. Energy flows in patterns. What you see as an object (a desk, a dog, a tree) is really a pocket of dense energy. All events in the physical world affect the flow of energy. In turn, all shifts in energy affect the physical world.

The energy in the mind is not separate from the energy in the rest of the world. When a person visualizes an event (sees it as a detailed picture in the mind), he or she forms energy into patterns. A person can focus his or her mental power to move and direct energy. By moving that energy, a person's mind can affect events or conditions in the physical world.

By visualizing events in the mind, a person can direct energy and shape the physical world. That process is called *magic*.

Inviting Deity: Wiccan magic

Magic itself is not religious or spiritual, it is a natural force. Magic is a process of moving and directing energy. However, all energy flows from and is part of Deity. For Wiccans, magic is spiritual or religious because the Divine is involved. Wiccans invoke or welcome the presence of Deity when they do magical work. Wiccan magic is different from other forms of magic because it often is done in sacred space in a ritual setting.

Ritual is a ceremony that a person does for a specific purpose. The purpose of a religious ritual is to understand, experience, or feel the connection to Deity. Wiccans often work magic during a ritual because they want to invoke or invite the Deity. Wiccans have varying ideas about the role that Deity plays in magic, including the following:

- ✔ Magic is an act of personal will and power, and magic happens without Divine intervention. Deity may or may not be present during magical work.

- ✔ Magic is an act of personal will and power, but Deity is present for the magic, and the presence of the Goddess and/or the God may magnify the power of the person doing the magic.

- ✔ Magic is an act of personal will and power, but Deity may actively oversee the magic and intervene to stop or aid in the magical work, if necessary.

- ✔ Magic is a cooperative act between an individual and Deity. The Divine participates in the magical work, but the individual must do his or her part, too.

- ✔ Magic is a focused or directed power, prayer, or petition to Deity, and the Goddess or the God may or may not meet the need or grant the request.

Working magic

Some rituals are just for celebrating and developing a person's relationship with the Goddess and the God. At other times, Wiccans work magic during ritual.

Wiccans generally use the same area, altar, and set of tools for all rituals, including those performed for the purpose of working magic. See Chapter 11 for advice on setting up an altar and creating sacred space. The basic design of the ritual remains the same when Wiccans decide to work magic as part of a ritual.

The following steps show one way to work magic within a ritual. If you want to work magic, you may adapt these steps to your own needs and circumstances. This is not a step-by-step list of instructions; it's one possible pattern among many.

1. **Decide why you want to conduct a ritual.**

   Make sure that your intention is clear.

2. **Decide how you want to perform your ritual**

   If you want to cast a spell, write the words of the spell in advance. (The next chapter offers detailed instructions for writing effective spells.) Gather whatever special materials you need for the magic. These may include candles, stones, herbs, or special tools (such as a bell or a mirror).

3. **Decide when to do the magic.**

   Many Wiccans work magic during the Full Moon. (See the following section, "When Do Wiccans Work Magic?")

4. **Decide where to do the magic and set up an altar.**

   See the section, "Where Do Wiccans Work Magic?" for more information.

   Arrange the tools on the altar and add any special materials you need for the spell or other magic. For example, place the specific candles, stones, or herbs.

   Don't forget to assemble whatever you need to raise personal power (see Step 8). Many people sing, dance, or chant to raise power. If you need music, place your CD player near the altar.

5. **Purify the space.**

   See Chapter 12 for information on purification.

6. **Purify yourself.**

7. **Cast a circle to create sacred space.**

   See Chapter 12 for a detailed explanation of circle casting.

8. **Invoke, evoke, or welcome Deity, according to your beliefs.**

   See Chapter 12 for information on invocation.

9. **Conduct a ritual observance; for example, celebrate the Full Moon.**

10. **Raise the power for the magical work.**

    Power is the subtle force that shapes energy. When working magic, a Wiccan raises personal power until it peaks at its strongest and most intense. Then the person releases the power, and it moves energy to accomplish a goal.

A Wiccan raises power in any one or more of the following ways: listening to or beating a drum, chanting, singing, dancing, stamping, pounding the ground, or clapping. Any activity that grows in intensity (stronger, deeper, louder, or faster) may be used to raise power.

When the power reaches its maximum intensity, the person releases the power and directs the energy by using visualization or symbols.

Using visualization: The Wiccan visualizes (or sees a detailed vision in his or her mind) the desired result, after the energy reaches its target and makes changes.

For example, a Wiccan needs money in order to pay a medical bill. He beats a drum and chants, "By Earth, Rain, Wind, and Fire, I have the money that I desire." The power begins to build. He increases the intensity, pushing himself physically and mentally until the power peaks. He releases the power and directs (or projects) energy toward his goal by visualizing himself standing at a counter in the hospital and happily paying off the balance due.

Using a symbol: The Wiccan raises power to its peak and sends energy into an object.

For example, a Wiccan casts a spell to protect her home. She raises power to its highest intensity. She speaks the words of a protection spell and directs the energy into a small bell. She hangs the bell on her door. The bell represents the power that she raised and the energy that now protects her living space.

11. **Earth the power.**

    See Chapter 12 for a detailed explanation of Earthing or grounding.

12. **Thank (or dismiss) Deity.**

13. **Take down the circle.**

    See Chapter 12 for instructions for taking down a circle.

For the best possible result, Wiccans invest all their physical and mental resources in their magical work.

Recognizing when to turn to magic

Turn to magic when you have a genuine need. Need (or desperation) fuels the effort to raise power and move energy. Being fed up with a stressful job or afraid because you don't have health insurance or angry about the pollution of a local river can all magnify power.

Working magic is physically and mentally demanding, and it requires the expenditure of a great deal of effort for an outcome that is not guaranteed. Wiccans generally see magic as a last resort or as a supplemental effort. For example, if you need a raise at work, make every effort in the physical world to get the increase in your salary. Get additional training or take a couple of courses. Add magic as an additional strategy or use it after other efforts have failed.

Magic also may be used for self-development (for example, to enhance self-esteem or concentration) in order to become more effective at meeting goals and enjoy greater achievement in the world.

Using magic for any of the following reasons is a bad idea — because the intention is negative, and the energy may return to the sender in an unexpected and unpleasant way — and violates Wiccan ethics:

- ✔ To cause harm (for example, as retribution)
- ✔ As a public display of power, especially to intimidate or manipulate others
- ✔ To override someone's free will, even if you think that you know what's best for him or her
- ✔ To create change in the life of someone who is unaware of your efforts

If you feel strongly about helping someone without his or her knowledge (for example, someone who is seriously ill), work the magic but don't aim the energy directly at the individual or toward a specific result. Instead, send the energy into the cosmos with a prayer or request for the best possible outcome for the person.

Generally, the results are better when people do magic for themselves. Each person knows his or her own life situation best, and each person has access to the power of his or her own unconscious mind. In many cases, teaching people to do their own magic is a better strategy than doing it for them. By working their own magic, people become more empowered; they deepen their relationship with the Divine and nature; and, generally, the outcome is better over the long-term.

Adopting the right magical mentality

People in the Craft sometimes refer to the Witches' Creed — also known as the Witches' Pyramid, the Four Powers of the Sphinx, the Four Powers of the Magus, the Four Words of the Magus, and many other names — to represent the mind-set necessary to effectively work magic.

The origin of these words is unclear. Regardless of their source, many Wiccans consider these words to be important guides in working magic.

These are the Four Words of the Magus (singular for Magi): To Know, To Dare, To Will, To Keep Silence. Wiccans tend to interpret these ideas as follows:

✔ **To Know** means that you know in your heart that magic works and that your actions are the result of study and intelligent analysis. This term also may refer to a specific magical working. In each working, you must know exactly the outcome that you are attempting to produce using magic.

✔ **To Dare** means that you are willing to take a risk and are persistent in your effort.

✔ **To Will** means that you are using your own unyielding will power and strength of character. You establish a course and follow through, regardless of inner fear or outward obstacles.

✔ **To Keep Silence** means that you are using sound judgment and self-protection that can't be corrupted or distracted. After you finish working magic, you consider the matter closed. Do not talk about your efforts to work magic. If you talk about it, you dissipate the energy, making the magic less likely to work. You also give others the opportunity to will you to fail (which erodes the energy of the magic) or to persecute you.

Traditionally, these four concepts are linked with the four elements, Air, Fire, Water, and Earth. In some traditions of Wicca, these elements also are associated with the four quarters (East, South, West, and North) of a ritual circle and to the four parts of the Self:

✔ To Know (Air): East, the mind
✔ To Dare (Water): West, emotions
✔ To Will (Fire): South, energy
✔ To Keep Silence (Earth): North, the body

According to the Four Words of the Magus, a Wiccan should practice magic with knowledge, conviction, and empowerment — and then walk away with calm assurance that energy will move, and the result will be the best possible outcome.

Getting results, or not

In the preceding section, I said that, in order to effectively work magic, you must know in your heart that magic works. That's true. As a force, magic does work. Effective, successful magic is possible. However, that doesn't mean that you can always expect to immediately get the outcome that you desire. People experience any one of the following results:

- ✔ The magic works, but not in the way that the person expects.
- ✔ The magic works, but not instantaneously; the situation slowly changes over time.
- ✔ The magic doesn't seem to work at all.

An individual is afloat in a vast sea of energy. Sometimes one person can move and direct enough energy to make change. Other times, the waves of the surrounding energy are moving too strongly in another direction, and even the most powerful magic can't alter the flow.

Many other reasons may explain the failure of magic to achieve the desired outcome. For example, Deity or the person's own unconscious mind may intervene because the desired result isn't in the individual's best interest.

When Do Wiccans Work Magic?

Timing is one of the factors that can contribute to the success or failure of magic. Wiccans try to choose the best time to do specific types of magic. Many books have been written about magical timing, but the best strategy is to pay attention to intuition. Does the time feel right?

Personal factors play a key role in magic. Physical illness, fatigue, depression, worry or anxiety, or preoccupation all hamper a person's ability to work magic. Before attempting magic, get a good night's sleep, eat a healthy meal, and do some quiet meditation. See Chapter 21 for information on developing a healthy lifestyle in order to have the stamina for effective spiritual and magical practice.

Some Wiccans use various methods of astrology to time their magic to the positions of celestial bodies (the planets, the Sun, the Moon, and the stars). Some Wiccans work magic on the Wiccan *Sabbats* (holy days, which are the solstices, equinoxes, and the cross-quarter days). Sabbats are based on the solar (the Sun's) cycle. However, the majority of Wiccans use these times for celebration rituals rather than magical work.

Most commonly, the people of the Craft time their magic to the phases of Earth's Moon. Traditionally, Wiccans work magic on the Full Moon and, sometimes, the New Moon.

Celebrations and magical work based on the lunar cycle are called *Esbats*. Traditionally, when Wiccans refer to an Esbat, they are talking about the Full

Moon, or possibly the New Moon. However, some Wiccans refer to any nonsolar, non-Sabbat ritual or magical activity as an Esbat. See Chapter 13 for more information about the cycles of the Moon.

The New Moon or Dark Moon

The New Moon or Dark Moon is the first phase. It occurs when the Moon is between the Earth and the Sun, with its dark side toward the Earth. This Moon phase symbolizes the time between death and rebirth.

The time of the New Moon is appropriate for working magic associated with change and new beginnings, and also secrets and solitude. The New Moon also is a good time for *banishing* (sending away or removing undesired energy).

The Waxing Moon

The Moon is waxing at any time after the New Moon and before the Full Moon. It's called waxing because its illuminated area is increasing.

Power increases as the Moon waxes. The time of the Waxing Moon is best for magic involving accumulation, expansion, growth, increase, or productivity. The Waxing Moon is associated with *invoking* (calling in or summoning desired energy).

The Full Moon

During the Full Moon, the Moon is on the opposite side of the Earth from the Sun. The Full Moon is the time when the whole disk of the Moon is fully illuminated.

When the Moon is full, power is at its maximum. The time of the Full Moon is appropriate for magic associated with achievement, completion, conclusion, fruition, fulfillment, or love. The Full Moon time also is good for healing. The Full Moon is associated with *invoking* (calling in or summoning desired energy).

The Waning Moon

The Moon is waning at any time after the Full Moon and before the New Moon. It's called waning because its illuminated area is decreasing.

Power decreases as the Moon wanes. The time of the Waning Moon is best for magic involving endings, inner secrets and wisdom, and the death of ideas or projects. The Waning Moon is associated with *banishing* (sending away or removing undesired energy).

Where Do Wiccans Work Magic?

A person can work magic anywhere.

Many Wiccans choose to work magic in sacred space (within a ritual circle). The circle helps them raise their energy and retain their power, so the magic can be more directed and possibly more effective. Wiccans work magic in a ritual setting so they can invoke or invite Deity to be present.

Any area, indoors or outdoors, is acceptable for working magic, as long as it is private, so that interruptions don't weaken the power of the magic. If you're going to do a magical ritual outside, make sure that your location is secluded (to avoid trouble with the public or authorities).

During a ritual to work magic, many Wiccans chant, sing, dance, or listen to drumming in order to raise energy. Make sure that you select a space where you can make a reasonable amount of noise without complaints from the neighbors or others.

Also, select a location that is large enough to accommodate an altar and allow the casting of a ritual circle.

Chapter 11 offers suggestions for transforming an area into sacred space and establishing an altar.

Why Do Wiccans Work Magic?

Most Wiccans would not work magic for frivolous reasons — their favorite sitcom is a rerun, or they're bored with the winter weather. Generally, Wiccans don't cast a spell or engage in divination as an experiment, just to see whether they can get a cool result. Because Wiccan magic involves Deity and also because it requires stamina and the investment of resources, most Wiccans approach magic seriously and respectfully, and they don't engage in empty ritual.

Wiccans work magic for many reasons, including:

- **Self-improvement and empowerment:** Many Wiccans do magical work not to accomplish a specific goal, but for self-development, so that they can become more effective, productive, creative, compassionate individuals in the world.

- **Problem-solving:** Wiccans work magic to reveal the best course of action or clear the path of obstacles. Many Wiccans believe that they are on Earth to learn specific lessons, gain wisdom, or engage is certain experiences for their own spiritual growth and evolution. Some work magic, especially divination, to determine whether they are following the best path.

- **Meeting physical, mental, and emotional needs:** Wicca is not a spirituality that encourages self-sacrifice or self-denial. Magic is a means to empower Wiccans to meet their own needs. The Goddess helps those who help themselves.

  Most Wiccans work magic in their own self-interest, as long as they act according to Wiccan ethics. See Chapter 4 for information on Wicca's ethics.

- **Serving Deity and community:** Most Wiccans are keenly aware that all of existence is interconnected and that Deity is the source of all life and is all-present (immanent) in the world. Many people of the Craft work magic in order to make positive changes in themselves and the world. Magic is a means to honor and deepen their relationship with the Divine and heal the Earth and its inhabitants.

Chapter 16

Spellcasting: The Poetry of Wicca

In This Chapter

▶ Grasping the poetry and promise of spellcasting

▶ Working with spells

▶ Understanding the ethics of spellcasting

Spellcasting has been used from antiquity. A good spell can help you meet your needs and cope in the world. At times when people feel the most helpless, a spell can offer empowerment. By spellcasting, people build trust in their own power to make change in themselves and the world.

Spells put people in touch with their deepest conscious and unconscious minds, providing a means for self-development, personal growth, and profound creativity. Spells are a blend of poetry and function, and they offer a great gift: the power of change.

Spellcasting: Matter-of-Fact Magic

To understand spellcasting, you need to grasp the idea of magic. Magic is a natural force. All of reality is a web or grid of vibrating energy. Energy flows in patterns. The energy in the mind is not separate from the energy in the rest of the world. When a person visualizes an event (sees it as a detailed picture in the mind), he or she forms energy into patterns. A person can focus his or her mental power to move and direct energy. This mental shift in energy may then affect events and conditions in the physical world. The bottom line: *Magic* is the process of moving and directing energy in order to achieve a desired result or outcome.

Casting a spell is an act of magic. A *spell* is a set of words and actions that represent the change or result that a person wants to achieve. These words and actions focus the mind and help the person casting the spell to move and direct the energy, causing the desired change to occur in the physical world.

Spellcasting is practical magic. Some Wiccans consider it to be lesser magic. The greater magic is performed during ritual with the purpose of developing the relationship with the Divine. However, by spellcasting, people develop the ability to use visualization and symbols, necessary tools for all ritual and magical work, and they cultivate trust in their own abilities to make change in themselves and the world.

So how do you cast a spell? As with all magic, creating your own spell is more apt to be effective than using a generic spell from a book or the Web. A spell that you craft yourself reflects your own needs and your own situation, so it has a greater chance of moving and directing the specific energy necessary to affect your own circumstances.

Before you begin to craft a spell, clearly define the change that you intend to bring about by using magic. Writing out the words of the spell before beginning the ritual provides a time to organize thoughts and create poetry or text that appeals to you. It's up to you whether you memorize these words, use them as a template for organizing your thoughts (and then let the words flow spontaneously during the ritual), or read them from a piece of paper during the ritual. The spell doesn't need to be long and complex; in general, the most effective spells are short, concise, and rhyming. Most people chant spells when they cast them. The key point is that the spell clearly states your intention and your desired outcome.

Focusing on Intention

If you want to create a spell, carefully examine your intention before you attempt to craft it. First and foremost, be very clear in your mind that the spell cannot cause harm to you, to other people, to animals, or to the Earth. Then, consider the following issues:

✔ **Decide exactly what you want to achieve or bring about by using spellcraft.**

When you cast a spell, have a very specific result or goal in mind. However, don't limit the possibilities by specifying exactly the way that outcome should happen. You don't want to close the door on positive events that you can't begin to predict. This strategy allows for wonderful happenstance to occur in your life.

For example, suppose that you are lonely, and you want to bring friends and good times into your life. When you cast the spell, picture the end result: yourself spending time with compatible friends. See yourself laughing, talking, and sharing warm friendships. Just don't make any assumptions about the way that you will meet these people and form these relationships.

Remember that your ability to move and direct energy is limited by physics. As much as I want to stop global poverty and deprivation, it's highly unlikely that I, alone, could cast a spell and end world hunger. I would have to move way too much collective energy. However, I may be able to cast a spell to help an unemployed single mother get a scholarship to a university, opening the door for future opportunities and more financial security.

✔ **Know why you want to accomplish your goal.**

You must examine your motivations before you attempt to cast a spell. For example, do you want to get that new job so that you can grow as a person and in your service to Deity and community? Or are you secretly satisfied in your current position? Perhaps you don't really want the extra responsibility, and your only goal in taking a new job is to show up your snobby and condescending sister, whose financial success wins her praise from your parents?

If you have hidden motives for your magic, you will project those with the energy of the spell. The spell may not be effective, or it may not achieve the desired goal — and possibly even a negative outcome. Knowing what you truly want is a key step in being able to define the change you will bring about with your spell.

✔ **Identify who you are trying to help.**

You can use magic to serve your own interests, as long as you don't harm anyone else. Wicca does not encourage self-sacrifice or self-denial. Magic is a means for Wiccans to empower themselves to meet their own needs, as well as the community's. Unfortunately, many people don't feel comfortable working magic for their own benefit, and they may need to convince themselves that a spell is really on behalf of someone else.

For example, do you want your friend to find a job for his own well-being and security, or do you just want the slacker to finally get his own place and stop sleeping on your couch?

In the latter case, your first priority is yourself, not the irresponsible slug who's drooling last night's tequila shots on your couch cushions. In this scenario, you may want to gear the spell toward your own self-development, not the drooling slug's. Maybe what you really need is to learn to say no? A spell may help you set healthy boundaries in your life and protect your own interests. Such a spell may not only help you to compassionately remove the current couch dweller but also avoid future exploitation by other people.

Healing spells, in particular, often require honest and sometimes agonizing self-evaluation. Remember that targeting magic at people who are unwilling or unaware is unethical, even if the magic is for their benefit. (See the last section, "Staying Mindful of Ethics.")

✔ **Make sure that you're using magic in conjunction with action in the physical world or as a last resort.**

Magic requires a considerable investment of physical, mental, and emotional resources. If you are in any type of negative situation, you may be better served by taking immediate action. For example, if you need a job, devote your energy to preparing and sending resumes.

Work magic as a supplemental strategy or use it after other efforts have failed. Action in the physical world is the best way to get results in the physical world.

Spellcasting is one type of magic. Wiccans often work magic during ritual. At a minimum, all you need to do is raise power in order to cast a spell, but most Wiccans work within a sacred circle in a ritual setting.

Spellcasting during Ritual

Ritual is a ceremony that a person does for a specific purpose. The purpose of a religious ritual is to understand, experience, or feel the connection to Deity. Wiccans often work magic during a ritual because they want Deity to be present or involved in some way. You don't have to perform a full ritual in order to cast a spell, however, but many Wiccans prefer to cast a sacred circle before working any magic.

Wiccans cast the circle to welcome the presence or involvement of Deity in the magic and/or because they want the protection of the circle to filter out unwanted energies. In addition, in sacred space, many Wiccans feel that they are at the threshold of the astral plane or Otherworld, providing them access to information and resources for the magic.

Chapter 12 describes the basic ritual steps in detail. If you don't know how to cast a circle, turn to that chapter to find the instructions. The following section gives a more detailed account of the actual spellcasting.

Casting a spell

Cast a circle and welcome Deity, if you desire, and then follow the steps described in the following sections for raising power, releasing and directing the energy, and binding the spell.

Raising power

The first step in spellcasting is to raise power. (Power is the subtle force that shapes energy.) When working magic, a Wiccan raises personal power until it peaks at its strongest and most intense. Then the person releases the power, and it moves energy to accomplish a goal.

A Wiccan raises power in any one or more of the following ways: chanting, listening to or beating a drum, singing, dancing, stamping, pounding the ground, or clapping. Any activity that grows in intensity (stronger, deeper, louder, or faster) may be used to raise power.

When casting a spell, the best way to raise power is to chant the words of the spell. Chanting the spell to raise power is especially effective if the words are poetic and they rhyme. For example:

By Earth, rain, wind, and fire,

I have the _____ that I desire.

Fill in the blank with a word that applies to your desired result, for example, money, job, home, answer, or patience. Notice that the spell doesn't say, "Send me the ___ that I desire" or "Give me . . ." Spells are more effective if you assume and the words reflect that the goal has already been reached or the desired result has already been achieved. Concentrate on the outcome, not the process, during spellcasting.

The chanting of the repetitive, rhyming lines of the spell takes on a sing-song, powerful rhythm that becomes mesmerizing and induces alpha brain waves. Alpha waves occur when people are awake and alert, but deeply relaxed. Most people feel at ease and calm. The alpha state has been linked to creativity (test subjects show alpha waves when they come to a solution for a problem) and mental work. Magic and healing are most effective when people are in this state. Alpha waves appear to act as a bridge between the conscious and the unconscious minds. People generate alpha waves when they are in a light trance state. (See Chapter 18 for more detailed information about the power of trance.)

Releasing and directing the energy

The act of raising power brings on a state of light trance. You may lose awareness of your physical surroundings. You may be unaware of your physical body, or your body may feel different. Some people experience tingling or a feeling like a rush of adrenaline. You may lose track of the passage of time. (Chapter 18 offers a full explanation of the trance state.)

When you feel the shift in consciousness and suspect that the power has reached its maximum intensity, release the energy and direct it toward your goal by using visualization and symbols.

When you release the energy:

1. **Visualize what you want.**

   In your mind, picture your desired result. Concentrate on the simplest and most powerful image or set of images possible. Try to use symbolic images that your unconscious mind understands. If you have had powerful dreams about the situation, use those dream images that apply. You may try using images from nature, if possible. Primal images, such as fire or animals, often are effective.

2. **Engage as many of your senses as possible.**

   Don't limit your experience to visual images. Try to hear, smell, taste, and feel the event that is occurring in your visualization.

3. **Repeat the words of the spell (if you have written any).**

   The standard procedure is to chant the words of the spell in order to raise power. Then, as you release the energy to cast the spell, you speak the words forcefully, one last time.

4. **If possible, act out your spell using symbols.**

   Actions speak louder than words in spellcasting. Use your power to focus or project energy through a symbol: Light a candle or ring a bell. Project energy into smoke, water, stones, herbs, or cords. Use poppets, talisman's, and amulets. (The next chapter provides instruction for using all of these symbols.)

A *symbol* is an image or object that represents something else, in this case, the desired goal or outcome. Symbols help focus the mind. You project energy through the symbol. For example, if you are casting a spell to improve your financial situation, you may carve a dollar sign on a candle and light it as you visualize your new prosperity.

When I am having trouble saying no or maintaining my personal boundaries, I visualize in my mind or look at an actual photo of a cougar. Big cats are adept at defending their own boundaries, and, for me, they are a symbol of that particular trait; they represent my goal of taking care of myself.

Remember that the *symbol* you use during the magic (for example, a candle, a stone, or a piece of art) is not the actual spell. It's the object that helps the mind to focus and to project energy toward your goal. The magic happens in the mind. The mind moves the energy and directs it into new patterns, reshaping reality.

The next chapter includes sample spells and explains how to use symbols to engage the unconscious mind and make magic more effective.

Binding the spell

After you release the energy, bind or set the spell, that is, give it a defined parameter and ending. Many people include a line asking that the spell not harm anyone or return on the sender (the person casting the spell), and then they end the spell with traditional language, such as, "As I so will, so mote it be" or a similar construction. If the "so mote it be" language is too archaic for you, you can say, "As I do will, so be it" or "As I so will, so shall it be." Use a format that seems right to you.

Repeating the spell

Moving and directing energy is not an exact science, yet anyway. Magic rarely works instantaneously, and the result may not be immediate. The situation may change slowly over time.

If, after some time, your desired result has not been achieved, you may want to consider casting your spell again. Some Wiccans repeat all their spells several times, choosing different conditions, times (for example, phases of the moon), or techniques.

Occasionally, no matter how many times you repeat a spell, the magic may not work the way you expect. You may get a different result or no apparent result at all. Many reasons may explain the failure of a spell to achieve the desired outcome. The energy may be moving too strongly in another direction, and even the most powerful magic can't alter the course. Deity or your own unconscious mind may intervene — perhaps because the expected result wasn't really in your best interest.

A critical element of spellcasting is trust. To effectively cast a spell, you must have a fundamental trust (in your own empowerment, in Deity, or in the cosmos) that the desired change will occur. After you bind the spell, walk away with assurance that the spell will work. Much of the time magic does.

Exploring how spells work

Combined with relaxation and focus, the chants, visualizations, and symbols (for example, candles, stones, or art) of spellcasting trigger the unconscious mind. They bypass the filters of the conscious mind and draw images directly into the unconscious. The unconscious mind absorbs that information and then influences you to make your spell work and achieve your goal.

In other words, the spellcasting awakens the unconscious mind, and then the unconscious mind goes to work to help you create the desired outcome in your life. This is the power of suggestion, and it's one way that spells may work. (See Chapter 3 for more information on the conscious and the unconscious parts of the mind.)

The energy of the mind isn't separate from the energy of the physical world. When a person visualizes an event in the mind, he or she forms energy into patterns that may subtly shift the energy in the physical world, thereby changing the events and conditions of life.

Another possible way that spells work is through the collective unconscious. The collective unconscious is the inherited part of the mind shared by all beings. When you cast a spell, the visualizations and symbols enter your unconscious mind and may become part of the collective unconscious that is common to everyone. Scientists can't confirm the true nature of the collective unconscious, but possibly, your images and symbols become part of the collective human experience. Subtly changing the energy patterns in the collective unconscious may be an effective way to direct energy and create change in the world outside yourself.

Clearly, spells are powerful ways to make changes happen. The next section shows you how to make sure that you are clear about your motivations and ethics before you cast a spell.

Staying Mindful of Ethics

When Wiccans work magic, including spellcasting, their ethics prohibit them from causing any harm to themselves or others. Nearly all Wiccans try to follow the Wiccan Rede:

> *"Eight words the Wiccan Rede fulfil,*
>
> *An' it harm none, do what ye will."*
>
> —Doreen Valiente, *Pentagram,* Volume One,
> 1964 (published by Gerard Noel)

Following the Rede means to carry out your own will but act in ways that cause the least harm to yourself, others, the Earth, and all beings.

In addition, Wiccans heed the other guiding principle, the Threefold Law. In general, the law means that whatever you say or do returns to you with three times the intensity. Everything that exists is connected and is part of nature's web. So when a Wiccan sends out energy — especially intentional, powerfully directed energy during a spellcasting — that person's intention and essence remain in the Self, are a part of the energy being sent, and are in the outcome (the energy that travels through nature's web and eventually returns to the sender). That's why this principle is called the Threefold Law.

Casting a spell for any of the following reasons is a bad idea:

- to cause harm
- to impress, intimidate, or manipulate others
- to create change in the life of someone who is unaware of your efforts
- to override someone's free will, even if you think that you know what's best for him or her

These ethical principles sound simple, but following them can pose many dilemmas for spellcasting, especially for healing and love spells.

Healing others

Healing spells require the most rigorous self-examination.

If you want to cast a healing spell, get the suffering person's permission. People sometimes have complex reasons for being ill. In some cases (not all), the illness may be serving the psychological or even the physical needs of the person. For example, a raging fever may be the body's effort to fight, or burn up, an infection, so using magic to stop the fever may be a negative (harmful) act.

Do you want to heal your 90-year-old grandmother for her own benefit, or for the family members who will miss her after she dies? Consider that your grandmother may be fully ready to move on to the Summerland and be free of her pain and suffering, and she may not want a healing spell performed. A healing spell in this situation would be negative.

If the person is unable to communicate and ask for or give consent for the spellcasting, think carefully before doing it. If you strongly believe that a healing would be a positive act, cast the spell but don't aim the energy directly at the individual. Instead, send the energy out as a focused prayer or petition to Deity, or send it into the cosmos. In either case, don't demand recovery from the illness, but simply ask for the best possible outcome for the person.

Remember that magic is not a substitute for medical care. Use magic in conjunction with sound, compassionate medical treatment. Never claim or promise that you can heal someone. Magic has no guarantees, and this type of claim is both dangerous and a violation of Wiccan ethics.

Looking for love

People get goofy when they fall in love. All those buzzing endorphins and hormones can cloud the mind. However, love spells require some critical thought.

Don't work a love spell on a specific person. Period. You may think that he or she is absolutely right for you, that you can make him or her blissfully content, and that you will live happily ever after. Here's the problem: To try to control someone and override his or her free will is negative (harmful) magic, even if you're sure that you know what's best for the person.

A better strategy is to work on your own self-development. Make sure that you are ready for love and commitment. Resolve any trust or abandonment issues. Work out any residual bitterness from your last relationship. Stop throwing darts at that picture of your ex. Focus on being a strong, independent person who's comfortable with him- or herself. That's what usually attracts others.

If you feel that you are happy, healthy, fine, and dandy and you're ready for a good relationship, try creating a spell to attract love into your life, but don't focus on a particular person. Visualize the type of person who meets your needs. Create him or her in your mind. Don't use love spells from books or the Web; make your spell specific. If you're political, visualize a mate with similar interests and values. If you enjoy music, picture a musical person. Create an image of a mutually satisfying relationship and then cast your spell.

Chapter 17

Boosting Magic with Fire, Stones, and Herbs

A woman bends over a cauldron, cackling wickedly as she boils up some eye of newt and other unsavory ingredients, with the obvious plan of using her evil potion to wreak havoc in the lives of the innocent townsfolk.

A woman squeezes a small cloth doll (which looks disturbingly like her ex-husband) and prepares to stick sharp pins into its unsuspecting anatomy.

A woman ignites a roomful of candles, clutches her crystals, and gushes some flaky New Age babble about unicorns, light, and creating your own reality. This pronouncement is met with eye-rolling contempt from her intellectually superior friends.

Those are some of the stereotypes of Wiccans and the objects that they use in magical practice. So why *do* Wiccans and other Witches hoard and use candles, stones, herbs, and other objects? This chapter explains why and how the people of the Craft use these materials, and, as usual, the truth isn't anything like the stereotypes.

Gathering Magical Materials

Most Wiccans don't worship stones, crystals, herbs, or any other objects. Wiccans are drawn to these gifts of nature because they are part of the Divine energy. Nature unfolds from Deity. Most Wiccans worship the Deity that is manifest within all creation, not the actual physical elements.

When Wiccans look at nature's beauty, for example, the flame of a candle or the elegance of a crystal, they feel the presence of Divinity or the life force in the universe. The objects may trigger a response deep within the mind or soul. Wiccans use these objects as tools during ritual, especially ritual that involves the working of magic.

Magical objects aren't necessary to do rituals, but they are helpful. Actions speak louder than words during the practice of magic. Using objects, a Wiccan may act out the goal or outcome that he or she is trying to accomplish. The object serves as a symbol of the desired result. A symbolic object helps the mind to focus on and project energy toward the goal.

Magical objects as symbols

To figure out how nature's gifts work as tools, you need to understand the following ideas:

- ✔ *Magic* happens when a person visualizes a desired change or outcome, and then focuses mental power to move and direct energy to bring about that result. The mental energy affects conditions in the world. Magic is possible because all of reality is a web or grid of vibrating energy, and the energy in the mind is not separate from the energy in the rest of the world. (Chapter 15 explains more about magic.)

- ✔ *Casting a spell* is an act of magic.

  A spell is a set of words and actions that represent a desired change or outcome. These words and actions focus the mind and help the person casting the spell to move and direct the energy, causing the desired change to occur in the physical world. A Wiccan may use a physical symbol to help project energy toward the goal. (For more about spells, see Chapter 16.)

- ✔ *A symbol* is an image or object that represents something else. In magic, a symbol represents the desired change or outcome. For example, a dollar sign carved onto a candle may represent financial security.

Wiccans use symbolic objects during rituals for working magic. However, keep in mind that Wiccans also may use symbolic objects during ritual for worshiping or honoring Deity. For example, a white candle on the altar may represent the Goddess.

Magical objects as triggers for the unconscious mind

For magic to be most effective, the unconscious mind must participate in bringing about the desired change (see Chapter 3 for more information about the conscious and unconscious parts of the mind). One reason that the unconscious mind is so important is that it drives some of a person's behaviors and emotions; so to make positive change in yourself, you need to trigger activity in your unconscious mind. The unconscious mind communicates mostly in images (pictures), instead of language. It uses and understands symbols.

Here's the important point about Wiccans and their magical stuff: Ancient and primal images, sounds, smells, and textures help to activate the unconscious mind. If you use fire, stones, herbs, and other natural materials during magical work, the unconscious mind rouses and says, "Hey, I recognize these symbols; I get the idea!" The objects help the unconscious mind understand your intention, so it goes to work to help you accomplish the desired outcome that you visualized.

The following sections explain the use of these objects in ritual for worship or for magic.

Kindling the Magic Spark with Candles

Flame appeals to the primal Self and triggers the unconscious mind. Fire is one of the most the most fundamental of magical materials. The deepest, most ancient parts of the human brain are aroused by the image of fire.

Candles are a big part of Wiccan practice; Wiccan used them for the following purposes and more:

- ✔ Candles on the altar often symbolize the Goddess and/or the God.
- ✔ Candles located in each of the four quarters (North, East, South, and West) of a ritual circle mark the boundary of sacred space.
- ✔ Candles are available in many colors and serve as a way to introduce different colors and their associated energies and symbolic meanings during ritual worship and magic.
- ✔ Candles provide the light by which Wiccans perform ritual or work magic.

This section provides information on using candles during the working of magic.

Fire and spirit: Candle magic basics

Candle magic is an ancient and simple form of magic. It's powerful and moving, but it doesn't demand a great deal of preparation or ceremony.

Candle magic generally involves speaking or chanting a spell and lighting a candle. The flame helps to focus the mind as well as to build and project the energy of the magic.

Candle spells are a good initial exploration for people who are new to magic.

Setting the goal

If you want to work a candle spell, you must first decide what you want to accomplish with your magic. Set a specific goal. Candle spells are good for practical issues, especially long-term or ongoing concerns, such as:

- ✔ Changing behavior, such as breaking addictions
- ✔ Personal growth, such as letting go of anger, fear, or loneliness
- ✔ Meeting basic needs, for example, career or housing issues

Set your goal and write your spell (see Chapter 16 for help in wording an effective spell).

Preparing for the magic

Choose an appropriate candle. Many Wiccans consider that a spell is complete after the candle burns completely down (the entire candle has melted), so size matters. If you want to cast the spell only once, buy a very small candle. If you want to repeat the spell several times on different days, buy a large candle. (Be sure to see the next section about when to snuff a candle.)

For many Wiccans, the color of the candle also matters. The best approach is to select a color that seems appropriate to you and to the spell that you are casting. (Appendix B offers some traditional suggestions.)

Many Wiccans choose candles that are made of natural substances. Some select unscented candles, but burn incense that is appropriate to the spell. Natural beeswax candles are a good choice, although they have a very mild scent. Alternatively, choose a scent that you feel is fitting for your particular spell. Make sure that you don't buy candles that contain lead or other harmful substances; many of them do.

Determine when, where, and how you want to work the magic. Traditionally, Wiccans time their magic to the phases of the Moon. Many Wiccans work magic on the Esbats (the Full or New Moons), and they cast spells in a ritual setting, which means that they do one or all the following: Set up an altar, purify Self and space, cast a circle, invoke or evoke Deity (according to beliefs), and raise power. The preceding two chapters offer detailed explanations and instructions for casting a circle and other stages of ritual. However, some people don't go through all (or any) of those steps for a simple candle spell.

The next section describes the specific steps for casting a candle spell.

Casting the spell

Follow these steps to work candle magic:

1. **Wash the candle with salt and water from your altar, and dry it thoroughly.**

   You may want to charge the candle by one or more of the following methods:

   - Carve a few words or a symbol into the candle. The phrase or symbol should be relevant to the spell. Choose a knife from your altar. Some Wiccans use an athame; others use a boline (or boleen or bolline), if they have that tool.

   - Many Wiccans anoint spell candles with an appropriately scented oil. Anointing oils are made by steeping herbs in oil. If you choose this option, make sure that you use an anointing oil that is safe for this purpose.

   - Speak, chant, or sing your spell as you cleanse and prepare it. Direct your voice into the candle to project energy into it. The candle becomes charged with your goal or desire.

2. **Place the candle in the candleholder, and then clearly speak, chant, or sing your spell as you light the candle.**

   In your mind, picture your desired result. Concentrate on the simplest and most powerful images possible.

3. **Watch the flame for several minutes.**

   As the candle burns, it releases and directs the energy toward your desired outcome. The spell is finished after the candle is completely melted. (See the next section about snuffing the candle flame.)

If you want to cast the spell again on another day, don't let the candle burn completely away. Instead, extinguish the flame with a candlesnuffer. To repeat the spell, once again speak, chant, or sing the spell as you re-light the candle and concentrate on your desired outcome. You may cast the spell as many times as you wish, but always visualize your goal as you re-light and snuff out the flame.

The number of repetitions depends on your goal and your preferences. For example, you may repeat a spell every day for seven days; or on the third, seventh, and ninth days; or perhaps once a week for seven weeks. You must decide when and how often to cast the spell. Magic is not an exact science. Follow your own heart.

After the flame is out, some Wiccans bury the remaining candle wax or dispose of it in running water because magical energy may remain in the wax. I suspect that the energy has already dispersed during the burning, but you can decide for yourself. I don't put candle wax down my sink because it may damage the plumbing or block the pipes. Another option is to keep the wax and reform it into candles that you make yourself.

To snuff or not to snuff?

Some Wiccans believe that a candle must be left burning after a magical working and that the flame must always die on its own. They think that to deliberately extinguish candles, especially by blowing them out, diminishes the power of the magic. They let large candles burn for hours and even days, and return to the flame periodically to repeat the spell.

I'm going to defy Craft custom and urge you to follow this advice:

Don't leave a burning candle unattended after magical work.

Even if you leave a burning candle in a safe place, you can never know what may happen to topple it over or to blow hot embers onto the carpet or other flammable materials. Candles are one of the most common causes of residence fires in the United States.

I always use a candle snuffer to extinguish the flame before I go to sleep or leave the room. If I know that I want to let a magical candle completely burn out on its own, I use a very small candle (for example, a tea light), and I stay in the same area with it until it winks out and stops smoldering. If I want to repeat a spell, I use a larger candle, but I snuff it out and re-light it later when I'm ready to cast the spell again.

Some Wiccans may consider this advice to be too cautionary, as well as in defiance of conventional Craft wisdom. But ask yourself: Is the spell worth burning down the house? Does your Deity want you to risk injury to yourself and to others?

Here are some more suggestions for staying safe when using candles:

✔ Place candles on a steady surface and in sturdy holders that won't tip over and ignite carpet or other materials. If your altar is rickety, fix it or find a safer foundation for your magical work — no matter how beautiful your altar is.

✔ Many Wiccans wear robes, especially with bell sleeves, during ritual. Take care not to touch your robe to the candle flames. Also, keep the flames away from your Book of Shadows.

✔ Make sure that your altar candles aren't too close to draperies or other fabric; most people don't realize how hot a candle flame can burn and from how far away it can ignite cloth and other materials.

> ✔ Confirm that the candle holder is big enough to collect the dripping wax.
>
> ✔ Keep candles away from children and animals.

I've always had a very healthy respect for the power of fire. After all, that power is why people use candles in their magic.

Finding Power in Stones and Crystals

The world's ancient stone structures still give people goose pimples today. Every year thousands of tourists and pilgrims visit Stonehenge and similar stone wonders. Like fire, stone is an archetypal material. Stones arouse the unconscious mind and awaken the primal Self, which is why Wiccans are drawn to them.

Stones and stereotypes

Many Pagans, including many Wiccans, believe that different types of stones have distinct energy patterns that may be valuable in magic. Some believe that *crystals* (which are actually mineral formations) contain unusual energy or vibrate at unique frequencies.

Now, that idea may sound like a bunch of New Age hooey to skeptics. However, crystals play a critical role in modern electronics, and some highly esteemed scientists in many fields of research are fascinated by crystals. The atoms and ions in crystals behave very weirdly. They arrange themselves in repeated, orderly patterns in three dimensions — just like a honeycomb.

Scientists are discovering remarkably strange forms of crystals. *Quasicrystals,* also called *impossible crystals,* are an example. They are so bizarre that, before they were discovered, researchers thought that their structure was impossible. The explanations are complicated, but suffice it to say that some of these discoveries are enough to make a top scientist's head swim. So maybe believing that crystals have some unexplained but potent energy isn't so far-fetched.

Stones and magic

Wiccans use stones for many reasons, including the following:

> ✔ To surround candles during candle spells, adding the stone energies to that of the flame as the light reflects from their surfaces.
>
> ✔ To use as charms (see the later section, "Making and Using Charms.")

- ✔ To stuff into poppets (see the later section, "Working with the Mommets and the Poppets").

- ✔ To place in the home, car, or office, for example, for protection.

- ✔ To wear in jewelry to attract or repel specific energies.

- ✔ To use for divination, such as rune stones.

- ✔ To signify a role in a coven. Some High Priestesses or other coven leaders wear amber or jet.

- ✔ To help focus the mind and project energy during spell casting. (During spell casting, the stone serves as a symbol of the desired outcome.)

When you find or purchase a new stone that you intend to use for magical work, cleanse and purify it by placing it under cold running water. You may decide to consecrate the stones during ritual as you do an altar tool (see Chapter 12 for instructions).

A sample spell using stones: The worry stone

Worry stones have been popular in many cultures and times. A *worry stone* is a smooth, polished gemstone that a person rubs between his or her thumb and fingers in order to release anxiety. Traditionally, these stones have a natural, smooth indentation on one side for the thumb to rest in.

Find a worry stone for yourself. Look for just the right shape and texture that encourages you to rub your thumb over its surface.

The first time that you cast this spell, you may want to cast a circle, invoke or evoke Deity according to your beliefs, and raise power. (Follow the steps in Chapter 12 for working magic during ritual.) After the initial ritual, you can carry the stone with you. Repeat the words of the spell and rub the stone any time that you feel overwhelmed by stress and tension.

Follow these steps to cast the spell:

1. Take a few minutes to fully relax.

2. Place the stone under cold, running water to cleanse and purify it. Ideally, cast the spell on the bank of a creek or a natural spring. A garden fountain also is a nice setting.

3. Hold the stone firmly in your hand. You may want to rest it on your forehead or your heart. Chant the words of the spell:

   Stress and worry I release.

   I am calm; my mind's at peace.

   From needless fear, I am free.

   As I will it, it shall be.

4. Project all your stress and tension into the stone. In the presence of true danger, stress and fear are appropriate responses, but most people weaken their bodies, minds, and spirits by holding onto generalized, causeless fear and anxiety. That's the unnecessary energy that you want to release into the stone. Picture yourself happy and content, free of needless worry and nagging doubt.

5. Once again, hold the stone under the running water in order to dissolve the negative energy.

If you choose to carry the stone after the ritual, periodically cleanse it in running water, preferably a natural source, in order to dissolve the accumulated energy.

Reaching Back to Our Roots: Herbs and Other Botanicals

People of all times and places have used all parts of plants for their magical as well as medicinal powers. Knowledge about plant magic and medicine has been handed down from wise people of ancient cultures all over the world.

In this book, the word *herb* is defined loosely to mean all plants that are used for medicinal or magical purposes. The word *herb* also refers to all parts of the plant: the root or bulb, stem, leaves, dried flowers, seeds, fruit, berries, bark, juice, and so on. Physicians, herbalists, and researchers use much more precise terms and definitions for the various types and parts of plants.

Pagans, including the people of the Craft, have been using herbs in their ritual and magical practices since antiquity.

Herbal magic

Wiccans use herbs for medicine and for magic. Herbs serve many purposes:

✔ As medicine to heal physical, mental, and emotional illnesses. Herbs have enormous potential for healing the mind and body. Plants have supplied the starting material for the development of hundreds of modern pharmaceutical medicines.

✔ As ingredients or tools in the working of magic. Uses for herbs in magic include the following:

- **To make anointing oils.**

  Anointing oils are made by steeping herbs in oil. Traditionally, mint was crushed and steeped in olive oil.

- **To use as charms.**

  The later section, "Making and Using Charms" offers some advice on herbal charms. Also, turn to Appendix B to find suggestions for choosing the appropriate herbs for spells.

- **To stuff into poppets.**

  See the later section, "Working with the Mommets and the Poppets" for information.

- **To adorn the altar.**

  Chapter 14 gives suggestions for using herbs to decorate your altar and home during the Sabbats, the Wiccan holidays.

- **To sprinkle in ritual baths.**

- **To burn as incense.**

- **To sprinkle in the house, car, office or other places for magical purposes, for example, for protection.**

    Traditionally, Wiccans use rosemary to protect the home.

    Some Wiccans heat herbs in water and use the solution to ritually cleanse and purify a space.

- **To help focus the mind and project the energy during spell casting.**

    The herbs serve as a symbol of the desired outcome.

Like any medicine, herbs can be toxic and can produce unintended and sometimes dangerous effects, especially if used incorrectly. Using herbs safely and effectively as medicine requires dedicated study and knowledge in order to understand the appropriate uses, the potential benefits, and the possible side effects. I'm not trained in herbalism, and I offer no advice for using herbs medicinally. When I discuss herbs in this book, I'm talking about their use in magic (for example, in charms), not their medical use. Do not eat or drink medicinal herbs or apply them to the body (in poultices, ointments, creams, lotions, oils, and compresses) without seeking the advice of a trained professional.

If you use herbs topically (you apply them to your body) in your ritual or magical work, for example in anointing oils or bath solutions, purchase products made for that specific purpose and labeled as safe for external use. If you make your own herbal products, consult a reputable source (person, book, or Web site) for information about the use and handling of the specific herb.

The next section offers advice for acquiring and storing herbs used for magical work.

Buying, drying, reaping, and keeping herbs

You can use fresh or dried herbs in magic. Gathering wild herbs is a nice way to get out and experience nature. Or your can grow your own herbs. If you don't have access to forest or countryside and you don't have a green thumb, dried herbs are widely available for purchase.

A sample spell using herbs: Rolling in clover

Some people aren't comfortable doing magic for personal gain. Certainly, enjoying gain at the expense of another person violates Wiccan ethics. But as long as you aren't harming someone else, Wiccan tradition encourages using magic for meeting your own needs. Wicca is not a spirituality that glorifies suffering and deprivation. A Wiccan holds respect for the inherent worth of all people, including him- or herself.

"Rolling in clover" is an old expression that refers to living in abundance, with all basic needs comfortably met. This joyous expression is the basis for this sample spell to ensure financial security.

To cast the spell, you may want to cast a circle, invoke or evoke Deity according to your beliefs, and raise power. Don't forget to take down the circle and Earth the power after the spell is cast. Follow the steps in Chapter 12 for working magic during ritual.

For this spell, you need to gather or purchase some clover. Clover is a common herb, and different varieties grow wild in many areas. Both fresh or dried forms are fine. Ideally, you can cast the spell in a field of growing clover. Follow these steps to cast the spell:

1. Take a few minutes to fully relax.

2. Pour the clover into your hand or lie down in the field of clover. Begin to chant the spell:

   My days of struggle are over.

   My needs are met; my bills are paid,

   and I am rolling in clover.

3. Throw the clover over you like confetti. If you are in a field of clover, roll around like a child and enjoy the scent of the sweet herb. Repeat the spell with all the power that you can muster. Visualize yourself living in abundance, free of fear and struggle.

With the empowerment of the spell, take practical steps to move toward financial security in your life. Seek help from a someone who can offer knowledgeable advice.

Buying herbs

You can purchase dried herbs from herb suppliers, both local and on the Web. Both dried and fresh herbs also are available at farmers' markets, occult stores, and many grocery stores. Buy high-quality produce, because the magical properties are stronger in fresh, healthy plants. Note these suggestions:

- Aromatic herbs should have a strong, specific scent.

- Buy brightly colored herbs. Dull, drab herbs are probably old or improperly stored and won't have much magical oomph.

- Don't buy herbs that have been stored in clear containers in direct sunlight. Oxidation occurs under these conditions, and the herbs are not as fresh and powerful as those stored more carefully.

- Look for dried grass, insects, or other infestation and avoid purchasing any herbs that contain such debris.

Store the herbs immediately. See the later section, "Storing herbs."

Gathering herbs from the wild

If you have access to forest land or countryside, you may want to gather your own wild plants, flowers, leaves, seeds, roots, fruits, and berries. The plants and trees around the world differ according to climate and location, so the best idea is to find a Web site or purchase an herb book that identifies the habitat, ecology, and growth cycles of the plants in your immediate geographic area. Here are some tips for gathering wild herbs:

- ✔ Confirm that you can legally harvest wild plants in your location. In some locations, removing any plants from public or wild areas is illegal and can carry stiff penalties.

- ✔ Make sure that you can identify the plants that you harvest. Carry a field guide or other book that identifies your local flora. If you don't know poison oak from a honeysuckle vine, you may want to do some studying before you head out into the wild.

- ✔ Take only common plants from the wild, and never take more than you can use. The taking of rare species often is prohibited. Even if the act isn't illegal, don't remove rare or uncommon species of plants from their wild habitats. To do so endangers the species' survival.

- ✔ Go herb gathering in dry weather and wait until the morning dew is gone.

- ✔ Wear gloves to avoid injury or allergic reaction. Cut plants with a sharp knife or scissors (you don't need to use a ritual knife, such as an athame or a boline) in order to reduce damage to the plant. Keep handling of the plant to a minimum.

- ✔ Harvest mature plants because the active constituents are more concentrated and the plant's magical properties are stronger. Collect flowers as they start to bloom, leaves in spring or early summer when the plant begins to flower, fruits when they are ripe, and roots in the autumn when the plant's power has seeped back into the ground. Harvesting bark is a delicate operation that risks killing the tree. Only harvest bark from your own trees, not from public places, and take the bark from outlying limbs that can be pruned, if necessary.

- ✔ Choose healthy plants that are not growing in overcrowded conditions. Take plants that don't have disease, insect damage, or bruising. Remember that dangerous herbicides, pesticides, and chemical waste are widely used on farmland, along highways, and other public areas, so be careful not to gather herbs that have been treated with toxic chemicals. Don't collect plants near factories.

Growing your own herbs

Growing your own herbs eliminates the dangers of unknown chemicals. Everyone's options for growing herbs are different, depending on location, climate, soil, and growing conditions. The decision also depends on how many woodland creatures, such as rabbits or deer, are around to help themselves to the lovingly grown herbs. The best approach is to consult a local nursery for advice.

Hardy plants can grow outside directly in the ground. Some plants may need to move indoors for the winter months (for example, rosemary) or get protective burlap covers. Other plants, such as peppermint and bay laurel, can grow in container gardens (in pots or window boxes). The ambitious gardener may want to grow herbs, especially more exotic herbs, in a greenhouse or other sheltered environment. Some herbs, such as sage, thyme, and aloe vera, thrive indoors.

The following is some very general advice for growing herbs:

- Most herbs prefer sun and fairly well-drained soil.

- Spring is the best time for planting most herbs, even indoors.

- Sandy soils drain easily but need fertilizer. Clay soils can be too wet and require drainage by mixing in sand, peat moss, or other organic matter. Consult with a nursery professional or an experienced gardener on the best ways to amend your specific type of soil. Try to add only natural, chemical-free materials to your soil.

- Keep herb beds free of weeds. Weeds weaken the plants and reduce their power. Except for sandy soils, most herbs don't need fertilizer.

- Water herbs well after planting and then, usually, once a week after that. Most herbs are more potent if their soil is kept on the dry side.

- Use organic methods to get rid of pests and diseases. Banish aphids by watering with soapy water or soak garlic skins in the water for two days.

- Some herbs can be grown from seeds; others get the best start from cuttings from another plant or by dividing a mature plant from an established bed.

- Some herbs (especially mints) grow vigorously and can quickly overtake an entire garden. Plant invasive herbs in containers or in a boxed-off area of your garden. Ask a nursery worker or experienced gardener or consult online resources to see whether an herb is invasive.

Storing herbs

Proper storage is necessary in order to preserve the power of herbs.

Storing dried herbs

Store dried herbs (leaves, flowers, seeds, and roots) in clean, dark glass containers with airtight lids. You also can store them in a brown paper bag. The key is to keep herbs dry and in the dark. Dried herbs may be kept for approximately 12 months in a cool, dark location.

Make sure to label the container with the herb name and, if possible, the source and date of harvesting or storage. Remember that the herbs, especially those stored in paper bags, may draw uninvited critters, including cockroaches! Keep a watchful eye.

Drying and storing fresh herbs

Fresh herbs must be allowed to dry before they are placed in dark glass containers or brown paper bags. Some Wiccans use food dehydrators to dry herbs, although other people may feel that this high-tech method violates Craft custom. These guidelines may help:

Stems and leaves

Harvest the plant by cutting the stems above ground about 2 to 4 inches (higher for perennials) when the plant begins to flower. Remove large flowers for separate drying. Bunch 8 to 10 stems together and hang the plants upside down in a warm, well-ventilated, dark place.

After the plants are dry and brittle, take them down and rub them with your hands over a large sheet of paper. The dried leaves, small stems and flowers, and seeds will fall onto the paper. Pour this dried material into a dark glass container or a brown paper bag. Rather than breaking the stems up like this, some people suggest storing the herbs flat between sheets of brown paper.

Large flowers

Pick flowers just after they open in spring or summer. Cut the flower heads from the stems and clean the petals of bugs and soil. Place the flowers on clean, absorbent paper on a tray in a dry place. Leave enough room on the tray for air to circulate between the flowers. After the flower heads are dry, store them in a brown paper bag or a dark glass container.

Fruits and berries

Harvest fruits and berries when they are ripe but still firm. Place the fruit or berries on clean, absorbent paper on oven-safe trays. Turn your oven to the lowest temperature or the "Warm" setting. Warm the oven and then turn it off. Place the tray of fruit or berries in the warm (but not hot) oven with the door slightly open for 3 to 4 hours. Then move the trays to a dry, warm, dark place. Turn the fruits or berries over once in a while. Throw out anything that becomes moldy.

Roots, bulbs, rhizomes, and tubers

Gather the underground parts of plants in autumn after the above-ground part of the plant is withered. Definitely harvest before the soil freezes. Dig around the root and lift it out of the ground. Shake off the clinging soil. Make sure that your specimens aren't rotting. Wash the root, bulb, rhizome, or tuber in warm water. Chop it into small bits with a knife, and spread out the pieces on clean, absorbent paper on an oven-safe tray.

Warm the oven and then turn it off. Place the tray in the warm (but not hot) oven with the door slightly open for 2 to 3 hours. Then move the trays to a dry, warm place.

Seeds

Gather ripe seeds in summer before they have scattered. Collect the plant stems that hold the seed heads. Bunch the stems together and hang them upside down over a tray lined with clean, absorbent paper, or you can place them in a paper bag.

After the plant is dry, shake the stems so that the seeds fall onto the paper or they disperse in the paper bag. You can remove larger seeds by hand. Store the seeds in dark, clean glass containers or in paper bags.

Remember that drying plant materials may attract bugs or rodents (who especially love seeds).

Working with the Mommets and the Poppets

Wiccans use poppets to aid in the working of magic, but they didn't invent the idea. These simple dolls have been used for thousands of years by many cultures.

Today, most people refer to these figures as poppets, and the term usually applies to both male or female figures. Historically, in the British Isles, the word mommet was used for figures of both sexes. Some modern Wiccans call a male doll a poppet and a female doll a mommet.

Positive poppets

A *poppet* or *mommet* is a human figure made out of cloth, wax, clay, paper, plant materials, or any other substance. It's a simple doll with the basic shape of a person. A poppet represents the person that the magic influences. Wiccan poppets often are made of cloth and stuffed with herbs, stones, or other items appropriate to the magical goal. The poppet's stuffing may include a hair or fingernail of the person it represents.

Now don't start to squirm. Wiccans don't use these dolls for evil intent. They don't stick pins into them or otherwise mistreat the little folks. Remember that Wiccans have a strong system of ethics (see Chapter 4), and they don't work negative magic. These simple figures serve only as a way to focus the mind during magical work to create positive change. They are an image that the deep, unconscious mind understands.

During a magical ritual, a Wiccan uses the poppet to act out the desired outcome or result. Wiccans commonly use poppets for indirect magic, for example, to heal someone who can't be physically present for the magic (always get the person's permission before attempting to heal).

Poppet construction

To make a cloth poppet, choose two small pieces of cloth. You may want to select a color that is appropriate for the spell that you are working. (Appendix B offers some suggestions for pairing colors with magical goals, but following your own intuition is the best approach.)

Place one piece of cloth over another. Draw the basic shape of a person about 4 to 6 inches tall on the cloth. You can trace around a cookie cutter that you use for gingerbread men and women. Use scissors to cut out the form, and then sew around the edges to connect the two pieces of cloth. Leave a hole at the top.

Stuff the poppet with cotton balls, material from an old T-shirt, foam from an old pillow, or any other appropriate stuffing. Many Wiccans insert herbs, stones, paper, or any symbolic objects or material that is relevant to the goal of the spell. You may choose to include a hair, an eyelash, a fingernail, or toenail of the person that the poppet represents. You may even include some saliva or a drop of menstrual blood. However, hurting yourself or anyone else to get material for poppet stuffing is unacceptable.

Sew up the hole after you finish stuffing the poppet. You may paint or use magic marker to define the face. Use string, ribbons, and so on for hair. Write the person's name on the poppet and possibly a symbol or word that exemplifies the spell. Some people believe that investing energy in detailing the poppet results in enhanced power for the magic.

The poppet is now ready for use as a component in a spell. Prepare and charge it as you would other tools for magical use. When the spell is done, either cleanse the poppet or dispose of it appropriately. See Chapter 12 for instructions on cleansing, charging, and consecrating tools.

Pocketing magic: Plackets

Plackets are small cloth pockets or bags that are used for magic. A placket is used much like a poppet, but it's a simple square shape rather than a human shape. When you select the cloth for the placket, choose a color that is appropriate to the spell. (Appendix B offers some suggestions for pairing colors with magical goals, but following your own intuition is the best approach.) Like a poppet, label the placket with the name of the person being affected by the magic. Although poppets usually represent someone else, plackets often represent the individual who is working the magic.

Inside a placket, Wiccans insert a photograph of the person, a handwritten letter, or some other identifying words or image. Place the placket on your altar and project energy through the placket in the same way that you work magic with a poppet or any symbolic object (see the preceding sections).

Making and Using Charms

A four-leaf clover for luck. The suit that you always wear to job interviews for success. The ring you never take off because it represents your love for another person. The pendent you wear around your neck every day for protection. The small statue hanging from the rearview mirror of your car for safe travel. These items can all be considered charms. Magic is alive and well throughout modern society.

The people of the Craft have always used and appreciated charms. In general, a charm represents the change or outcome that a person intends to magically bring about. However, Wiccans use the word *charm* in two different ways:

- ✔ **Definition 1:** An *object* that represents a desired change or outcome. The object focuses the mind and helps the person casting the spell to move and direct energy, causing the desired change to occur in the physical world. The object may be carried on the person, left in the home or other space, or used during magical or other ritual workings. Don't create a charm for someone else before getting his or her permission. You may give a charm as a gift, but generally Wiccans give charms only to other people in the Craft.

- ✔ **Definition 2:** *A set of words and actions* that represent a desired change or outcome. These words and actions focus the mind and help the person casting the spell to move and direct the energy, causing the desired change to occur in the physical world. In this context, charm is a synonym for the word *spell*.

For the purposes of this book, a charm is an object (Definition 1). That's probably the most common Wiccan usage of the word.

Alternatively, some Wiccans may say that they use charms to repel or attract specific energies, but if you think about it, that definition means the same as the above: to magically bring about a desired change or outcome.

Wiccans cleanse, charge, and/or consecrate their charms before they use them (see Chapter 12 for this ritual).

Several types of charms are common in Wicca. Amulets and talismans are popular types. Unfortunately, like the word charm, Wiccans aren't real precise about the meanings of these two words, either. Sigh. . . .

Charming basics

The following are steps for making an easy charm bag (turn to Appendix B if you need help in selecting appropriate colors, herbs, or stones for the charm; however, trusting your own intuition is best):

1. Find a small square or circle of cloth. Plain cotton is fine, but you can also use silk or velvet if you want to spend the money. Choose an appropriate color.

2. Pour any combination of the following onto the center of the cloth: herbs, stones, coins, seeds, fossils, or other materials that are relevant to the magical goal.

3. Bring up the edges of the cloth and tie with a natural vine, some string, or a ribbon.

4. If you desire, decorate the bag with words or symbols that reflect your magical intent.

5. Charge or consecrate your charm (see Chapter 12 for this ritual).

Amazing amulets, nature's gifts

The following is probably the most common Wiccan definition for the word *amulet:*

> An *amulet* is a natural object used as a charm. Amulets may include: stones, crystals, fossils, bird feathers found on the ground or in trees, four-leaf clovers, pieces of wood, nuts, shells (especially cowrie shells), dried flowers or other herbs, and seeds.

A good example of an amulet is a holey stone, also known as a hag stone, which is a stone with a natural (not a human-made) hole through it, as shown in Figure 17-1. Holey stones have long been carried as charms. The holes are considered doorways or portals through which someone can draw or repel energy. For example, the holey stone can bring luck or send away misfortune, bring wealth or banish deprivation, and so on. Many people look at the Moon through the holey stone in order to charge it with lunar power. Many cultures use holey stones for divination. To divine with a holey stone, the holder of the stone peers through the hole to see visions and gain wisdom.

Some fossils, such as the sand dollar, also have natural holes in them and assume the same magical qualities as a holey stone. Sand dollars have special meaning because they are natural pentacles (see Chapter 11 and 12 for more information about the significance of pentagrams and pentacles.)

Amulets may be found by accident or deliberately acquired.

Crafting talismans

The following is probably the most common Wiccan definition for the word talisman:

> A *talisman* is a human-made or manufactured object used as a charm. Talismans may have natural elements, but they are incorporated into a human-created design.

A talisman is a magical tool, and the magic is more powerful if the person being affected by the spell is the one to make or acquire the talisman. In other words, magic is more effective if the person with the need makes the talisman and casts the spell. Making your own talisman is considered better than purchasing a manufactured one.

Many Wiccans wear or carry their talismans at all times. A common talisman is a piece of metal, wood, stone, or paper with words, symbols, or objects that are engraved, carved, painted, printed or attached. The words and/or symbols reflect a person's magical goal or intention. A common talisman is a metal disk (often made of copper) worn on a chain around the neck. If you want to wear or carry a talisman:

✔ **Identify the talisman as yours.**

   Put your name on it (your common name or a Wiccan name). Possibly mark it with your birth date or astrological signs, or some other symbol that clearly represents you.

✔ **Add words, symbols, or objects that represent your desired change or outcome for the magic to the talisman.**

   For example, if your goal is to overcome depression, write the word joy or optimism on your talisman. You may want to use an alphabet or symbol system from your cultural heritage, instead of the language you use every day. Or you may use an image or a symbol instead of words, for example, a butterfly emerging from a cocoon or a Phoenix bird rising from the ashes. You may attach (using glue, solder, or other means) a meaningful object, such as an appropriate stone or a found bird feather.

If your talisman has two sides (for example, a metal disk), place the identification on one side and the desired magical outcome on the other.

In addition to charms, which are used for magical purposes, many Wiccans own personal and/or ritual jewelry or other items that serve as a reminder of Deity, the Otherworld, or their own personal power or goals.

Maintaining Perspective

Objects, such as charms, symbolically represent a desired change or outcome. They offer a way for the person working magic to focus the mind, trigger the unconscious, and move and direct energy — causing the desired change to occur in the physical world.

Crystals, stones, and other objects may be imbued with strong natural energies of their own and should be respected as part of nature flowing from Deity. It's easy to become attached to a beautiful amulet. However, the initiative, the will, and the power to work magic flows from the human mind and soul. The mind, not the object, moves the energy and directs it into new patterns, reshaping reality.

Chapter 18

Working with Trance and Dreams

This chapter is about those times when the mind stops paying attention to the usual stuff. The brain checks out of ordinary time and space and goes inward, tapping into the unconscious mind. This is the world of trance and dreams. These states of consciousness are natural and very common. In fact, most people experience both every day.

Wiccans intentionally enter trance during ritual, either to work magic or to experience or communicate with the Divine. This chapter takes a closer look at what trance really is and the key role it plays in ritual worship and magic. The chapter also explores dreams and potential ways to learn from them, creating positive change in your life and enhancing your spiritual practice.

Giving Trance a Chance

REMEMBER

The word trance sometimes scares people. It brings up images from horror films, when the ominous Dr. Whoever uses trance to make zombie-like victims do his evil bidding. The truth is that people shift in and out of trance frequently. Trance is a natural part of everyday life.

De-mystifying trance

If you have experienced situations like any of the following, you have been in a state of light trance:

> ✔ You were driving down the road and missed your exit because you were thinking about something else.

✔ You lapsed into a daydream during a meeting, only to suddenly realize that your boss was asking you a question.

✔ You were reading a riveting novel or watching a compelling movie and were surprised to find that two hours had expired without your being aware of the passage of time.

People can experience many types and levels of trance, from very light to very deep.

Daydreaming, hypnosis, and meditation

Most people spontaneously experience light trance on a regular basis. Daydreaming is a very common form of light trance, and so is extreme concentration.

During episodes of peak performance, athletes experience trance, as do performing artists (such as dancers and musicians). Mental health professionals use trance, in the form of hypnosis, to help people change self-destructive behaviors or to recall and work through memories of traumatic events. Meditation is a form of trance used for stress reduction and/or spiritual advancement. Some people use trance to control physical and psychological pain.

Some people can achieve very deep levels of trance, dramatically slowing their own breathing and heartbeat, and reportedly, some people have been able to undergo surgery without pain while in the trance state.

Defining trance

You may not look different when you're in trance, but a big difference actually exists between ordinary consciousness and trance.

Ordinary consciousness is when you're fully aware of your surroundings and you go about your everyday activities. Your mind handles an onslaught of sights, sounds, smells, and sensations. You hear the buzzing alarm clock. You feel hungry. You smell the brewing coffee. You see the dog pleading at the back door and let her out. In this state, you can handle multiple tasks, writing a report for your boss, secretly listening to your favorite soap opera, and keeping an eye on the clock. The key point is that your mind focuses broadly on life's little details.

Trance is the opposite of ordinary consciousness; it's a state of narrowed and heightened focus. Your attention narrows until it's drawn to events happening inside your own mind, in your imagination (or some other plane in the brain). You're unaware of your physical surroundings; you may be unaware of your physical body or the passage of time.

People might say that you are "a million miles away" or "out in space," but you've really just shifted your awareness inside. This turning inward is a *change in consciousness*. Some people call it an *altered state of consciousness*.

Entering into trance spontaneously

How do you know when you're in trance? How does it happen during the course of everyday life? Here's how:

1. Your attention is restricted or limited to one task, activity, or problem.

2. Your thoughts become repetitious; your mind is stuck in an endless loop of the same pattern occurring over and over.

3. Part of your mind continues to pay attention to the repetitive activity or task, but part of your mind steps out of the loop of repeated thoughts and turns inward, to events happening in your imagination.

Here are two simple but very different examples of this process:

✔ **You're performing a boring, monotonous activity.**

You've been driving for four hours on a boring stretch of interstate, watching the lines in the center of the highway and listening to the rhythmic sounds of the car's engine. Or maybe you are working on an assembly line in a factory, attaching the same two parts, over and over again.

Your mind desperately looks for something more exciting to engage it. The mind is demanding, and if it finds only dull repetition, it gives up and turns its attention inward, detaching from the physical world and shifting into the imagination. For example, you continue to drive your car, but your mind is planning your vacation or daydreaming about a person you're attracted to. You're still standing on the assembly line, but your imagination is picturing a beach or a potential love connection (or both!).

Soon, you're no longer consciously aware of your driving or your work. A light state of trance while driving is called *highway hypnosis,* and you can continue to function. You probably can snap out of it and respond if a car suddenly veered in front of you (although you'd take longer to hit the brakes than you would if you were paying attention).

✔ **You're completely engrossed in an interesting activity (such as watching a movie, reading a book, taking an exam, or creating artwork).**

You're watching TV. You look at the TV screen, and your mind processes what you see. You look at the next TV scene, and your mind processes the new image. You look and process, over and over. Even though the TV program is interesting, the activity is repetitive. Your focus is narrow.

Your mind becomes bored with the repetitive loop of looking at the TV and processing the image, so your imagination takes over and suddenly you're absorbed in the scene that you're watching. Your concentration is so complete that you cease to be aware of your physical surroundings or the passage of time. If someone tapped you on the shoulder, you may startle and spill your popcorn.

Extreme boredom and intense concentration are seemingly opposite situations, but the results are the same for the brain: It's locked into one activity or task, so your mind frees itself by shifting its attention away from the everyday, mundane world to an inner world.

Trance occurs naturally in day-to-day life, but many people, including many Wiccans, deliberately enter into trance, and they reap a variety of benefits.

Entering into trance intentionally: Getting a little R and R

To *induce* trance means to deliberately cause one's self to enter into a trance state. The key here is that the person enters trance intentionally.

People of virtually every culture and time have explored the benefits of the trance state. Humans enter into trance in order to communicate with Deity, gain knowledge, enhance personal power, and restore physical, mental, and emotional health and well-being for themselves and others.

In this book, the phrase *trance work* means to intentionally and voluntarily induce a simple trance for a positive, healthy, and beneficial reason. (Some conditions — including mental illness, physical disease, addictions, drug use, and repetitive work — can produce dangerous or extreme trance states, but that type of trance is not what this chapter is about.)

To do trance work, you need to:

- ✔ Set a goal for the trance work. For example, are you looking for a solution to a specific problem?

- ✔ Induce the trance state, and observe the images, events, and information that flow from your unconscious mind. You don't need to plan on ending the trance with a specific action or trigger. You will return to ordinary consciousness automatically.

- ✔ Interpret the trance experience, sometimes called a *journey,* gain insight, and apply it to your life.

In order to bring about trance, people create the same conditions that cause a natural shift into the trance state: *relaxation* and *repetition*.

Just relax . . .

Anxiety and tension are obstacles to effective spiritual practice of any kind, including trance work. So the first step to insightful trance work is to relax.

A common relaxation exercise is to sit or lie in a comfortable position with your eyes closed. Breathe deeply and focus on and relax each of the muscle groups in the body, one at a time (the hands, and then the arms, and then the shoulders, and so on).

Over and over and over . . .

When you feel relaxed, begin some form of repetition. Have you ever heard the phrase "bored out of your mind"? That's the goal here. You want to bore your conscious mind and force it to let go of your physical surroundings and turn inward for something more exciting. Here are some ways to deprive the mind and force it to let go:

- Listen to repetitive drumming. You want a steady, monotonous, rhythmic beat. This technique is the traditional Shamanic way to induce trance. Tribal people of nearly every time and place have used drumming to enter trance. Sometimes a rattle is used instead. If a drumbeat or a rattle doesn't work for you, substitute any repetitive sound, such as the sounds from a bell, chimes, gong, or rainstick.

  You need a CD or tape, or someone to actually beat the drum or shake the rattle for you, because you can't do it yourself after you enter the trance state. Traditionally, the tempo speeds up as the person nears the trance state.

- Focus on the sensation of each breath as it moves and out of your body.

- Speak, chant, or sing a word, phrase, or prayer.

- Dance in a circle. Rhythmically stamp your feet or wear bells or some other noisemaker on your ankles.

- Scry, or stare, into some object, for example, a bowl of water, a black mirror, a stone, a crystal ball, or a flame.

I have entered into a trance state by staring at one portion of the night sky. I happened upon this method one night when I was watching for meteors. I have also reached trance by staring at a Full Moon. However, if you remain motionless for too long in the summer, the mosquitoes can eat you alive.

Jump-starting the trance state: Visualization

Traditionally, Shamans and others have used *visualization* (picturing a scene in your mind) to sort of jump-start trance. This practice is very common among Pagans, including Wiccans, today.

The following are some suggestions for encouraging the shift in consciousness. The options are endless, and most people develop their own favorite. Picture yourself:

✔ going through a tunnel

✔ descending into a deep cave

✔ going down a large rabbit hole

✔ diving into the ocean

The trance journey begins. You cannot predict what you may encounter in this state of consciousness. The conscious mind is no longer calling the shots, although it's available. You're no longer intentionally deciding what you are going to see or experience. You aren't consciously deciding to imagine or visualize something. Material is flowing from your unconscious mind, and your conscious mind must process it.

Try to remember everything that you experience, even small details. The more you remember, the more success you will have in interpreting your journey and finding meaning for your life.

You may see, hear, smell, taste, and/or feel the events occurring in your trance consciousness. However, those sensations aren't coming from your actual senses (your eyes, ears, nose, mouth, and skin); they're emerging from your mind.

Benefiting from trance

Here's the interesting idea about trance: It doesn't matter whether you are perceiving an event in reality or you are imagining it in your mind during a trance state; the brain reacts remarkably the same. You use virtually the same parts of the brain whether your mind is focused outward or inward. That's why the trance state is powerful and offers vast potential to help people make changes in their lives.

When you picture images during trance, your brain processes the images as though they were real, so the power of suggestion is more effective during trance. By focusing on a desired goal as you enter the trance, you can influence the experience in order to help you make the internal changes that you desire. For example, if you want to stop smoking, induce trance and picture yourself throwing out your cigarettes or declining a smoke from someone else. The conscious mind sets the agenda, and the unconscious mind takes over and produces results.

Most Wiccans believe that the mind must change before behavior can change. What begins in the imagination can happen in reality.

Why do you need to induce a trance state? Simply deciding to make changes in your life may not get results. In other words, changing your rational (or conscious) mind may not always be enough to make long-term, positive change in yourself. If that were sufficient, people wouldn't have to struggle so mightily with behaviors, such as smoking, that the conscious mind clearly knows are self-destructive.

Sometimes, the conscious mind isn't completely in charge. The unconscious mind drives certain behaviors and emotions. It may even play a role in directing a person's future.

A meeting of the minds

Trance is a primary way to tap into the unconscious mind to affect emotions and behavior. The conscious and the unconscious are the two distinct parts of the mind:

- ✔ The *conscious mind* contains everything that you're presently aware of. It is the rational mind, and it can think and communicate using language.

- ✔ The *unconscious mind* holds information that was once in your conscious mind, including memories that are easily recalled, as well as those that have been deeply buried. It also holds material that has never been part of the conscious or aware mind, for example, inherited and instinctive human drives and behaviors.

The unconscious mind doesn't use much language. It has a special way of thinking that uses images and symbols instead of words, so the conscious, rational mind cannot easily communicate with it.

When people are in a trance state, they generate alpha brain waves. Alpha waves act as a bridge between the conscious and the unconscious minds, allowing them to communicate. The rational mind can influence the unconscious mind, as well as receive information from it. When the conscious and the unconscious parts of the mind connect, powerful images and ideas flow, and a person can more easily solve problems, direct his or her future, and make lasting personal change.

Ritual, especially for the working of magic, is most effective when it triggers the unconscious mind, and that is the key to why Wiccans induce trance.

Trance, Wiccan style

Trance plays a major role in magic. Most Wiccans raise power in order to cast spells or work other types of magic. Raising power induces a light trance state because it engages the unconscious mind and creates alpha brain waves. (Chapters 15 and 16 describe raising power.) Some Wiccans may use trance to accomplish other spiritual goals.

Wiccans induce trance during ritual for several reasons, including the following:

✔ **To work magic, including physical and emotional healing.**

Since antiquity, Shamans have healed themselves and others while in the trance state. Some Wiccans also work healing magic during trance.

One of the reasons that Wiccans work magic is to bring about personal change, so they can grow and develop as people or enrich their lives (see the earlier section "Benefiting from trance"). Trance is a means of exploring the mind and personal obstacles.

✔ **To journey to places or communicate with beings that are outside of ordinary time and space, for example ancestors.**

Other beings or spirits may have an opportunity to communicate with people while they are in trance and the unconscious is active. Likewise, during the trance state, a person's consciousness may be able to journey to the Otherworld.

Wiccans draw inspiration and information from the Otherworld (other planes of existence, states of consciousness, or dimensions of reality). Trance is a way to experience the Otherworld.

✔ **To worship or honor Deity.**

Trance arouses the unconscious mind and may make someone more open to communication from or attunement with the Deity. In trance, Wiccans receive Divine revelation.

✔ **To experience psychic awareness, for example, astral projection, clairvoyance, precognition, and telepathy.**

Shamans of all cultures and times have reported psychic experiences during trance, including:

- Astral projection: leaving the physical body. The consciousness or spirit separates from the physical body and travels to other places or planes.

- Clairvoyance: perceiving or gaining information about something that is not in physical sight.

- Precognition: perceiving events or conditions before they happen (foretelling the future).

- Telepathy: communicating with another live person without having to make physical contact.

Exercising caution during trance work

Generally, the conscious mind is available during trance and can become active quickly in response to an emergency, a threat, or an inappropriate suggestion. If a person in trance is asked to do something that he or she truly doesn't want to do — an action that endangers the person or violates personal ethics — the conscious mind rejects the suggestion and stops the behavior.

However, trance work is not a game. Think carefully before you decide to induce trance in order to work magic or to journey for self-exploration or some other purpose. If you feel that you may be experiencing emotional or mental problems of any kind, seek treatment with a competent, caring professional before engaging in any type of rigorous spiritual or magical work — and that includes trance work.

When you induce trance, choose a place where you are safe and you aren't vulnerable to interruption or danger. Remember that you are less alert to your physical surroundings during trance. Cast a sacred circle before inducing trance and take down the circle after you finish the trance work. Those actions can help you to create a clear beginning and end for your work. (Chapter 12 offers instructions for casting and taking down a circle.)

Guidelines for trance work

The following recommendations may help you to exercise reasonable caution when you do trance work. Before inducing trance, make sure that you have:

- ✔ **Clear intention:** Trance work requires a considerable investment of energy, to induce the trance as well as to interpret the results. Don't induce trance for magic or for journeying and self-exploration unless you have a clear reason for the work. Don't engage in trance simply as a form of mental or emotional escape, and don't induce trance so often that you develop an unhealthy dependence on it (trance may release pleasant brain chemicals). Trance work should never interfere with your normal functioning. If it does, stop immediately.

- ✔ **Control:** Effective trance work has a definite beginning and a definite end. You shouldn't experience prolonged fuzzy periods of time when you don't know whether you are in ordinary consciousness or a trance state. Everybody lapses into daydreaming or periods of deep concentration sometimes. However, if you enter deeper states of trance involuntarily and at inappropriate times, seek help.

- ✔ **Realistic expectations:** When you induce trance, be prepared to encounter powerful images from the unconscious mind. Remember that trance side-steps some of the conscious mind's filters. During trance, you may possibly bring up disturbing material in some form. You may need to confront your fears, traits that you don't like about yourself, or images from upsetting memories. Remember that the conscious mind represses or banishes thoughts and images into the unconscious mind. It gets rid of this stuff for a reason: Your rational mind may resist dealing with some thoughts, ideas, images, and memories.

Trance may be a liberating way of working through personal obstacles. However, don't try to handle very traumatic issues alone. Get help if you need it.

Trance and ethics

Trance may be remarkably beneficial, providing a means for both deep insight and positive change. However, not all trance states promote well-being. Some professionals in corporate management, advertising, politics, and religion effectively use techniques that encourage light trance because trance makes people more open to the power of suggestion. This suggestibility is good when you are using it to make positive change in yourself. It's bad when others use it to manipulate you for their own interests.

People who do personal trance work may be less vulnerable to these common forms of public manipulation because they are able to recognize others' attempts to induce trance and they are able to control their own responses. Use your knowledge to avoid manipulation by others but never attempt to use trance techniques to influence someone else. To do so is a big violation of Wiccan ethics.

Like trance work, working with dreams is an empowering way to access the unconscious mind. The next section offers information about dream recall, interpretation, and control.

Dreaming Big Dreams

All humans dream, although some people are better at remembering their dreams than others are. Dreams must be critically important, given that everybody has them, every night. They are a doorway to multiple levels of consciousness and dimensions of reality, and they may hold the key to life-changing insight and information. All you have to do is pay attention.

What are dreams, where do they come from, and why does everyone experience them?

A *dream* is a sequence of images, thoughts, and sensations occurring in the mind of a sleeping person or other animal. Most dreaming happens during a stage of light sleep called *rapid eye movement* or *REM*.

Many people in the field of psychology believe that the material for dreams comes from the unconscious mind. The conscious mind may provoke the dream with thoughts about the events of your life, and after the unconscious creates the dream, the conscious mind also may contribute language and interpretation. However, the images, the nitty-gritty of a dream, spring from the unconscious mind.

Dreams allow the unconscious mind to communicate with the conscious mind. Despite years of dream research, scientists don't know for sure why people dream. The sidebar, "Why do people dream?" (at the end of the chapter) offers some contemporary ideas about the psychological purpose of dreams. This section, however, is about dream work as a spiritual practice.

Using dream energy

Dreams are a natural part of life, and they no doubt serve a valuable psychological function. But why are they important to Wiccans and other Pagans? Well, many Wiccans believe that dreams serve as a portal to the unconscious mind and perhaps to other realms of consciousness or dimensions of reality. They are a key to exploring both the inner landscape and the outer realms. They offer vast potential for personal empowerment and even Divine revelation.

A Wiccan may believe any one, some, or all the following spiritual ideas about dreams.

Dreams as resources for personal change

Wiccans try to interpret dreams because they carry messages from the unconscious to the conscious parts of the mind. When you pay attention to your dreams, you get information from your unconscious mind. The unconscious mind drives some behaviors and emotions. Efforts to make changes in your life may be more successful if you can get a hint of what's going on in your unconscious.

Dreams may not only reflect past experiences but also may point to the future. Carl Jung, the eminent psychologist, believed that the unconscious mind is more than just a storehouse of information (instincts, memories, and so on). Jung insisted that the unconscious mind is able to study the experiences, emotions, and other information that it stores, and then creatively draw conclusions about the direction that a person is heading.

The roles and challenges in a person's dreams indicate the goals of the unconscious mind and the path it intends for the dreamer to follow. The way that the mind decides to present dream symbols and imagery may offer insight into the dreamer's future. Dream material that springs from the unconscious carries valuable information to the rational mind.

Dreams as portals to the Otherworld

Like trance, dreams may serve as a portal to places outside of ordinary time and space. Other beings or spirits may have an opportunity to communicate with people while they dream. Likewise, during the dream state, your consciousness may be able to journey to the Otherworld.

If dreams can be links to other dimensions, then all kinds of dreams are possible, including:

- Astral projection dreams, when the consciousness or spirit completely separates from the physical body and travels to other places or planes.
- Clairvoyant dreams that enable the dreamer to perceive or gain information about something that is in a different location, out of physical sight.
- Precognitive dreams that enable the dreamer to perceive events or conditions before they happen.
- Telepathic dreams during which the dreamer can communicate with another live person without having to make physical contact.

During dreams, the consciousness is not bound by time. In dreams, people may be able to witness events from "past" or different lives. Some people may be able to access the future.

Following dreams

Harriet Tubman is famous for her courage, her dedication to her people, and her trust in her dreams. Tubman was held in slavery on a plantation in pre-Civil War Maryland. During a confrontation between an overseer and an enslaved man, she was struck on the forehead with a metal weight. After the blow to the head, her dreams became powerful and prophetic. She often unexpectedly fell to sleep in the middle of a task, and during these involuntary naps, she experienced vivid, instructive dreams.

According to her own accounts, Tubman received reliable guidance and information during her dreams. After her own escape from slavery, she made at least 19 harrowing return trips to the South to guide others northward to the free states or Canada. Her dreams helped her to successfully evade slave hunters and navigate the way to freedom for more than 300 enslaved people.

Dreams have played an immeasurable role in the evolution and history of humankind. They have often served as a call to action or as inspiration. They have directed or powerfully influenced countless leaders in religion (Muhammad, Buddha, and Joseph Smith), government (Alexander the Great and Julius Caesar), art (Henri Rousseau, Salvador Dali, and William Blake), literature (Jack Kerouac and Robert Louis Stevenson), and science (Descartes and Carl Jung).

Probably most important to Wiccans, dreams may make people more open to the Divine. When people turn off the conscious mind's filters, they may be more able to connect deeply with Deity and receive guidance or comfort.

Dreaming the night away

In order to take advantage of dreams, you need to understand how dreaming works. The following section provides a quick look at dreams and the physical body.

When do people dream?

All people dream. Scientists don't know for sure, but many think that all mammals dream because nonhuman animals experience the same type of sleep stage that causes dreaming in people. Birds probably dream a little bit. Reptiles don't dream at all. I guess snakes just don't have anything to dream about.

During an average night, a person alternates between two different sleep states:

- **Non-REM.** This stage breaks down into four separate stages:
    - Stage 1: The sleeper is just on the edge of sleep, either beginning to fall asleep or to wake up.
    - Stage 2: Light sleep.
    - Stage 3: The beginning of deep sleep.
    - Stage 4: Deep sleep.
- **REM sleep.** This stage, sometimes called Stage 5, is when people go a little wild. Breathing becomes more rapid, irregular, and shallow. Heart rate increases, and blood pressure rises. Underneath the eyelids, the eyes jerk rapidly. The large skeletal muscles become temporarily paralyzed, although some muscles (such as the face, fingers, or leg muscles) may twitch.

People do most of their dreaming during this REM stage of sleep.

When you lie down to go to sleep, you begin in non-REM sleep, descending through the four stages from drowsiness to deep sleep. Then you quickly backtrack back up to Stage 1. However, instead of waking up when you hit Stage 1, you go into REM sleep and begin to dream. (Stage 5 is the fifth distinct level of sleep during the night, but doesn't follow Stage 4 in sequence.)

Scientists watching the dreaming brain have found that one of the busiest areas during REM sleep is the limbic system, which controls emotions. The prefrontal cortex, which is associated with logical thinking, is much less active. That's why dreams sometimes cause mighty emotions, such as fear, but don't make much sense at all.

How long do people dream?

Humans start the night with about 80 minutes of non-REM sleep, followed by about 10 minutes of REM sleep. One complete cycle lasts about 90 minutes, including both non-REM and REM sleep. This 90-minute cycle repeats from four to six times during the night. A sleeper alternates back and forth between non-REM and REM sleep.

The first sleep cycles each night have relatively short REM periods and long periods of deep sleep. As the night progresses, REM sleep periods increase in length, while deep sleep decreases. By morning, people spend nearly all their sleep time in Stages 1, 2, and REM.

Longer and more vivid dreams usually occur in early morning, when the REM sleep period is longest.

People spend 20 to 25 percent of the night in REM sleep. The first REM period of the night may be less than 10 minutes in duration, but the last period may last more than 60 minutes. Here's how the percentages average out over the night for adults: 50 percent of sleep is spent in Stage 2, 20 percent in REM sleep, and the remaining 30 percent in the other stages combined. Stages 3 and 4 sleep are thought to be the most restorative.

The bottom line: You dream away about 20 to 25 percent of each night. That's a big investment of time, and it makes dreams worth exploring.

Recalling and interpreting dreams

If you are an introverted, creative person, you probably often remember your dreams. If you are an objective, practical thinker, you probably don't often recall them. However, most people can become better at remembering their dreams, just by clearly stating their intention to recall them.

Enhancing dream recall

If you are interested in dream work, you have to get enough sleep so that you have time to dream. That fact is obvious, I guess, but many people don't get a full 8 hours of sleep every night, and they fail to experience natural sleep patterns that enable healthy amounts of dream time.

The best approach to remembering dreams is simple: Purchase a notebook or a tape recorder and record your dreams *immediately* upon awakening. People lose recall of dream content very rapidly as soon as they wake up, so have paper and pen or electronics ready and waiting at bedside. This is one time when a computer may not be an asset. By the time you reach your machine and open the proper program, the dream may be long gone.

You also may want to keep a flashlight near the bed, so that when you wake up during the night, you can record your dreams without having to struggle to turn on lights or awaken a partner. Keeping a dream journal is essential for dream work.

Here are some other tips for encouraging meaningful and helpful dreams and their recall:

✔ Before you go to sleep, review the recent events of your life. Are your physical needs being met, such as the need for health care, safe shelter, or nurturing relationships? Are you stressed about basic issues such as losing your job or your home? Are you mentally stimulated or is your life boring? Do you have people and activities that enrich your life? Are you emotionally upset? What emotions are you feeling? Are you feeling your emotions at all, or shutting them down? The idea for this self-reflection is to determine whether your concerns show up in your dreams. You may want to record these observations in your dream journal to compare with the dreams that you experience.

✔ Firmly tell yourself, "I will remember my dreams!" Ask the Divine and/or the Self to give you clear dreams that shed light on your life and point the way to overcoming obstacles and gaining wisdom and fulfillment.

✔ Upon awakening, don't move. Keep your eyes closed. Try to remember the details of your dream. Pay attention to locations, people, activities, sensations, and emotions. Reconstruct the events, working backward through the dream. Relive it in reverse. What was happening when emotions and actions were most intense?

✔ Open your eyes and immediately record the dream in your dream journal. Record even dull dreams.

If you find that recalling dreams remains difficult, try setting an alarm clock to wake you up at a time when you most likely will be dreaming. See the preceding section to determine the best time.

Interpreting dreams

At regular intervals, read through your dream journal. Examine each dream and give it a title that reflects the events. The following are some additional ideas and questions for dream interpretation.

Did your dream relate to events in your life? Was any object or character emphasized in the dream? Was anything distorted? The qualities of an emphasized person, place, or object may shed light on recent events in your waking life. For example, was someone lost or angry or lonely? Did confusion permeate the dream? Did the dream offer solutions to any problems?

If you are an artist, try drawing the images in the dream to reveal the underlying themes. If you're a writer, try writing short stories or poetry rooted in your dreams. Artistic expression of any kind may help draw out insight from the dream.

Psychologist Carl Jung promoted an approach to dream analysis called *amplification*. In general, the process works like this:

1. **Recall one powerful image from the dream.**

   Ask yourself what the person, place, or thing represents to you. Describe it as if you were explaining it to someone who had no prior knowledge of that person, place, or thing. Note how the image made you feel emotionally. Keep peeling away the layers until you get to the core essence of what this image means to you mentally and emotionally.

2. **Place the image in context of your larger culture and society.**

   If a coyote appears in a dream, the image may have one meaning for a country dweller who actually sees coyotes on a regular basis. The meaning may be vastly different for an urban dweller living in the heart of a sprawling city.

3. **Look for deep, primal, archetypal themes.**

   An *archetype* is not a specific image, but a tendency for humans to represent certain ideas with a specific symbol. These archetypal symbols appear in religions, dreams, myths, and fairytales. The Earth Mother is an example of an archetype, so is the Hero.

4. **After you explore the separate images, put the information together to see what combining all the parts reveals about the message of the full dream.**

5. **When you review your dream journal, look at your dreams together.**

   Study the sequence of your dreams. They may come together like episodes of a soap opera. The story may bounce around in time and from character to character, but you may see a clear connection and be able to follow the story. Pay close attention to any recurring themes or common content that may illuminate ongoing problems or concerns in your life.

Certain dream imagery appears to be common. Most people have had dreams of falling, flying, being chased, being attacked, losing teeth, or appearing nude in public, but researchers haven't settled on a common interpretation for these dreams that applies to everyone. The truth seems to be that age, culture, gender, geography, and individual circumstances all influence dream content. No dream image means the same thing to every person.

You may notice that this book doesn't include a list of dream symbols and their interpretations. These lists give the dream image (dog, lightning, little gray alien) and then the meaning of the image. These lists are very entertaining but not very accurate or illuminating. Dream images represent something different for each individual. If you want to seriously explore your dreams, a method such as Jung's amplification technique gives you deeper and more valuable insight into your own life.

The way that you interpret dreams depends largely on your theory about the reason for dreams — why *do* people dream? If you think that dreams are caused by random, meaningless signals bouncing around the brain, then you may reject the idea that dreams are valuable. You may dismiss dream interpretation as either an amusing diversion or a flat-out waste of time. If you believe that the Divine speaks directly to people through dreams, then you are going to take dream recall and interpretation very seriously indeed. Your interpretations will expand beyond the idea that dreams only re-hash everyday life.

The sidebar at the end of this chapter, "Why do people dream?", offers some current scientific theories about the nature of dreams, so that you can examine your own beliefs.

Interpreting dreams would be easier if people could stay awake during dreams, even ask questions and participate in the action. Some people say that this type of dreaming is possible. The next section outlines the idea.

Mastering lucid dreaming

When you wake up in the morning, you may remember that you were dreaming, even if you can't vividly recall the dream. Unfortunately, people ordinarily aren't aware of the dream process while it's going on. That awareness may be possible, though.

During a *lucid dream,* the dreamer is consciously aware that he or she is dreaming. The person participates in the dream events but also recognizes that he or she is asleep and dreaming. The conscious mind remains able to think, remember, and make decisions, while the dream unfolds. The experience is sort of like a split-screen view on a television or the image in Figure 18-1.

Figure 18-1: During lucid dreaming, the conscious mind can react to dream images and make decisions.

Discovering lucid dreaming by accident

Many people report that they have experienced a lucid dream. Most people appear to experience lucidity by accident, meaning that they didn't try to have a lucid dream. The following is a common scenario: The person is dreaming. Something weird or illogical occurs in the dream, although the characters may accept it as normal. For example, people fly, a clock runs backward, or a little gray alien walks through the wall. The conscious mind kicks in, and says, "That doesn't make sense, you must be dreaming!" From that point, the person is lucid.

A number of major universities conduct research into the possibility of lucid dreaming, although some scientists poo-poo the idea that it even exists. Techniques have been developed to deliberately cause lucid dreaming. They require training and motivation. If you want to explore the idea, start by firmly declaring your intention by saying, "The next time I dream, I will realize that I am dreaming."

Trying too hard and too often to dream lucidly isn't a good idea. Read the cautions in the earlier section, "Exercising caution during trance work," because most of them also apply to lucid dreaming. If you become confused, stop trying to dream lucidly. Don't sacrifice a good night's sleep because you're trying to induce lucid dreaming.

Lucid dreaming and Divine revelation

Researchers differ about how much control the lucid dreamer has over the dream's events, also called the *dreamscape*. Many agree that a person's conscious mind can't control the content flowing from the unconscious, but the lucid dreamer may direct his or her reactions to events in the dreamscape. That's why lucid dreaming may be beneficial. If a person is lucid during a dream, he or she can ask questions of the other characters and possibly get information for problem solving and self-development in waking life. The dreamer also can safely confront deep-seated fears and phobias.

Lucid dreams often are reported to be vivid, intense, and profoundly spiritual. Many lucid dreamers report feeling elated, blissful, or ecstatic. Some Wiccans believe that lucid dreaming offers the best opportunity to interact with the Divine.

Why do people dream?

Dreams have always been a subject of research and speculation. Sigmund Freud didn't discover the unconscious mind and its link to dreams, although he often gets the credit because he included dreams in his groundbreaking and controversial theory of psychology.

Freud thought that dreams are rooted in sexual conflict, and he is known for interpreting almost all elements in dreams as sexual symbols. To Freud, a *symbol* is an image or object that substitutes for something else. For example, in a dream, any long objects (such as a tree trunk or an umbrella) may be symbols for a penis. (Really, Sigmund, sometimes a cigar *is* just a cigar!)

Today, the scientific explanations for dreams vary wildly. Researchers can't confirm why people dream, where dreams come from, or which parts of an individual's personality a dream represents. The following are some general, and often competing, theories:

✔ **Dreams guard sleep and make sure that it isn't interrupted.**

This was Sigmund Freud's theory. For Freud, dreams served as:

Wish fulfillment: Dreams express unfulfilled wishes — wishes arising from the unconscious or wishes that the mind forced into the unconscious because they were unacceptable and cause anxiety. These desires often stem from childhood. A simple wish of the conscious mind may be a beginning for a dream, but it isn't enough. Only the stuff held deep in the unconscious mind can drive a dream.

Censorship: The mind has a barrier between the conscious and the unconscious mind. A censor stands guard and keeps sexual, violent, or otherwise taboo thoughts and urges buried in the unconscious. During sleep, the mind's censor gets lazy. Highly upsetting and unacceptable material sometimes gets past the barrier and bubbles up from the unconscious mind into awareness.

Dreams disguise and distort these fugitive nasty thoughts and urges, so they don't cause people too much anxiety. The images in dreams serve as symbols for this forbidden, unthinkable stuff. Dreams are a way for the mind to release or repress all the bad

(continued)

(continued)

images and impulses that creep into the mind, cause anxiety, and wake a person up.

In addition, by working out these nasty thoughts and impulses during a dream, people may drain off all of the psychological tension built up over the course of the day.

✔ **Dreams serve as a bridge between the conscious and the unconscious parts of the mind.**

Dreams may be a way to express the material in the unconscious mind, the part of the mind that contains everything that the person is not consciously aware of. The unconscious mind doesn't have much language, so it uses the images of dreams to communicate with the conscious mind.

The unconscious mind contains inherited, instinctive human drives and behaviors that have never been part of the conscious or aware mind (the *collective unconscious*). It also contains material that the person was once consciously aware of (the *personal unconscious*). Unacceptable and disturbing material produces anxiety, so the conscious mind refuses to deal with it and banishes, or *represses*, it into the unconscious mind.

Dreams represent this inner content of the mind, such as a person's deepest needs or traumatic memories.

✔ **Dreams are a way for the human psyche to evolve.**

Although Freud believed that dreams are a primitive effort to hide or disguise negative stuff arising from the unconscious mind, noted psychologist Carl Jung believed that dreams reveal helpful information, encourage self-development, and point to the future.

Dreams provide situations and circumstances outside the boundaries of daily, mundane existence. They force people to face their deepest fears and feel peaks of euphoric joy. In dreams, people are failures and heroes.

In dreams, people make the archetypal journey, confronting archetypal roles and challenges. Archetypes are the universal symbols that rise from the collective unconscious, the inherited, ancient part of the brain that contains basic human instincts and patterns of behavior. An *archetype* is not an image, but a tendency for humans to represent certain ideas with a specific symbol. The Hero and the Earth Mother are two examples of archetypal figures. Fire and water are primal, archetypal elements.

A key role of dreams is to help people face the Shadow archetype. The Shadow is all the primitive, animal drives and behaviors (unbridled sexuality, aggression, and so on) that modern humans inherited from ancient ancestors and have remained within humans since the days in the caves. Dreams help people cope with the Shadow and use its energy positively, rather than deny and repress it, leading to guilt or inappropriate behavior.

Dream symbols are a way for the ancient, collective unconscious to communicate with the rational mind. These messages may even be creative and insight-provoking ideas that move people toward future personal development and growth. Dreams can reveal the goal of the unconscious mind. The roles and challenges in a person's dreams may shed some light on the path that the unconscious mind intends for the dreamer to follow. "Following your dreams" isn't just an empty expression.

✔ **Dreams force people to deal with the major emotional or mental issues that the conscious mind is grappling with on any given day.**

Are you puzzled by a problem, for example, whether to pay off your student loans or buy a house? Are you worried, scared, jealous, or angry about a personal situation? Your mind may search for a dream scenario or symbol that reflects your problem. Dreams may even be a way for the mind to work on solutions to problems. The conscious mind passes the buck to the unconscious mind, saying "I give up; you work on this mess for a while!"

✔ **Dreams are associated with learning.**

Dreams help people process information that they have acquired during the day and file it in the brain. They help people store information so that they can remember it, retrieve it, and use it later.

✔ **Dreams are the mind's way of dumping useless information that people take in daily.**

People forget dreams so rapidly that some researchers believe that dreams are a way of releasing material that people don't need to keep. For example, you probably don't need to maintain a complete transcript of the 97 television commercials that you watched today. Dreams are a way for the brain to clean house, throwing out the mind's clutter.

✔ **Dreams are the mind's interpretation of random, meaningless signals from a primitive part of the brain.**

Dreams may be the desperate effort of the more evolved part of the brain (the cortex) to try to make sense of neural chatter seeping up from the primitive, less sophisticated, and dumber part of the brain (the brain stem). In other words, dreams may not be valuable, mysterious wisdom from the unconscious mind; they're only stories that the cortex creates from the mind dust of the day's events.

Even if this theory is true, exploring and interpreting the dream itself is an interesting endeavor. After all, the cortex went to a lot of trouble to put the dream together in a certain way, and a person may gain valuable insight by looking at the cortex's spin on his or her current state of affairs.

Chapter 19

Daring to Divine

Most Wiccans practice divination in some form. The most common is the tarot. The general public, though, is often a little uncomfortable about divination. The popular misconception is that it indicates a person's sealed and unchangeable fate. However, that's not what divination is at all.

Divination gives people the opportunity to gain wisdom and knowledge from deep within their unconscious minds and to expand their awareness in order to see their present and future possibilities and potential. This chapter provides an overview of what divination is and isn't, as well as introducing several of the most common forms.

Understanding Divination

Divination is an attempt to receive unknown information about the past, present, or future. The process requires two steps. A person:

1. Uses a tool or method (tarot cards, for example) to produce symbols.
2. Interprets the symbols in a way that is meaningful to his or her life.

A Wiccan uses divination when he or she seeks wisdom, insight, guidance, or direction. Divination offers a way of seeing new possibilities that are not readily apparent in current, ordinary reality.

Divination is not fortune telling or predicting the future, in the way that most people think of these terms. Wiccans don't believe that the future is predetermined. In other words, people can change the future by their choices, behavior, and so on. Divination shows how the energy is flowing in a given situation and indicates a possible future if the energy continues in the current pattern. Divination can point to how the future (limited to a year, at most) will look if no significant changes are made. It gives a person an opportunity to take a reading of the current situation so that he or she can decide what to do next. It does not seal a person's fate.

Revealing how divination works

The vast majority of Wiccans believe that divination is a way of tapping into an individual's unconscious or subconscious mind. Some believe that divination allows a person to access the universal (or collective) unconscious that is common to all people. Some believe that divination is also a means of receiving communication directly from Deity, for example, as an answer to a prayer.

Drawing knowledge from the sea of energy

Successful divination is possible because everything is interconnected. All of existence is an unbroken circle of energy, and everything is merged into one living organism flowing from Deity. People come from and are a part of the Divine energy, and the Deity is within everyone and everything. Because all energy is linked, a person can receive information from deep within the unconscious mind, from all planes of existence, or directly from Deity.

Divination allows the conscious mind to draw relevant information out of this sea of energy. Divination is a way of heightening awareness or expanding consciousness so a person can perceive this information.

Recognizing Carl Jung's contribution

The theories of Carl Jung, a Swiss psychiatrist who lived from 1875 to 1961, offer a possible explanation of why divination works.

You may already be familiar with the idea of the conscious and unconscious or subconscious mind:

- ✔ The *conscious mind* holds the thoughts, sensations, emotions, and experiences that you are aware of. The conscious mind is the rational mind that analyzes and organizes. The conscious experiences the world and communicates with language (words and numbers).

- ✔ The *unconscious* (or *subconscious*) *mind* is the location of everything that isn't presently conscious but can be, including memories that you could call up easily and those that you have buried deep in your mind.

Carl Jung went one step further and described the unconscious mind as having two parts, the *personal unconscious* and the *collective unconscious*. The collective unconscious holds the accumulated knowledge and experiences of all humankind (and possibly animals). It is the inherited part of the brain.

The collective unconscious mind doesn't have many language skills. It experiences the world and expresses itself in images, emotions, sensations, and dreams. It uses symbols. A *symbol* is an image or object that represents something else.

The collective unconscious contains human instincts, which are patterns of behavior. Instinct tells a bird to build a nest, and a turtle to go to water. *Instincts* are ways of acting. The collective unconscious also contains *archetypes,* which are ways of perceiving. An archetype is a tendency for humans to represent certain ideas with a specific symbol. These archetypal symbols appear in religions, dreams, myths, and fairytales throughout all of human history. The Earth Mother and the Hero are examples of archetypes.

For some, Jung's theory explains the power and effectiveness of dreams (which can be a form of divination), scrying (staring at a reflective surface, such as a crystal ball), tarot cards, and other divination systems that use archetypal symbols. The symbols, combined with focus and relaxation, bypass the conscious mind. The symbols and the practice of divination temporarily turn off the filters of the conscious mind and draw information directly from the unconscious, providing a person with valuable insight and knowledge. Your unconscious mind has information about your individual experiences. It uses that information with the symbols from any divination method in order to create a meaningful message.

Divining is a two-way process. The divination method triggers or activates the unconscious mind, and then the unconscious mind plays a role in the divination session.

Some people consider divination to be what Jung termed a synchronicity. A *synchronicity* occurs when events happen at the same time, but seem connected and appear to influence each other — a meaningful coincidence. In the case of divination, the divination method draws energy from the unconscious mind, and the unconscious mind affects the result of the divination session (the content of the dream or the particular tarot cards that appear, and so on).

Choosing a divination system

Hundreds of divination systems are available, and the choice is up to the individual. Books are devoted to the use of each system. Many divination systems are inexpensive. This chapter focuses on those methods and is only meant as a very basic introduction to these techniques. For more information, seek out a title devoted to the type of divination that most interests you.

If you're making a decision about whether to add divination to your personal spiritual practice, avoid spending a great deal of money on a system until you know whether you like it.

You can test a divination system. Ask two versions of the same question in order to check for consistency of the answers. Record the uses of the method and the outcomes in your Book of Shadows (see the next chapter for information on Books of Shadows). That way, you'll have a record of its effectiveness.

Divination is probably as old as humankind and is common to most cultures around the world. Before you use a system, make sure that you know its history and culture of origin, so you understand its symbolism. You may want to investigate systems from the cultures of your ancestors. Or, if you're drawn to a particular aspect of the Goddess or the God (for example, Artemis of Greece or Bast of Egypt), you may choose a divination system from that culture.

Settle on a system that feels comfortable for you, provides you with clear information, and isn't a struggle for you to learn.

Divining

Divination is especially useful when you need to be aware of all the options and possibilities available to you. It can be an invaluable psychological and spiritual tool when you are at a crossroads and need direction, when you want to examine your own strengths and weaknesses, or when you want to focus your efforts toward a goal and be more productive in life.

Sometimes the very act of using divination can clarify your own desires. You may find yourself hoping for a specific result during the divination session. For example, you are doing a tarot reading to help you make a decision about whether to move across the country, and halfway through the reading, you find that you are fervently hoping that the cards will tell you to stay put. You already have your answer.

Here are some tips for making divination more successful and meaningful:

✔ Cast a circle before you begin a divination session. The circle filters out distractions and improves focus. Casting a circle isn't necessary; you may choose only to relax, center, and ground yourself. (See Chapter 12 for information on circle casting, centering, and grounding.) Casting a circle allows you to welcome or invite the presence of Deity for the divination session.

✔ Do your own reading, instead of going to someone else. Doing the reading yourself builds your understanding of your own unconscious mind and puts you in touch with your own inner resources. It expands your consciousness as well as enhances your perception and builds your self-reliance.

If you do the reading yourself, you don't have to face the dilemma of finding someone trustworthy to do it for you. Some very reliable and skilled people perform divination for others as a service for free or for a fee. A reading with one of these people may be invaluable. However, some people set up divination services as deliberate scams. The con artists don't invest sufficient skill, effort, or ethics into the practice. Exercise common sense, just as you do when you hire someone for any other service, such as tax preparation.

✔ If you believe that you have received information from Deity or another positive source during a divination session, be sure to express gratitude.

Avoid getting hooked on divination. Divination becomes meaningless if it is used daily. Wicca encourages the healthy development of the conscious mind, and self-sufficiency depends on the decision-making abilities of the conscious part of the brain. Don't rely too heavily on the symbolism from the unconscious. When you need to make a decision, work with the information you receive from all sources (conscious and unconscious). Balance is the key.

Scrying with Water, Mirrors, Copper, or Crystal

Scrying is gazing into any reflective surface in order to see images. Scrying may be the oldest of divination techniques. It is certainly the simplest and least expensive. Scrying may have begun when early humans first gazed into pools of water and watched the images and reflections.

The most well-known form of scrying involves looking into a crystal ball, but any reflective surface works, including the following:

✔ black mirror (a mirror that is reflective because of its black rather than silver surface)

✔ bowl (or tumbler or other container) of water

✔ candle flame

✔ copper (a highly polished sheet)

✔ crystal pendant or stone

- ✔ fire or smoke
- ✔ moving stream
- ✔ pool of ink
- ✔ random patterns on a TV or computer screen
- ✔ slab of onyx or obsidian
- ✔ waterfall

When some Wiccans scry, they see actual images in the object or substance. However, most Wiccans see images or impressions in their minds. Some may see symbols, for example, seeing an animal with bared teeth may be a warning not to pursue a particular course of action.

The following steps offer one way to practice scrying:

1. Fill a bowl with water and place it on a dark cloth in front of you on a table. You may want to choose a clear bowl or a black bowl.

2. Light a candle and place it behind you (keep it away from your hair and clothing). Turn off electric lights.

3. You may want to cast a circle and/or center and ground (see Chapter 12 for instructions on casting a circle, centering, and grounding).

4. Focus on a specific question you need to answer or a situation you need to resolve. Clear your mind, and relax deeply.

5. Stare down into the water. Gaze directly into the water, blinking normally. The water should fill up your field of vision. Don't try to force images to be visible. Remember any images or symbols that appear in the water or in your mind. If you don't see anything after 10 or 15 minutes, give up the effort.

6. Write down anything that you saw. You may want to record your observations in a Book of Shadows.

7. If you receive information from Deity or another positive source, be sure to express gratitude.

If the image that you see is symbolic, take some time to consider possible interpretations. Ask yourself what the specific symbol means to you.

Using a Pendulum

A *pendulum* is a weight hanging from a cord. The swinging motion of the weight is used for divination. Using a pendulum is another easy and very inexpensive method of divining information. You can purchase beautiful pendulums in stores and on the Web. However, almost anything that hangs from a chain, cord, ribbon, string, or thread may serve as a pendulum, including a button, charm, crystal, key, locket, needle, pendent, or ring

The following steps show one method of using a pendulum:

1. Find a quiet place. You may want to cast a circle and/or center and ground (see Chapter 12 for instructions on casting a circle, centering, and grounding).

2. Seat yourself at your altar or a table.

3. Draw up a question or a list of questions. The question(s) must require a yes or no response.

4. Hold the string, and suspend the weight of the pendulum about 7 inches beneath your fingers. You may suspend it about 2 inches over the table or over the open palm of your other hand. You can rest your elbows on the table if necessary.

5. Hold the string so it moves as little as possible.

6. Ask the pendulum, "What is your direction that means yes?" Note which way the pendulum swings (side to side or to you and away from you). Ask the pendulum, "What is your direction that indicates no?" Note which way the pendulum swings. Let the pendulum come to a stop.

7. Hold the pendulum as still as possible, and ask a question.

8. Although you are holding the pendulum as still as possible, it will begin to swing. Involuntary movements of your hand cause the pendulum to move. Don't actively try to control the movement. Let your unconscious mind control it. Note the direction and whether the answer is yes or no.

9. Make sure to let the pendulum come to a complete stop before asking another question.

10. If you receive information from Deity or another positive source, be sure to express gratitude.

Your unconscious mind controls the pendulum's movement. Divining with a pendulum, like all other forms of divination, is a way to override the conscious mind and let the unconscious speak to you.

If the pendulum swings wildly (not in either of the directions that you identified as meaning yes and no), it cannot answer the question as framed. Try to be more precise. For example, if the question is, "Should I move?", the mind may have trouble processing the word "move." But if you say, "Should I sell my current home and buy a house in Bloomington, Indiana?," you may get a better result.

If you want to answer a question about location, such as locating where to place a well for water, you can dangle a pendulum over a map. Methodically suspend the pendulum over different areas of the map. When the pendulum is over the correct area, it begins to move and circle.

Divining with a pendulum is related to *dowsing* or *water witching*. A dowser finds water, oil, or other substances and materials in the Earth. He or she uses a pendulum or a forked wand or wire. The dowser concentrates on water or another substance or material and walks, holding the pendulum or the forked ends of the wand out in front of the body. Eventually, the pendulum will swing, or the wand will turn downward and point to the area in the Earth where the water or other material lies. Many people have used this method to determine where to dig wells.

Casting Lots

Another very old form of divination is sortilege, or casting lots. Objects (such as stones, bones, beans, shells, dice, I-Ching coins or sticks, or dominoes) are thrown on the ground or other surface. Interpretations are made based on where and how the objects land. Flipping a coin (resulting in heads or tails) is a very simple form of casting lots.

Many Wiccans cast runes. A rune is a letter of the alphabet of the old Norse or Germanic (Teutonic) cultures. Many different versions of the runic alphabet have been used over the centuries. The Norse and Teutonic peoples used the runes for writing, magic, and divination.

Today, many Wiccans buy tiles made of stone, wood, metal, or clay with the characters of the runic alphabet painted on them (or they make their own set of runes by collecting materials and painting, carving, or burning the alphabet symbols on them). Most modern sets include 24 runes and one blank tile.

The ancient Shamanic meanings for the specific stones have been lost. But the system of divination has been revived, and various authors have developed new meanings for the runes. If you're drawn to runes, look at some of the available sets, and buy or make the system whose meanings most appeal to you. Visit your local library or bookstore and browse the books on the subject or check out some Web sites devoted to the subject.

The runes generally are kept in a drawstring bag. The runes are shaken inside the bag, and then a specific number are drawn for interpretation, in much the same way as tarot cards are drawn and interpreted.

Reading Tarot Cards

The most common divination method for Wiccans is reading tarot cards. The strong symbolism of the images on the tarot cards appeals directly to the unconscious mind. After the unconscious mind has been triggered, it focuses on the question at hand and actively engages in the reading.

Selecting from dozens of decks

Dozens of different tarot decks are now available in stores and on the Web. Some are specialized for specific kinds of readings. Many Wiccans have several decks of tarot cards. One deck may apply to a given situation better than another deck. Numerous Web sites offer electronic readings with a wide selection of tarot decks, offering the opportunity to see and use various decks.

Many card decks are available that aren't traditional tarot cards, for example, spirit animal or spirit guide decks. Each of these decks has its own symbolism and system.

Some of the newer tarot decks are round, instead of rectangular. This shape allows more flexibility in the reading. The cards in a rectangular deck have an established meaning. Traditionally, for many decks, if the card appears upside down in the reading, the meaning of the card is the reverse of the standard meaning. In many decks, the upright meaning is positive, and the reversed meaning is negative. However, a round card may appear turned to any number of degrees between upright and upside down, so the meaning is a blend of positive and negative. The meaning varies depending on how much the card is tilted.

If you decide to purchase your own deck for tarot readings, look at several types, and review most of the cards in the decks. Also carefully evaluate the book that accompanies each deck and provides explanations for the meanings of the cards. The symbolism for the decks varies widely. Make sure that the symbolism of the deck that you choose appeals to you and is in keeping with your own values, principles, and beliefs. Decks can cost anywhere from a few dollars to over a hundred dollars; choose one that feels right to you.

You may want to cleanse, charge, and consecrate your tarot cards, as you would any Wiccan tool (see Chapters 11 and 12 for guidance). Store your tarot cards in a safe place, where other people won't be tempted to handle them. Many Wiccans believe that tarot cards are imbued with the owner's energy, which makes them more powerful.

Getting familiar with the Major and Minor Arcana

The tarot deck used for divination consists of 78 cards. The tarot card deck is divided into two parts: the Major Arcana and the Minor Arcana (also called the Greater and Lesser Trumps).

The Major Arcana

The Major Arcana consists of 22 cards. Each card offers a specific title and picture, and has a unique meaning. The Major Arcana represents major archetypes of the unconscious mind. The unconscious mind doesn't have language to express human behaviors and experiences. It only communicates in pictures, using symbols called archetypes. (See the earlier section, "Revealing how divination works" for more information on archetypes.) The Major Arcana signifies life's major passages.

The Minor Arcana

The Minor Arcana comprises 56 cards divided into four suits. The suits are often called: Pentacles, Wands, Swords, and Cups. These names correspond to the four elements, which are a running theme throughout Wicca.

The sacred circle, in which Wiccans perform ritual and magic, is divided into four quarters and the center. Each of the quarters of the circle corresponds to parts of the Self and the elements of nature. So when a person casts a circle, all aspects of the Self and nature are activated and unified. Each of the suits of the tarot also corresponds to these elements. The following shows a common system of these *correspondences:*

- ✔ Pentacles correspond to North, Earth, and the human body (health, work, and physical possessions).
- ✔ Wands correspond to East, Air, and the human mind (thought and communication).
- ✔ Swords correspond to South, Fire, and human energy (will, passion, and drive).
- ✔ Cups correspond to West, Water, and human emotions (love, moods, and intuition).

(The center of a sacred circle represents Spirit. Spirit corresponds to the Major Arcana of the tarot.)

Each suit consists of 14 cards: ace through ten and four court cards (Page, Knight, Queen, and King). In many decks, each card has a separate scene depicted on it, and the illustrations incorporate distinct symbols. The Minor Arcana represent everyday human experiences. In many tarot systems, each of the cards of a particular value has a consistent meaning. For example, all the two cards, regardless of suit, may have a similar theme, such as balance.

All the cards of the tarot together represent a complete picture of all the possibilities and potential of human consciousness.

Doing a tarot reading

You can read tarot cards for yourself or for someone else. The person doing the tarot reading is called the *reader*. The subject of the reading — the person asking the question — is called the *querent*. The reader makes interpretations of the cards for the querent. If you do a reading for yourself, you serve as both the reader and the querent.

During a tarot reading, the cards first are shuffled. When you shuffle the cards, the deck absorbs your energy, especially from your unconscious mind. (If you are doing a reading for someone else, he or she shuffles the cards.) Then the cards are laid out in a pattern or *spread*. Spreads can include very few cards or many. The relationship between the cards in these spreads reveals different aspects of the querent's life.

You can choose from a wide variety of spreads (see Figure 19-1). For example, in a very simple three-card spread, the three cards may represent the past, the present, and the future. Or the three cards may represent the present situation, the obstacles the person faces, and the possible outcome. Tarot decks generally are sold with a book that provides recommendations for potential spreads, as well as possible interpretations for the cards. In addition, many books are devoted to the long history and vast body of knowledge about the art of tarot.

The reader interprets the cards based on the standard meanings for the cards, as well as unique impressions from the cards' symbols and the cards' positions in the spread.

Follow these steps to do a tarot reading:

1. Find a quiet place with enough room to spread out the cards.

2. You may want to cast a circle and/or center and ground (see Chapter 12).

3. Light a candle to prepare your unconscious for the reading.

4. Ask a question

5. Shuffle the cards at least seven times. Choose the cards and lay them out according to the spread that you have chosen to use.

6. Make an interpretation of the cards.

7. Record your question, the date, the exact cards in the reading, and any interpretation. You may put this information in your Book of Shadows.

© The Cover Story/CORBIS

Figure 19-1:
Laying out
tarot cards
in a more
complex
spread.

Although you can read the standard interpretations spelled out in the book that accompanies the cards, feel free to deviate from these meanings. Everyone's unconscious mind responds and interprets symbolism differently, so make the reading individual. Look at the picture on the card and think about what it means to you.

Let the cards speak for themselves. When you interpret the cards, don't rely on information that you know about yourself (or the individual for whom you are reading) or the situation.

Surveying the Planets — Astrology Rules

Many Wiccans believe in and practice astrology. Astrology is the relationship between the changing positions of celestial bodies (the planets, Sun, Moon, and stars) and the characteristics, events, and personal development in a person's life.

In astrology, certain powers and attributes are associated with each celestial body.

Astrology is a form of divination. Astrology may give an individual a way to divine his or her feelings and understand his or her patterns of behavior, as well as the obstacles that stand in the way of possible futures. With will power, a person always may overcome astrological indications.

Astrology offers a way for individuals to link their lives to the cosmos and revere their interconnection with the universe. Astrology is archetypal, and the symbols appear throughout the cultures of humankind. Many people use astrology as a tool to describe themselves, others, and the relationships between them (see the earlier section, "Understanding Divination," for an explanation of archetypes).

In the West, astrology generally is based on the zodiac, which begins at 0 degrees Aries (where the Sun crosses the equator moving northward on the spring equinox). The following are the principal signs of the zodiac and the typical dates for each:

- Aries (The Ram): March 21 to April 19
- Taurus (The Bull): April 20 to May 20
- Gemini (The Twins) May 21 to June 21
- Cancer (The Crab) June 22 to July 22
- Leo (The Lion) July 23 to August 22
- Virgo (The Virgin): August 23 to September 22
- Libra (The Balance): September 23 to October 23
- Scorpio (The Scorpion): October 24 to November 21
- Sagittarius (The Archer): November 22 to December 21
- Capricorn (The Goat): December 22 to January 19
- Aquarius (The Water Bearer): January 20 to February 18
- Pisces (The Fishes): February 19 to March 20

Like tarot, astrology ties in with the elements. The signs of the zodiac correspond to the various elements, as follows:

- Fire: Aries, Leo, Sagittarius
- Earth: Taurus, Virgo, Capricorn
- Air: Gemini, Libra, Aquarius
- Water: Cancer, Scorpio, Pisces

Astrology has many different branches and methods. To learn to use it for divination requires considerable study. Check out your local library or bookstore. Many good sources are available online.

Other Types of Divination

Divination is as old as history. People can — and do — use almost anything to divine. This chapter doesn't begin to even scratch the surface of the divination techniques that humankind has devised.

Natural or *direct* forms of divination include interpreting:

- Dreams and trance (see Chapter 18)
- Contact with ancestors or others who have died (some Wiccans believe that death transcends time and space, so souls who have passed on may be able to provide information across time and space)
- The words of prophets (people who have natural ability to access information across time and space)

Indirect forms of divination include reading and interpreting events and patterns, such as behavior of animals and insects, comets, earthquakes, eclipses, flight patterns or songs of birds, meteors, smoke or flame, tea leaves, the lines of the palm or forehead, and weather (especially winds and cloud formations).

If the vast number of possibilities for divination overwhelms you, you can always choose the easy way: Just flip a coin!

Chapter 20

Keeping a Book of Shadows, a Sacred Record

In This Chapter

▶ Respecting Books of Shadows

▶ Choosing a book style

▶ Staying mindful of Book of Shadows ethics

*W*icca is a spirituality of discovery and personal experience. Although it is rooted in antiquity, it has no doctrine or holy book that has been passed through the ages for all Wiccans to follow. Each Wiccan creates his or her own book of teachings and practice. This sacred book is usually called a *Book of Shadows* and is sometimes respectfully abbreviated *BOS*.

A Book of Shadows reflects Wicca in all its depth and creativity. This chapter is about these personal volumes that serve as a record of the individual and collective evolution of Wicca.

Understanding the Importance of a Book of Shadows

A *Book of Shadows* is a written chronicle of Wiccan life. Today, almost every Wiccan has her or his own personal Book of Shadows, and the keeping of a Book of Shadows is one of the few universal practices in Wicca.

A personal Book of Shadows

Each Wiccan keeps and adds to a Book of Shadows throughout his or her life in Wicca. The book serves as a personal history, memoir, journal, sourcebook, and encyclopedia. The following is a list of some possible contents of a Book of Shadows (each entry usually includes the date, time, and Moon phase):

✔ Animal connections (encounters with or wisdom from familiars, spirit animals, or other animals)

✔ Astrology information

✔ Chants

✔ Class, workshop, or other study notes

✔ Deity information

✔ Divination records (for example, tarot readings)

✔ Dreams and interpretations

✔ Festivals attended

✔ Healing techniques

✔ History of Wicca

✔ Internet information (for example, sites related to Wicca)

✔ Invocations

✔ Poetry

✔ Political work (anti-defamation, environmental, or other work in the service of Deity)

✔ Prayers

✔ Principles and ethics of Wicca

✔ Psychic abilities, occurrences, or exercises

✔ Recipes

✔ Rites and rituals (for example, Sabbats, Esbats, or rites of passage)

✔ Songs

✔ Spells and their outcomes

✔ Stone, candle, or herb magic

✔ Synchronicities

✔ Thoughts, feelings, and questions about Wicca

✔ Tool list and altar diagram

✔ Trance work and results

Many Wiccans believe that a Book of Shadows should be cleansed and consecrated before it is used for the first time, just like other Wiccan tools. (See Chapter 12 to find out how to cleanse and consecrate tools.)

The title for the Book of Shadows appears on the first page, along with the date that the book was presented or created. Some Wiccans follow the title page with a blessing page.

The owner of a Book of Shadows may decorate the blessing page in any way that is pleasing. The blessing is customarily written by hand and usually includes a request for Deity to bless the book, a dedication to the owner's spiritual growth, and a request for protection of the contents. The blessing can be lyrical and poetic, or it can be straight to the point. It will have more meaning and power if the owner of the book writes it himself or herself, from the heart, instead of copying it from book or Internet resources.

Many Wiccans follow the blessing page with a section index, to give the book some organization. The sections begin after the index page.

The owner of the Book of Shadows decides what to put in his or her book. Wicca does not mandate any specific content. A Wiccan may decorate and organize the book according to his or her own needs. Even the name Book of Shadows is not required; any other name that is personally meaningful is fine. A Book of Shadows is a personal creation that reflects an individual's walk on the Wiccan path.

Collective Books of Shadows

Many traditions and covens require that a Wiccan create and maintain a personal Book of Shadows before he or she can be initiated into the group.

In addition to the books kept by individuals, each tradition and coven usually has a Book of Shadows that is held collectively by the group. Some groups require that the Book of Shadows be kept secret. It is only shown to initiates (members) or to students. However, the Books of Shadows from several traditions have now been published and are available for purchase by the general public.

If a new coven spins off from an older coven, the new group usually takes a copy of the original coven's Book of Shadows, to serve as a basis for the new volume.

In some traditions, an initiate receives his or her own copy of the Book of Shadows for the tradition and the initiating coven. This copy may be compiled by the student during training, or the initiator may make the copy for the new initiate.

No original Book of Shadows exists from before the modern period; no one Wiccan book preceded all others and has been handed down through the ages to serve as the source of all truth.

History in the shadows

Although most Wiccans use the name Book of Shadows, some refer to it as a Grimoire or a Black Book. The traditional definition of *Grimoire* is a book of magical knowledge, written between the late Middle Ages and the 18th Century. *Black Book* is also a historical term, used before Book of Shadows was popularized during the Wiccan revival. The term Book of Shadows was probably not widely used before the late Middle Ages, and most scholars believe that the name has been in common usage only since the mid-20th Century, after Gerald Gardner introduced the term.

All the Pagan religions were originally oral traditions, and unfortunately, much of the knowledge about those beliefs and practices has been lost through the ages. The Pagans of old couldn't read and write well enough to keep such records, nor did they have access to resources, such as quality paper. They certainly couldn't boot up the ol' computer at the end of the day and dash off an account of the latest harvest festival.

For the first time in history, Pagans, including Wiccans, have the freedom and the means to create detailed written records of their personal spiritual experiences. The creation of Books of Shadows began to catch on after the anti-Witchcraft laws were repealed in Britain, and legal recognition and protection increased in the United States. The name Book of Shadows reflects the fact that practitioners of the Craft have had to practice in the shadows.

The word "Shadows" can also refer to the shadow world (also called the Otherworld, the astral planes, or other universes or dimensions). The Book of Shadows is a written record of the relationship between a Wiccan and the world beyond ordinary reality, and the book serves as a link to that place.

Choosing a Style for the Book

Historically, a Book of Shadows was a bound book with a black cover. Any blank book could serve the purpose; today, the style is a matter of personal choice.

Content is more important than style, but if you decide to begin a Book of Shadows, choose the book with care. If you don't like the book's style, you may be inclined to neglect the contents, and the energy that you do put into the book will be less powerful.

Plain or fancy?

A Book of Shadows may be a blank book purchased from a local bookstore or online. Bookstores that cater to the Pagan community usually offer a wide variety of covers and styles in Wiccan themes.

Wiccans don't haggle over price when they purchase any spiritual or magical tool, including a Book of Shadows. During the haggling, the seller may unwillingly be forced to drop his or her price. This may constitute harm done to the seller, and is a violation of the Wiccan Rede (which says, "An' it harm none, do what ye will."). In general, tools — including Books of Shadows — should be kept free of any type of negative energy.

Some Wiccans construct their own Book of Shadows from scratch. The cover of the book can be any suitable material: cloth, painted or nicely grained wood, or leather, possibly hand-tooled (some Wiccans are vegetarians who object to the use of leather). Natural materials are preferred, and many Wiccans try to choose materials that are ecologically sound.

The owner may drill holes through the covers, so the book can be bound with ribbon, natural vines, twine, or other materials. High-quality paper goes between the covers; choose a type of paper that will last a long time and doesn't cause ink to run.

If a Book of Shadows has a cloth cover, the owner can sew a pocket into the cloth and insert stones, herbs, or other items that have meaning and power. My own book contains dried fern leaves from a wooded hillside that has extraordinary energy and is very special to me. My family has lived at the foot of this hill beside a winding creek for generations.

Notebooks of Shadows

Wiccans may begin their practice with beautiful and ornate Books of Shadows. But after some time, many switch to simple three-ringed notebooks. A ringed binder is more practical for several reasons:

- ✔ Individual pages can be temporarily removed for updating or use.

- ✔ The book can be reorganized as material is added. Index tabs may be inserted to organize the contents.

- ✔ You can add inserts to hold notes on sheets of paper of difference sizes and ones with pockets to hold other items.

- ✔ The book lies flat so the pages don't shuffle during worship or magical work. A book that keeps trying to close at critical moments destroys the momentum of a ritual or spell. (Some Wiccans place the book on a stand, such as a music stand. The stand holds the pages steady, and the book doesn't take up space on a crowded altar.)

Protecting the magical legacy: BOS ethics

Wicca doesn't have many rules, but a Book of Shadows presents some serious ethical challenges. If you are a new Wiccan, be aware of the following expectations related to Books of Shadows:

✔ Never list the real names, addresses, telephone numbers, or e-mail addresses of fellow Wiccans. Books of Shadows may contain Craft names (names that people choose when they make a permanent commitment to Wicca), but these names should not be linked to legal names or contact information.

✔ Be cautious about sharing your Book of Shadows with people outside of the Craft. Even if you are completely out of the broom closet, you don't want to violate the privacy of anyone else who may be referenced in your book. Be especially diligent if you decide to place your Book of Shadows on the Web. Make sure that you don't identify other Wiccans.

✔ Never touch another person's Book of Shadows without permission. Many Wiccans feel that a Book of Shadows is imbued with personal power that is disturbed or diminished if someone else touches the book. In addition, the book may contain private information about the owner and others, which should not be shared.

✔ If you are *oathbound,* meaning that you have promised to keep some piece of information secret, make sure that you note your promise in your Book of Shadows (if you choose to record the information). Otherwise, you may forget later.

✔ When you include material that you didn't write (rituals, spells, articles, poetry, and so on), make sure that you list the Craft name of the author in your Book of Shadows, or otherwise note that you didn't create the work.

✔ Make arrangements to have your Book of Shadows handled according to your wishes upon your death. Many traditions and covens require that a member's Book of Shadows be destroyed or given to fellow coveners at death. Whether you practice alone or belong to a coven, make sure that someone trustworthy takes care of your book after you die. If possible, protect your legacy and make arrangements to give it to a loved one or friend who will cherish it and safeguard its contents.

Shelves of Shadows

Wiccans who have been following the path for a while often purchase multiple ringed binders and dedicate each one to a separate aspect of Wiccan life (a binder for rituals, one for spells, one for dreams, one for tarot readings, and so on). The result is a *Bookshelf of Shadows,* a *File Cabinet of Shadows,* a *Trunk of Shadows* . . . you get the idea.

Handwritten or high tech?

According to tradition, a Book of Shadows should be entirely handwritten. A few Wiccans believe — fervently — that this should still be the case, and some traditions require it. They believe that the act of handwriting the contents imbues the book with the owner's personal power, and that power can be tapped during magic or ritual. The act of handwriting also aids in understanding and memory, because the writer must focus on each word.

The custom of handwriting information related to the Craft is rooted in history. In the past, Witchcraft was illegal, and persecution was widespread. People can be readily identified by their handwriting, so each person copied material in his or her own hand. That way, if someone was caught practicing Witchcraft, only he or she would be implicated. None of the written records could lead authorities to anyone else.

Wiccans of the 21st Century have the option of creating Books of Shadows by computer and other high-tech means. Because this material is not easily traceable to its source, Wiccans are actually more secure using digital means of creating documents than they are handwriting them. No one can argue with the fact that producing, organizing, duplicating, and storing information is infinitely easier using computer technologies. In addition, people with arthritis and other ailments may find keyboarding much less painful than writing by hand.

The old custom of carefully handwriting a Book of Shadows is doomed, although some in the Wiccan community valiantly try to preserve the old practice. Many Wiccans now have *Disks of Shadows (DoS)* or *CDs of Shadows,* and they even post their Books of Shadows on Web sites. Wiccans are notorious for their use of technology for spiritual purposes. The number of Wicca-related Web sites is increasing exponentially, enabling an unprecedented exchange of knowledge and support in the Wiccan community.

The digital age has vastly improved the quality of life for Wiccans, however, everyone knows that technology fails and is not always secure. Techno-Wiccans are wise to take precautions to preserve their Books of Shadows, such as the following:

- Store the contents on floppy disks, Zip disks, CDs, or other formats, instead of on a computer's hard drive, which may not be secure or stable.
- When upgrading to new software, convert old files to the new format so that you can continue to access them in the future.
- Maintain hard copies and/or create a backup of everything.

Remember that the key to an effective Book of Shadows is that it can be easily read. The font type used for spells or rituals should be large enough to see by candlelight or a Full Moon.

Part VI
The Part of Tens

"We should cast a circle, invoke the elements, and direct the energy. If that doesn't work, we'll read the manual."

In this part . . .

This part is the traditional *For Dummies* Part of Tens. These are three easy-to-read chapters that offer bits of practical information.

You can explore ten habits or techniques that may make you a more effective Wiccan — and person!

To avoid learning lessons the hard way, you can read about Wicca's unofficial code of conduct. These ten pieces of advice aren't rules of etiquette exactly; they're more about honor, mutual respect, and preserving the Craft.

You also can find out ten ways to avoid scams and recognize inappropriate behavior, in the Craft or any other religion or spirituality.

Chapter 21

Ten Habits of Effective Wiccans

In This Chapter

▶ Moving energy in, out, and away

▶ Using the mind to visualize, meditate, and relax

▶ Caring for Self and community

*P*eople of the Craft are wildly diverse. However, they are all human. Wiccans who are successful and effective, both in their spiritual practice and in their general lives, tend to have some coping skills and lifestyle choices in common.

This chapter takes a look at these skills and choices that improve spiritual effectiveness and quality of life.

Grounding

Grounding power or *Earthing power* means to connect personal energy with the Earth. Wiccans ground themselves *before* ritual or magic, in order to enable the energy to flow unobstructed through them. Wiccans ground *after* ritual or magic so the energy raised during the working dissolves or dissipates naturally. Lingering energy that isn't grounded may turn into tension or anxiety, and perhaps result in a headache or another physical ailment.

In times of stress or anxiety, grounding is a way to release excess energy from yourself. At times when you need energy, grounding enables you to draw it up from the Earth, offering a wellspring of power that can flow through you without exhausting your own resources.

To ground yourself and release energy, sit in a comfortable position and flatten the palms of your hands on the ground or floor, or lie down, placing your body flat on the ground. Take three deep breaths. Visualize (picture in your mind) the energy flowing through your hands or your body and *into* the Earth. If you need energy, visualize the energy flowing up *from* the Earth and into your body. Maintain the visualization until you begin to feel the desired result.

An alternative method is to sit or stand upright and imagine the excess energy flowing down your spine and deep into the Earth. Some people picture themselves as a tree with roots sinking into the Earth. If you need energy, imagine the energy flowing up from the Earth and traveling up your spine.

Centering

After you have grounded excess energy (see the preceding section), you may want to center your own energy or power.

Your physical center is your center of gravity, your place of balance, where your weight is equally distributed. It is usually somewhere between the breastbone and the navel, although for women it may be lower. You also have an energy center, the source of all your personal energy. It's probably in the same area as your physical center. If you don't know where your center is, try picturing something that you truly love (your dog or cat, a piece of music, and so on). When you bring up that loving, self-satisfied, serene, warm feeling, try to pinpoint its source in your body. That is your center.

To *center* yourself, relax your body into a comfortable position (the same position you used for grounding will work), and then rest your mental, emotional, and physical awareness at that spot in your body.

Shielding

Shielding is a technique to protect yourself from negative, counter-productive, depleting, or even dangerous energy. Shielding is a simple process.

In your mind, create a clear bubble or sphere of energy or light around your body. It moves with you and protects you. Instead of a bubble, you also may construct, in your mind, a shield of energy or light layered over your skin. With practice, you may become able to shield your car, your bed, or your entire living space.

Visualizing

Visualization is the ability to experience something in the mind, instead of in physical reality. If you can visualize, you can form a complete mental image of a person, place, object, or event. Visualization enables you to see, hear, touch, and taste in your mind. Most people can experience the senses in their dreams; visualization allows you to do it while you're awake.

This ability allows you to interact with or receive information from the non-physical world, including the conscious and the unconscious mind, or the Divine.

Visualizing something in the nonphysical world makes it much more obtainable in the physical world. For example, if you can visualize yourself as the author of a successful novel, you are more likely to achieve that goal in the physical world. During a working of magic, visualization enables you to fully perceive the goal or outcome of the magical work.

To get the idea about how to visualize, follow these steps:

- ✔ Remember a time when you were very happy or content.
- ✔ Close your eyes and breathe deeply.
- ✔ Picture yourself back at that scene in the past. Try to remember the event vividly (if possible, engage all of your senses: sight, smell, hearing, taste, and feeling).
- ✔ Try to practice visualization during the time just prior to or just after sleep. These times offer enhanced interaction with the unconscious mind.

Meditating

Meditation is a technique to turn off the mundane chatter of the mind and achieve profound contemplation or deep relaxation. Meditation is reported to have many positive effects on the mind and the body (reducing stress, lowering blood pressure, and relieving pain). Some people meditate only for the health benefits or as a means of relaxation. Other people incorporate meditation into their spiritual practice and use it as a way of gaining insight or communing with Deity.

For Wiccans, meditation is a way to clear the mind and prepare for ritual, magic, or divination.

The two basic types of meditation:

- ✔ **Concentration meditation** focuses the mind on a single image, sound, object, mantra (a repeated, usually sacred, word or phrase), or the body's own breathing.
- ✔ **Mindful meditation** doesn't focus on a single purpose; the goal is to remain aware of all the thoughts, feelings, sounds, and images that pass through the mind. A person trains his or her mind to notice each perception or thought that passes without stopping on any one of them.

The following is a simple concentration meditation:

1. Sit or lie in a comfortable position with your eyes closed. If convenient, change into comfortable, loose clothing and remove any restrictive jewelry or eyeglasses.

2. Focus on the sensation of each breath as it moves in and out of your body. An alternative is to focus your attention on the repetition of a word, sound, phrase, or prayer, doing this silently or whispering.

3. Every time your attention wanders (which occurs naturally), gently redirect it back, without judging yourself.

Many Wiccans select a specific meditation technique and build it into their daily routine. Some people start or end the day with meditation; others take meditation breaks throughout the day. The general advice is to start with 5-minute meditation sessions once or twice a day and work up to 20 minutes each time. Most people keep a clock nearby, or set an alarm that is not jarring when it sounds.

Meditation is not for everyone and has been known to produce negative side effects in some people. Consult a physician before beginning a regular meditation practice.

Relaxing

Anxiety obstructs the flow of energy. Stress and anxiety take a tremendous toll on physical, emotional, and mental health, and they erode quality of life. Stress has been linked to all the leading causes of death, such as cardiovascular disease, cancer, accidents, and suicide.

In terms of spiritual practice, stress diminishes the quality of ritual and negatively affects the outcome, especially of magic.

Many books teach techniques for relaxing the mind and the body. The best strategy for coping with anxiety and stress is to choose a method and stick with it. Practice relaxation for half an hour every day.

For Wiccans, relaxation may be part of the preparation for ritual. Relaxation aids focus and concentration.

A common exercise is to breathe deeply, and focus on and relax each of the muscle groups in the body, one at a time (the hands, and then the arms, and then the shoulders, and so on).

Exercising

Good health improves the quality of life, including spiritual life. Rewarding ritual, especially effective magic, requires stamina and concentration. A fulfilling spiritual practice is easier to achieve for someone in good health, physically and emotionally. Regular aerobic exercise benefits the body, as well as helping to reduce stress and protect against depression and other mental and emotional disorders. Everyone's exercise needs and abilities are different. Ask your doctor to develop the best plan for you, based on your age, fitness level, lifestyle, medications, available equipment, and so on.

Living Well

Many people regularly don't get enough sleep, and catching up on weekends doesn't work. Sleep deprivation diminishes physical and mental functioning. (It may also be dangerous. The National Highway Traffic Safety Administration estimates that sleepy drivers cause thousands of automobile crashes each year.) Lack of sleep reduces productivity, weakens concentration, and impairs memory.

Nobody can function at peak physical, emotional, and mental levels without proper nutrition: the right foods in the right amounts, as well as plenty of water. That's the goal, but few people even get close. Without sufficient vitamins, minerals, protein, fiber, phytochemicals (from fruits and vegetables), and water, no one can live up to his or her potential.

The bottom line? Ritual, magic, prayer, and other aspects of spiritual practice take dedication and effort. People who don't live wisely won't have the energy to sustain rich and fulfilling spiritual lives.

Serving

Many Wiccans find that serving the larger community encourages their own self-development, builds inner strength and empowerment, anchors their spiritual practice, and provides a deep sense of satisfaction.

Generally, Wiccans consider Deity to be immanent, or all-present in the world. All living beings come from and are a part of the Divine energy, and the Divine is within everyone. Everything is interconnected. All of nature is an unbroken circle or web of energy, manifested from Deity. Any action within the web of life affects everything else. For Wiccans, the concept of community encompasses all of the natural world, including people and animals. All people are equal in the web of life. Doing harm to anything, even by neglect or apathy, violates Wiccan ethics. Any energy that a person sends out into the world is ultimately returned to him or her with three times the intensity.

Based on these beliefs, most Wiccans share a sense of social responsibility, although they serve community within the framework of very different political positions, and as members and activists of widely diverse organizations and institutions.

The following are examples of Wiccan service, based on the commonly held beliefs in interconnection, immanent Deity, and expanded community:

- ✔ Preserving the Earth and its resources
- ✔ Protecting animals
- ✔ Ending poverty
- ✔ Ensuring equality of people of both sexes and all races and ethnicities
- ✔ Helping to sustain indigenous cultures
- ✔ Promoting conflict resolution
- ✔ Championing education
- ✔ Supporting the arts
- ✔ Working for legal freedom of religion and equal protection for the Craft

Laughing

All people seek pleasure; it's one common drive that reminds us of our interconnection. Humans desire and respond to pleasure, play, and laughter. Laughter is therapeutic, releasing endorphins (chemicals in the brain) that create a sense of well-being. Laughter also may boost the immune system, elevate mood, improve brain functioning, lower blood pressure, and reduce stress.

A need for laughter is part of the way that humans have evolved, and people are manifestations of Deity. Joy, laughter, delight, and bliss are expressions of the life force. Wicca is not a religion of sacrifice, self-denial, and repression of emotions. It is a spiritual path of celebration and satisfaction. To look at life and laugh is to show trust in Self and in Deity.

Chapter 22

Ten Wiccan Principles of Behavior

In This Chapter

▶ Keeping Craft confidentiality

▶ Showing respect at Craft gatherings

▶ Respecting boundaries: your own and everyone else's

*W*iccans generally are "live and let live" people. Wicca has no doctrine or dogma. It has no central leadership, no authoritative body that enforces standards and rules. In general, the people of the Craft try to be self-directed, self-reliant, self-controlled, and self-willed. They generally expect and respect the same traits in others.

Wiccans do have a sort of informal code of conduct that is mutually agreed on and followed by most. This unofficial code isn't about etiquette and proper protocol, or even civility. It's more about honor and respect for yourself, each other, and the preservation of the Craft. This chapter offers ten (or so) of the most important of these unofficial principles of behavior.

Don't Ask

Don't ask someone directly whether he or she is a Wiccan or a Witch — or try to find out covertly. Wait until the information is volunteered. If a person mentions the subject in conversation, show that you are open-minded and receptive, but wait for the person to confide in you.

Many Wiccans are comfortable talking about their religion. Although many speak freely about their spiritual path, many more Wiccans are guarded about disclosing their affiliation with Wicca. Even if you share information about your own spirituality, don't do so with the expectation that all Wiccans will be equally forthright. Discrimination and persecution are ongoing, and Wiccans continue to lose child custody, jobs, housing, and relationships with family and friends, as well as personal security.

Don't Tell

Try not to "out" anyone. Don't reveal to others that someone is Wiccan without first getting permission in private. This advice applies even if the person you want to tell is also a member of the Craft.

Be careful if you keep a Book of Shadows (a personal journal of Craft life), use group e-mail, maintain a Web site, or use other media and technologies that may not be secure. Don't write or post the legal names, addresses (e-mail or snail mail), telephone numbers, or other contact information of people in the Craft. Use Craft names and don't link them to identifying information. Likewise, don't gossip about who you saw at Craft events and gatherings.

Put That Camera Away!

Show restraint in taking photographs of the participants and public at Craft events, unless you have their explicit permission. Make sure that people in the background in your photos aren't identifiable. Even if you are behaving responsibly, you may make people nervous if you wave around a camera at a Craft gathering. This advice applies to public rituals, classes and workshops, lectures, and so on.

Show Respect at Public Rituals

If you attend a public ritual, where Wiccans cast a sacred circle, consider these recommendations:

- Make a decision about whether or not to take part *before* the ritual circle begins. If you don't want to focus, contribute your efforts, and fully experience the ritual, don't enter the circle. Half-hearted participation dampens the energy of the entire group and dishonors Deity. Don't feel pressured to join the circle, just make your decision before people begin to meditate and ground themselves (Chapter 12 offers detailed advice on preparing for a ritual). If you decide not to participate, be sure to respect the privacy of those who are involved. Some groups are comfortable letting people watch without actively participating; others aren't. Ask the advice of the organizers, if you aren't sure what's appropriate.

- Attend to personal needs before the circle is cast. Before you enter a circle, turn off beepers and phones, visit the restroom, and arrange for supervision of children and pets.

- Don't leave a circle except in the case of an emergency. Participants in a circle build and merge their energy and focus. If people walk in and out of a circle, other participants are distracted, and the energy of the circle rapidly diminishes. If you must leave a circle mid-ritual, cut a door in the circle. *Cutting a door* means that you symbolically and psychically create a door, walk through it, and seal it tightly before departing (see Chapter 12 for more explanation). If you don't have experience, ask an organizer or someone in the circle to cut the door for you.

✔ Respect the ceremony. Don't engage in talking or laughing at inappropriate times.

Be Wise with Alcohol and Drugs

Drug use and excessive use of alcohol are not a part of the Craft. Being drunk or stoned is unacceptable in a ritual circle. Cigarette smoking generally is prohibited in this setting, too.

Some traditions use a small amount of wine for grounding during a ritual. If you don't want to drink, either kiss the cup or hold it up in salute to Deity. Most large group gatherings have non-alcoholic alternatives available.

Care for Children and Animals

If you have children or pets and you plan to attend a Craft event or gathering, make arrangements early. Call the organizers and find out whether minors or animals are allowed on the premises. Find out exactly what will happen at the event and determine whether it's appropriate and legal for children to attend. Don't forget to ask whether there will be public nudity.

Supervise kids and pets at all times. Make sure that they don't harm the local environment, including the wildlife. Don't leave them with people you don't know well. Pagan space can feel so warm and welcoming that people often let down their guard.

Take Care of Yourself

If a person or group asks you to do something that you don't want to do, refuse. Walk away. Wicca encourages self-respect, critical thinking, and independent behavior. Wiccans expect others to assert healthy boundaries.

If you attend a Craft gathering or event, and the participants ask you to do something that you don't understand, ask questions. Seek explanations until you are comfortable with the answers. Most organizers hold a pre-ritual discussion before the actual event begins. That's the best time to ask questions and get clarification.

Just as you would with any group of people, be cautious about divulging too much personal information too fast at a Wiccan gathering. Don't automatically disclose your personal contact information just because the attendees are Wiccan or Pagan.

Don't Touch Others' Belongings

Don't touch other people's spiritual stuff. Wiccans cleanse, charge, and consecrate the spiritual objects that they use, which means that they devote time and effort to purifying the objects of outside energies and imbuing them with their own energy.

If you touch someone's belongings, you disturb and disperse the owner's energy and attach your own to them.

If you really feel the need to handle an object, ask permission. But be aware that this may put the owner in the awkward position of having to say no and appear rude. Spiritual objects may include:

- Altars
- Books of Shadows
- Jewelry
- Musical instruments (especially drums)
- Nature objects (stones, gems, crystals, shells, herbs, and roots)
- Ritual tools (pentacles, wands, brooms, cauldrons, ritual knives, bells, goblets, chalices, incense holders, incense, candles, and bells)
- Robes, cords, or other clothing

Be Tolerant

When the followers of most religions attend events or gatherings, they know what to expect. They usually have a history, a doctrine, and a liturgy in common. Wicca is different. Wicca is a group of loosely connected small groups, that operate and evolve independently. The Wiccan traditions are very diverse. Not everyone believes and practices the same way. Be tolerant of differences.

Chapter 23

Ten Warning Signs of a Scam or Inappropriate Behavior

*W*iccans are some of the most compassionate and ethical people on Earth. According to Wicca, every living being embodies Deity, so every being deserves care and respect. Wiccans are honor-bound to serve the community and the Divine. Wiccan ethics prohibit doing harm to anyone, and Wicca teaches that the negative energy will return to someone who does. However, unscrupulous or unstable people sometimes perpetrate scams or other manipulations under the guise of religion, and this situation is as true for Wicca as for other religious groups.

Many people desperately want to find and be part of a spiritual group of like-minded people. Don't let your need for companionship cause you to accept abuse, misconduct, or inappropriate activity. In addition, don't endure mistreatment in silence because you feel that you have to prove yourself to a group or because you are afraid of appearing ignorant of Wicca as a whole or of a specific group's traditions.

This chapter offers advice for carefully evaluating leaders and groups before becoming involved with them. Use this information wisely, think critically, and trust your own instincts, no matter which spiritual path you are pursuing.

Inflicting Harm

Any leader or group that encourages or inflicts physical, mental, emotional, financial, or sexual abuse is violating the sound tenets of Wicca and should be avoided. This includes harm to fellow coveners, to the general public, to children, or to animals. This also applies to self-inflicted injury.

Causing harm to anyone or anything violates the ethics of Wicca. The Wiccan Rede, which Wiccans almost universally accept, says, "An' it harm none, do what ye will." The Threefold Law, the other basic ethic of Wicca, states that whatever a person sends out into the world comes back to him or her three-fold. The law means that words and actions return to the sender with three times the intensity.

Abuse and violence include intimidation, harassment, pressure, bullying, destructive criticism, nit-picking, mockery, humiliation, threats of retribution, and outright physical harm. In Wicca, abuse and violence are never acceptable.

Demanding Control

Members of any group should be capable of confident, independent thought and action. Free will should be respected and encouraged. Members should have the right to say no, to change their minds, and to assert boundaries. In groups, especially in covens, everyone has the right to trust and construc-tively express their own feelings, judgment, and intuition.

A leader or a group's members should recognize that people may have legiti-mate reasons for leaving the group. The leader or the members should not assume that anyone who has left or who wants to leave is wrong or bad. Beware if former members of a group provide similar accounts of abuse or exploitation.

All members of a group should be able to relax and have fun when appropriate.

Exercising Inappropriate Authority

The traditions in Wicca have varying levels of democracy, but leaders should never have absolute authority over members of a coven or group. A safe leader shares power and decision-making, listens to the opinions of others, and admits when he or she is wrong.

A group should not depend on the leader to solve personal problems.

Encouraging Isolation or Dependency

True Wiccans do not ask you to sever ties with your family, friends, or other non-Wiccans. You are free to continue the family, career, and community activities that you pursued prior to your involvement in Wicca. Wicca doesn't require or encourage you to renounce or repudiate your former religion.

Members of a group should not be expected to put the needs of the group above their own. The group should encourage members to maintain a healthy balance between Wiccan and non-Wiccan activities. Members should not be asked to devote time and effort to the group to the exclusion of other areas of their lives.

In addition, some groups may rightfully require that members keep certain information secret, such as magical work or the personal information of coveners. However, you have no obligation to keep abuse or misconduct secret. Don't allow a group to segregate you from the rest of the Craft and pressure you to keep quiet about inappropriate activity.

Charging Inappropriate Fees or Demanding Undue Money

Money issues are a topic of debate in the Wiccan community. On the one hand, many say that until Wicca has paid clergy, just as other religions do, it will not get the leaders it needs nor achieve legitimacy and acceptance in mainstream society.

On the other hand, the law in Gardnerian Wicca, as well as in many other traditions, is: "You shall not teach the craft for money." So Wiccans, as a body, aren't sure when charging for their work is appropriate and when it isn't. Many agree that charging for classes and workshops taught outside the coven (for example, at colleges), for lectures given to the public, or for services (such as tarot readings) is okay. But most Wiccans also agree that for a group or coven to charge coveners for teaching, for entrance, or for initiations is a breach of ethics.

Within a coven, you should pay your share for the group's incidentals, such as meals, ritual supplies, photocopying costs, or room rentals, but you should not be asked to pay for your training or initiation.

The coven leadership should be thoroughly forthcoming about all financial records. If you are concerned about the money that a group is requesting, seek the advice of reputable Pagans in your community.

A true Wiccan leader or group will never demand that you give up your personal wealth to them, change your will, or make other significant sacrifices. In addition, no leader or group has the right to take or destroy your personal property.

Engaging in Sexual Manipulation

Sexual activity is not a part of standard Wiccan practice. Some Wiccans do practice skyclad (nude), but that is not a prelude to sexual acts. If someone tries to coerce you into having sex with anyone affiliated with the group, leave that group immediately.

Never allow anyone to convince you that you must engage in sex because sexual activity is:

- ✔ Necessary for initiation into Wicca
- ✔ An expected part of ritual
- ✔ Necessary in order to "become one of us"
- ✔ Required in order to become a student of Wicca
- ✔ A prerequisite for exploring Wiccan secrets or mysteries
- ✔ A way of opening up to magic, psychic ability, and so on

None of these claims are true, and no one should demand sex in exchange for anything.

Romance does occur in covens, where people are emotionally close, but even in that context, sexual activity should be considered carefully.

Wicca celebrates free will and encourages independence and self-determination. You are free to say no to any practice or request at any time.

Making Inflated Claims or Promises

Beware of leaders or groups that claim that they have old and powerful mysteries or secrets that can instantaneously solve all your problems and meet all your needs. No one has some hidden knowledge, passed through the ages, that can get you out of debt, break an addiction, or fix your relationship — not to mention enable you to win the lottery.

Wicca is a spirituality of profound wisdom. It can give you tools for transforming your life (for example, information about healing or rituals for personal growth and empowerment). Directing energy and working magic can enable you to make positive changes in yourself and the world. But no one in Wicca can bestow upon you a word, charm, or spell that immediately fixes your problems.

Using Illicit Drugs or Excessive Amounts of Alcohol in Spiritual Practice

Some Wiccan traditions may call for coveners to drink small amounts of wine during rituals. Given the current epidemic of addiction, many covens have switched to juice for these occasions; the decision is up to the individual coven or group. If drinking alcohol is a concern for you, be sure to talk with the ritual hosts about it beforehand so arrangements can be made.

However, excessive drug or alcohol use is not a standard part of Wiccan practice. Don't be pressured into taking drugs or using alcohol. Working toward physical, mental, and emotional health and strength is the best way to improve the results of your Craft practice.

Breeding Paranoia

Wiccans are well aware of the history of persecution of Witches and alleged Witches. They also are painfully aware that discrimination continues all over the world. However, question the motives of any leader or group that constantly focuses on the negative, breeding fear and anxiety, especially if the fear-mongering is to achieve some end, for example, to get you to sever ties with family or to give them money. Real Wicca is a spirituality that fosters personal strength and constructive action.

Recruiting and Proselytizing

Trying to convert people to Wicca or attempting to recruit people for coven membership is unacceptable in Wicca. Engaging in these activities is not in keeping with the teachings of any Wiccan tradition. Avoid anyone who tries to recruit you into his or her group. Legitimate Wiccan groups behave just the opposite; they are very selective and are very careful to make sure that people have sufficient knowledge and training before entering a group.

Appendix A

Wicca FAQ

*W*icca is a nature religion. The common public perception of Wicca is very different from the actual beliefs and practices. Wicca is shrouded in stereotypes, inaccuracies, propaganda, and bad press, most of which began during the hysteria of the Witch trials of medieval and Renaissance times.

This appendix answers the most frequently asked questions about the Wiccan path. It offers clear, honest explanations about Wicca and Witchcraft to help you sort out the truth from the hype.

Understanding Wicca

This section provides a look at what Wicca and Witchcraft are, and what they are not. In books and on the Web, you may find the words Wicca, Wiccan, Witch, and Witchcraft used in a variety of ways. The terms don't have clearly established meanings, even among Wiccans. This ambiguity sometimes makes Wiccan books difficult to understand, especially for people who are getting their first exposure to Wicca and Witchcraft. However, if you intend to study further, you need to know that the definitions of some terms are inconsistent, and words are used in various contexts.

Many authors explain, early in their books, their own usage of specific words. (See the Introduction for an explanation for this book.)

What is Wicca?

Wicca is a continuation, a revival, or a recreation of pre-Christian, primarily European, nature religion or spirituality.

Most Wiccans agree with one of the following definitions:

- ✔ Wicca is a continuation of a very old religion that has been passed down through families and groups since ancient times.

- ✔ Wicca is a return to or revival of an old, even ancient, form of religion. Because not a great deal is known about the original beliefs and practices, contemporary Wiccans must add to the old tradition.

- ✔ Wicca is a new form of spirituality that re-creates some very old practices and ideas. The modern form of Wicca began in the 1950s. (See Chapter 5 for a short history of Wicca.)

Put very simply, Wiccans generally agree on two basic principles:

- ✔ **A belief in immanent Deity:** A Wiccan's main spiritual goal is to grow in his or her relationship with Divinity. Almost all Wiccans believe in a Creative Being. Many, but not all, Wiccans honor Deity in both the male and female aspects, that is the Goddess and the God.

    Most Wiccans believe that the Divine is immanent in the world, meaning that Deity is right here, right now, and is all-present in the world. People come from and are a part of the Divine energy, and Deity is within everyone.

- ✔ **A belief in interconnection:** All of life — everything that exists — comes from and is a part of the Divine energy, so everything is interconnected. All of existence is an unbroken circle of energy. Human beings are not separate from the web of nature but are a part of it. Nature is a manifestation of the Deity, and people have an obligation to respect and protect the natural world.

Wiccans revere nature in all its forms. Wiccan spiritual practice is based on the cycles of nature. Rituals often are timed to the phases of the moon. Wiccans celebrate eight major holidays, the beginning and midpoint of each of Earth's four seasons (winter, spring, summer, and fall).

See Part I for a more detailed explanation of Wiccan beliefs.

What's the difference between a Wiccan and a Witch?

The answer to this question is complicated because these words don't have standard definitions, and people use them in different contexts.

Some people consider Witch and Wiccan to be synonymous, and they use the terms interchangeably. Some people use the word Witch as a collective term for many different groups, and a Wiccan is one type or sect of Witch. However, note the following:

✔ **Many Wiccans don't consider themselves to be Witches.** Some consider Wicca to be a separate system of beliefs and practices, different from all forms of traditional Witchcraft.

Some Wiccans reject the Witch label simply because it has such a negative and evil connotation in the culture. They have abandoned the word, believing that Wiccans can never undo the centuries of propaganda and bad press that Witches have endured. Other Wiccans are just as adamant that the word Witch must be reclaimed, and they use the label proudly.

✔ **Many Witches don't consider themselves to be Wiccan.** Although Wicca has its roots in ancient spirituality, the modern Wiccan revival occurred in the 1950s. Many Witches follow traditions that existed before — or are otherwise separate from — the traditions born during the Wiccan revival of the mid-20th Century. The followers of these traditions commonly are called _traditional Witches_ or sometimes _Hedgewitches_. Most traditional Witches don't consider themselves to be Wiccan at all.

Many traditional Witches focus on the oral teachings, literature, history, and folklore of a specific culture (for example, Celtic), and many traditional Witches have ancestry in their chosen tradition. Some Witches are from family (hereditary) backgrounds in Witchcraft. Some groups of Witches have well-defined spiritual beliefs, and others focus almost solely on practice (folk magic, healing, midwifery, and so on).

What is Witchcraft?

Outside of Wicca, there are a seemingly endless number of stereotypical and outlandishly inaccurate definitions of Witchcraft, even within credible sources (such as dictionaries). However, even within Wicca, the word Witchcraft has many different meanings and contexts. The following are some of the (sometimes contradictory) definitions and usages for the word Witchcraft:

✔ Wicca refers to the spirituality (the relationship with or worship of Deity). Witchcraft is the magical practice (for example, magic, healing, divination, and so on). This is a very popular definition.

✔ Witchcraft encompasses _all_ the practices of Wicca, including rituals for worship and for magic. Generally, Wiccans create sacred space by casting a circle. Within that circle, they worship or honor Deity and they also work magic. Some Wiccans consider everything that happens in that sacred space to be Witchcraft. For them, Witchcraft is spiritual ritual and magical art.

✔ Wicca is a sect or a specific form of Witchcraft. In this case, Witchcraft is an umbrella or collective term for the beliefs and practices of all Witches and Wiccans.

✔ Wicca is the modern-day revival religion, and Witchcraft is the old, pre-Christian religion of Europe.

✔ Witchcraft and Wicca are synonyms and are interchangeable.

The slang term, the Craft, is sometimes used as an alternative name for Wicca. Like the other terms, though, this one has many meanings. It may refer to all Wiccans and Witches (from the Old English *Wiccacraeft,* as well as the word Witchcraft).

Is Wicca a religion?

Whether Wicca is a religion or not depends on your definition of the word.

Wiccans believe in Deity, and they perform ritual in order to honor and develop their relationship with the Divine. They form small, independent, but closely knit groups (sometimes called covens) in order to practice in community. Many Wiccans choose to follow a tradition of belief and practice. Wiccans act within defined ethical and moral guidelines. Wicca provides a framework for addressing the same cosmic questions and universal concerns that other religions do (for example, life after death). So, in this sense, Wicca is a religion just like any other recognized faith.

However, Wicca has no official holy book or written doctrine, and no central authority or hierarchy of leaders who counsel people on how to live and enforce religious laws and obedience. The focus of Wicca is on individual discovery and personal experience of the Divine, which suggests that it is more of a spiritual path than a religion.

Is Wicca a cult?

Wicca is not a cult. In fact, Wicca is just about the opposite of a cult. Wicca has no central authority or leadership who tells people how to believe, practice, and live. The Wiccan path is focused on personal discovery and experience of the Divine. Every Wiccan is considered to be a Priestess or a Priest.

Wiccans practice alone or in very small, independent groups. The few Wiccan organizations that exist have no authority over individual practitioners. No leaders or groups in Wicca have large sums of money or the power that comes from wealth.

In addition, Wicca has a culture of self-determination and individualism; personal strength and independence are encouraged.

Wiccans do not try to convert others; proselytizing is unacceptable behavior. Wiccans are not expected to denounce their former religions, and they do not sever ties with their family and friends when they make a personal commitment to Wicca. People are free to leave Wicca at any time.

Worshipping Deity

Nearly all Wiccans believe in Deity; however, they hold wildly varying ideas about the nature of the Divine (see Chapter 2). Even Wiccans who practice their spirituality together may have very different views of Deity. The way that an individual perceives and interacts with the Divine is a personal decision.

It's probably safe to say that the majority of Wiccans worship or honor Deity in both the female and the male aspect or form, the Goddess and the God, but that's not true of all Wiccans. Some are Goddess-centered in their worship, and some don't recognize the God at all, or they acknowledge him only as coming from and contained within the Goddess.

Who — or what — do Wiccans worship?

Some Wiccans worship or honor a generic Goddess and/or God, others use various names for Deity. The following are a few of the possible ways that Wiccans perceive Deity:

- **The Deity is unknowable or unfathomable by the human mind.**

  In this case, the Divine is sometimes called *The All* or *The One* or *The All That Is One*.

- **The primal Great Goddess is the only or the primary Deity, and She is a supernatural, creative being.**

  She is the source of all life, and the life force flows from Her. If there is a God, He is the child, consort, or manifestation of the Great Goddess. She is known chiefly in the Mother aspect, sometimes called Great Goddess or Earth Mother.

- **The Goddess (or the God) is actually the life force, the core energy of all that exists.**

All of reality is an unbroken circle or web of vibrating energy, and this energy *is* the Goddess. The entire cosmos is the body of the Goddess (including physical and mental energy, as well as the forces of nature and the laws of physics). The Goddess may or may not transcend (be over or separate from) the universe, meaning that She is a supernatural, thinking, creative being apart from the cosmos.

✔ **The Goddess and the God are opposite poles of the Divine, and Wiccans honor or worship both the male and the female aspect or form of Deity.**

Many Wiccans honor the duality in nature (light and dark, life and death, and so on), and they see the Divine in the same way, sort of like the two poles on a battery.

✔ **The Deity is too complex and vast for humans to comprehend, so they perceive limited aspects, forms, or parts of Deity as Gods and Goddesses.**

In other words, the many Goddesses and Gods are various aspects or parts of one Great Source. Or, there's only one Deity, which takes many different forms.

✔ **The Goddesses and Gods are separate and distinct Divinities.**

They may be supernatural beings, nature spirits, or something else. Many different Gods and Goddesses exist, and each has His or Her own personality and realm. Sometimes Wiccans choose or feel called by a Goddess and/or God from an old Pagan pantheon for whom they feel affinity. Others choose or feel called by Deities of their personal ancestry (for example, Celtic).

✔ **Deity may be the Higher Self or the Deep Self (a person's spiritual essence), or a symbol arising from the unconscious mind.**

The unconscious mind has two parts:

- *The personal unconscious* is the location of everything that isn't presently conscious, but can be, including memories that you can call up easily and those that you have buried deep in your mind.

- *The collective unconscious* holds the accumulated knowledge and experiences of all humankind (and possibly animals). It is the inherited part of the brain. It holds our instincts, which are patterns of behavior. Instinct tells a bird to build a nest, and a turtle to go to water. Humans also have instinctive ways of behaving.

The unconscious mind doesn't have language to express these human behaviors and experiences. It communicates only in pictures. It uses symbols. A *symbol* is an image or object that represents something else. The collective unconscious uses archetypes, which are common to all humans. An *archetype* is not an image, but a tendency for humans to represent certain ideas with a specific symbol. These archetypal symbols appear in religions, dreams, myths, and fairytales. The Earth Mother is an example of an archetype.

Do Wiccans worship Satan?

Satan, as the opponent of God and the embodiment of evil, is a Christian concept. Wiccans don't believe in Satan. Wiccans don't worship Satan. Wicca is a revival of *pre*-Christian nature religion.

Historically, the Catholic and Protestant Churches regarded Witches as followers of the Christian Satan. During the widespread Witch hunts of medieval and Renaissance times, the churches falsely accused alleged Witches of consorting with and worshipping the Christian Devil. This historical link between Wicca and Satanism was unfounded, but remains deeply embedded in many cultures.

Wicca and Satanism were and are separate and entirely different systems of beliefs, practices, and ethics.

If Wiccans don't worship Satan, why do they use pentagrams?

A *pentagram* is a five-pointed interlaced star. It is an ancient magical symbol, and it represented mathematical and geometric principles, too.

In the United States, Satanists sometimes use an inverted pentagram as a symbol. In Europe, they sometimes use an inverted cross. The Satanist use of either of these symbols is irrelevant to Wicca.

The pentagram is a primary symbol of Wicca. The five points represent the four elements: Earth, Air, Fire, and Water, plus Spirit (the top point). The pentagram is also a symbol for humanity, and to some it means self-improvement. Historically, a person often is superimposed on the pentagram. The head is at the top, the middle points are outstretched arms, and the bottom two points are legs. See Chapter 12 for more information on pentagrams.

A *pentacle* is a disk with a pentagram inscribed on it. Inside a Wiccan ritual circle, pentagrams are drawn in the air in order to invoke or banish energy. When drawing a pentagram, a Wiccan may start at several different points, depending on the goal he or she wants to accomplish.

Evaluating Ethics and Morality

One of the most common and the most serious stereotypes about Wicca is that Wiccans don't have any ethics or morals. In actuality, Wiccans have a highly developed sense of ethics, and they devote considerable time and effort to figuring out what is right and wrong, and why (see Chapter 4). Two ideas form the basis for Wiccan ethics and morality.

- ✔ Wiccans view Deity as all-present in the world. All life comes from and is a part of the Divine energy. Each person has personal access to Deity and is able to seek direction and guidance. Wiccans communicate directly with the Goddess and/or the God. Instead of rigidly following religious dogma or obeying religious authorities, a Wiccan trusts in his or her own spiritual experience and ability to interpret the will of Deity for his or her own life. Wiccans believe that everyone comes from and is a part of the Divine, so to cause harm to anything or anyone is to act against the Goddess and/or the God.

- ✔ All of existence is an unbroken circle or web of energy. Human beings are not separate from the web of nature but are a part of it. Because people are connected to each other, Wiccans know that their own energy is never separate from the energy of other people, and doing harm to others eventually results in harm to the Self.

A Wiccan believes that his or her own personal energy is never separate from the energy of the rest of life and the cosmos.

Do Wiccans have morals and ethics? Who or what keeps a Wiccan in line?

The Wiccan Rede and the Threefold Law are the central ethics of Wicca, and almost all Wiccans agree with these principles.

The Wiccan Rede

The following words are known as the *Wiccan Rede:*

> *"Eight words the Wiccan Rede fulfil,*
>
> *An' it harm none, do what ye will."*

> —Doreen Valiente, Pentagram, Volume One, 1964 (published by Gerard Noel)

The majority of Wiccans try to follow the Wiccan Rede, sometimes called simply "the Rede," and consider it to be the guiding ethic for their lives.

Following the Rede means carrying out your own will but acting in ways that cause the least harm to yourself, others, the Earth, and all beings. Wiccans generally interpret the Rede to mean that a Wiccan should live and let live, while respecting the sacredness of all life. They should think critically about the consequences of their actions, before they act.

Many Wiccans have expanded the scope of the Rede. They think that apathy, neglect, and failure to act — to stop violence, abuse, suffering, or injustice — also are violations of the Rede.

The Threefold Law

Human beings are not separate from the web of nature but are a part of it. Everything that exists is linked together, and any action, no matter how small or insignificant, affects everything else. The behavior of every member of the web of life affects every other member. Negative or harmful energy not only harms the target of the energy, but the negativity and damage remains in nature's web and impacts all of life, including the sender.

The Threefold Law, sometimes called the Law of Return, is the idea that whatever a person sends out comes back threefold. In general, the law means that whatever you say or do — negative or positive, bad or good — will return to you with three times the intensity. Some Wiccans believe that this applies to words and actions, but others include thoughts.

When a Wiccan sends out energy — especially intentional, powerfully directed energy during magic — that person's intention and essence:

- ✔ Remain in the Self.
- ✔ Are a part of the energy being sent.
- ✔ Are in the outcome — the energy that travels through the circle of life, nature's web, and eventually returns to the sender.

That's why this ethic is called the *Three*fold Law. This principle is reflected in the old folk saying: What goes around, comes around.

Do Wiccans have clergy, denominations, and churches?

Because each Wiccan has direct access to Deity, each practitioner is considered to be clergy. Every Wiccan is a Priestess or Priest. Wiccans are expected to direct their own spiritual lives.

Wicca differs from most of the mainstream religions because it doesn't have a central authority with levels of clergy who make rules for all of Wicca. Wicca does have a few ordained clergy, but they are not associated with a centralized religious body that oversees the Craft. Instead, Wicca is made up of loosely connected and independent, small groups who define their own spiritual beliefs and practices.

Many of these small groups (called *covens*) have High Priestesses and/or High Priests, or leaders with some other title, who offer their skills to the group and direct its activities. Many Wiccan groups have levels of initiation; people advance as they study and grow in the Craft. Some groups have a council of elders who are a source of ongoing wisdom gained during their long experience in the Craft. However, in Wicca, leaders do not have control over the others. Wiccans independently decide how to believe and practice. No one in Wicca is obligated to follow the leader.

Wiccan churches do exist, and some have ordained clergy recognized by government, as well as tax-exempt status. In addition, Wicca has a few umbrella organizations or confederations of covens, by which small groups maintain their independence but join together in order to support ordained clergy, engage in advocacy for the legal rights and protections of Wiccans, and other collective activities.

People who practice Wicca, alone (as solitaries) or in covens, sometimes belong to a tradition. A tradition is a particular sect, subgroup, or denomination of Wicca. Specifically, a tradition is a framework or system for practicing Wicca, which usually includes spiritual principles, ethics, rituals, and magical practices. In other words, a tradition is someone's version of Wicca. (See Chapter 10 for more information on traditions.)

Do Wiccans believe in heaven and hell? What happens after death?

Nearly all Wiccans reject the idea of heaven and hell, as well as the need for absolution from sin. Most believe in some form of reincarnation.

All of life, everything in the cosmos, is made of one unbroken and unending circle of energy. Energy has no beginning and no end. It can be transformed, but it cannot cease to exist. Reality is a cycle of creation and destruction and re-creation — birth and death and rebirth. This pattern is repeated throughout the natural world, from the tiniest of cells to the most massive of stars; everything is in an endless cycle of regeneration. Most Wiccans believe that the same principle holds true for human lives.

Many Wiccans believe that when a person's physical body dies, the soul or the consciousness goes to the Summerland (also called the Land of Eternal Youth, the Land of the Young, or the Shining Land), located in non-physical, non-ordinary reality. Some Wiccans perceive the Summerland as a literal place of overwhelming natural beauty, unspoiled and pristine. Other Wiccans interpret it as the place where a person's essence or life force re-joins with the energy of Deity, the Great Source.

Many Wiccans believe that the soul engages in a life review while resting in the Summerland. Most reject the idea of a punishment for sins committed in life. The review is to help the soul learn lessons and evolve. After a time, the soul then has the opportunity to reincarnate. Some Wiccans believe that the soul has a choice about whether to return to physical life or move on to some other plane of existence.

Each new lifetime is viewed as a gift from the Deity, not a banishment into suffering and drudgery. Some Wiccans believe that after sufficient lifetimes or *incarnations,* the soul will reach a state of perfection and return to the Divine Source.

Wiccans have varied ideas about the afterlife, and some are complex. Some philosophies take into account that time is not linear, and people may be living many lives at once. Some believe in Oversouls that branch off and manifest in many physical lives. Regardless of the nuances, most Wiccans do believe in reincarnation.

Working Magic

First and foremost, Wicca is a spiritual path or a religion. The central goal of Wicca is to grow and develop in relationship with Deity. Magic is a natural act that is not inherently religious or spiritual. However, many Wiccans work magic within sacred space in a ritual setting, and welcome the presence or involvement of Deity during magic. Wiccans work magic for a variety of reasons, including self-improvement and empowerment, problem-solving, serving Diety and community, and meeting physical, mental, or emotional needs of Self and others. See Chapters 3 and 15 for more information on the premises and practices of Wiccan magic.

What is magic, and how do Wiccans use it?

All of reality is an unbroken web or grid of vibrating energy. Energy flows in patterns. All events in the physical world affect the flow of energy. In turn, all shifts in energy affect the physical world.

The energy in the mind is not separate from the energy in the rest of the world. When a person visualizes an event (sees it as a detailed picture in the mind), he or she forms energy into patterns. A person can focus his or her mental power to move and direct energy to shape events or conditions in the physical world. That process is called *magic.*

Magic itself is not religious or spiritual; it's a natural force. Magic is a process of moving and directing energy. However, all energy flows from and is part of Deity. For many Wiccans, magic is spiritual or religious because the Divine is involved. Wiccans often welcome the presence or involvement of Deity when they do magical work, and they often work magic in a ritual setting.

Do Wiccans work black magic?

Presumably, the terms white and black magic harken back to a time in early human history when the night, the dark, was associated with fear and danger. The daytime, the light, represented safety. However, some Wiccans, including this author, don't use the terms black magic and white magic. The terminology smacks of racism (designating that white is good and positive and black is evil and negative reinforces racial stereotypes). In addition, the usage isn't accurate. Magic is a tool, like mathematics or computer technology. Magic follows natural law, like gravity. The ethics of its use depend on the intention of the user.

Wiccans don't practice negative magic, what is sometimes called black magic. Black magic is any magic that is performed to coerce someone into doing something; is aimed at someone against his or her will; is aimed at someone without his or her knowledge; or is used to produce a restrictive, unwanted, unethical, or objectionable outcome.

The Wiccan Rede, the guiding ethical principle, prohibits Wiccans from doing harm. The Wiccan Threefold Law states that the energy that a person sends out into the world ultimately comes back to that person with three times the intensity. A Wiccan would not want to pay the karmic consequences of negative or "black" magic.

Do Wiccans curse or hex people?

Most Wiccans don't engage in hexing, cursing, and other negative practices. Wiccans know that their own energy is never separate from the energy of other people, and harm to others eventually results in harm to the Self. In addition, all people are connected to Deity. Harm directed at someone also is directed at the Divine.

The Wiccan Rede, the guiding ethical principle, prohibits Wiccans from doing harm.

Wiccans may try to banish (send away) or bind (make ineffective) someone who is dangerous or is guilty of inflicting violence or abuse.

Would a Wiccan turn someone into a toad?

Not unless the person *really* wanted to be toad.

Magic works within the natural laws of physics. I suspect that turning someone into a toad is beyond the bounds of both magic and scientific possibility, and such an act certainly violates Wiccan ethics. This magic myth is the stuff of stereotypes and fairy tales. See the next section to dispel a few more negative stereotypes about Wicca.

Dealing with Negative Stereotypes

Ugly hags with long, crooked noses and pronounced warts. Orgies in the woods. Depraved sexuality. Ritual abuse of children. Human and animal sacrifice. Blood rituals. Wicca is steeped in stereotypes. Some may be comic; others aren't funny at all. This propaganda is deeply embedded in the culture and continues to fuel discrimination and persecution of Wiccans. The following section dispels the most common stereotypes about Wicca and Witchcraft.

What about sexuality? Do Wiccans engage in ritual orgies?

Sexual activity, as part of ritual, is not a standard practice in Wicca. Wiccans do not engage in public or group sex as a religious or spiritual act. The stereotype of wild orgies under the full moon has no basis in truth, at least in modern-day Wicca.

Wicca as a fertility religion

Historical evidence suggests that the early Pagans engaged in various fertility rites at certain times of the year (especially at Beltane, the festival celebrated on April 30 or May 1). For example, couples are reported to have made love in the fields in order to encourage a good growing season and a bountiful harvest. However, these were Pagan festivals of antiquity, and making ritual whoopee among the peas and carrots is not a part of contemporary Wicca.

True to its ancient roots, Wicca is considered by most Wiccans to be a fertility religion. Fertility has many meanings, including the birth of ideas (creativity, art, and self-development). However, procreation also is part of fertility, and Wiccans celebrate sexuality. Healthy, safe, respectful sexual activity between adults is a sacred part of life and is not viewed as sinful, dirty, or prohibited. Sexuality is sacred energy, a gift from Deity. Violence or abuse associated with sexuality is not only a violation of Wiccan ethics, it is sacrilege and dishonors the Divine.

Because Wiccans celebrate sexual and creative energy, some traditions include sexual symbolism in ritual. Within the sacred circle, during ritual, some Wiccans perform the *Great Rite*. At the appropriate time during the ritual, the person conducting the ceremony says something like, "as the cup is the female and the athame is the male, together they are one." The person then thrusts the athame into a chalice filled with wine, juice, cider, or other drink. This act consecrates the wine, designating it as holy. (An athame is small knife used symbolically during ritual; a chalice is a cup or goblet.) The Great Rite is *symbolic* sex and does celebrate the sexual and creative energy in the universe.

Some couples may engage in the traditional Great Rite, actual sex, as a private act done at home. However, Wiccans do not engage in public or group sex as part of their religious or spiritual experience.

Ritual nudity

Today some Wiccans do perform ritual *skyclad,* which means nude. This is more common in solitary practice (when someone performs ritual alone). However, covens (closely knit, small groups of Wiccans) who belong to some traditions of Wicca perform ritual skyclad. The ritual nudity is not sexual, however, and it is done for a few reasons:

- When participants in a ritual are nude, clothing can't be used as a sign of social class or status. Nudity is thought to reflect the equality of all people. Every person embodies Deity, and all people are equal before the Goddess and the God. Economic wealth is not readily apparent when people are free of clothing and the rest of society's entrapments.

  Nudity is a way for all participants in a ritual to gather as equals. Many Wiccans believe that this tradition has continued from feudal times or earlier, when peasants resisted the values of class division.

- Ritual nudity is a way for Wiccans to reject current societal values. Wiccans celebrate the human body as a beautiful and miraculous manifestation of Deity. They reject the notion that the nude body is sinful, shameful, or vulgar.

- Nudity is sometimes incorporated into specific rituals to signify rebirth.

- Some Wiccans believe that clothing interferes with the flow of energy between people.

- Some Wiccan traditions prescribe ritual nudity.

However, many Wiccans don't practice skyclad; this is far from a universal practice. Instead, many Wiccans wear ritual garb, such as a cotton robe tied with a cord. Ritual nudity is a matter of personal choice, and the individual's choice must be respected.

Do Wiccans ritually abuse children?

To abuse a child — physically, sexually, and/or emotionally — would be a profound violation of Wiccan ethics (see the section "Evaluating Ethics and Morality"). No true Wiccan would condone such an abomination.

The Wiccan Rede, the guiding ethical principle, demands that Wiccans harm no one. The Wiccan Threefold Law states that the energy that a person sends out into the world ultimately comes back to that person with three times the intensity. No sane Wiccan would want to face the karmic consequences of such a heinous act as child abuse.

Do Wiccans engage in animal or human sacrifice?

Wiccans do not perform human or animal sacrifice. Period. Ever. Ritual sacrifice would be the ultimate violation of Wiccan ethics, which prohibit Wiccans from doing harm to others.

Sometimes Wiccans may set aside a portion of a feast or the wine (or juice) and cakes used in ritual, as an offering for Deity or ancestors. But Wiccans have no need or use for the blood of others, human or animal. In fact, Wicca probably has a greater percentage of vegetarians and vegans than most other religions or spiritualities. Some Wiccans argue that eating meat violates the Wiccan Rede, the guiding ethical principle of Wicca.

The Wiccan Rede states that Wiccans must "harm none." Vegetarian and vegan Wiccans make the case that eating animals, by definition, is harming them. The eating of meat is a matter of debate in the Craft. Certainly, ritual sacrifice of animals is not promoted or condoned.

The Pagan festivals of history were timed to the agricultural cycles and the seasons. Some of these festivals marked the slaughter of the livestock. The early Pagans prepared for the long, bitter cold winter by slaughtering livestock and storing the meat. They knew from experience how many animals they could feed over the long winter, and they slaughtered the rest to prevent their starvation and to store the meat for food to sustain the community over the winter. One such festival was called the Blood Harvest.

Most cultures have kept livestock for use as food. Today, millions of animals are slaughtered annually, and I suspect that the practices of the early Pagans were far more humane than those used today. Regardless, the Pagan animal slaughters of old were a traditional farming practice, and hardly could be considered ritual animal sacrifice.

Looking at Lifestyle

Some cultural trends indicate that Wicca is growing — fast. Many people have questions about just who Wiccans are and how they live. Unfortunately, not much hard data is available. This section answers some of the questions about Wiccan demographics and lifestyles. (See Chapter 6 for more information on Wiccan lifestyle and passages.)

How do Wiccans become Wiccan?

Some Wiccans believe that all one needs to do to become Wiccan is to declare the intention, to vow to honor Deity, and to follow the ethical principles of the Craft.

Others believe that an initiation is necessary. Some Wiccans perform a self-initiation, a ritual during which they make an official commitment to Wicca. Others believe that a group or coven ritual initiation is necessary. (See Chapter 9 for more information.)

How many Wiccans live in the United States and Europe?

No one knows for sure the total population of Wiccans. Recent surveys by groups outside of Wicca, sales of books about Wicca, and other indicators suggest that Wicca is growing rapidly. No one really knows how many Wiccans there are, who they are, and what kind of lives they lead. Wicca doesn't have large institutions that can provide this kind of collective information. Out of fear of persecution and desire for privacy, many Wiccans lead very low-profile lives. Many don't disclose their affiliation with Wicca to people outside of the Craft.

Are all Wiccans women?

No one is really sure about the demographics of the Wiccan population. It's fairly obvious that more women than men are Wiccan. (The numbers aren't unusual; women members outnumber men in most mainstream religions, at least in the United States.)

Most people assume that the disparity is because Wicca, unlike most other religions, offers women the opportunity to worship, honor, and/or celebrate the feminine aspect of the Divine. Some groups are women-centered, and some are women-only.

However, recent surveys indicate that men also are well-represented in Wicca, and the percentage of men in Wicca may be growing. (See the book *Voices from the Pagan Census: A National Survey of Witches and Neo-Pagans in the United States*, 2003, by Helen A. Berger, Evan A. Leach, and Leigh S. Shaffer.)

By the way, men are called Wiccans or Witches. They are not called warlocks, and most Wiccans take offense at that term. Many believe that the word *warlock* comes from an Anglo-Saxon word meaning traitor, deceiver, or oathbreaker. Some think that during the Witch trials of medieval and Renaissance times, a warlock was a Witch who betrayed others to Inquisition authorities. Today, someone who has turned against the Craft may be called a warlock.

Some Wiccans believe that the term warlock actually derives from an Old Norse word meaning spirit song, however, the term generally is not accepted as a word for a male Wiccan or Witch.

Do Wiccans legally marry?

A Wiccan couple may be handfasted, legally married, or both. *Handfasting* is the Wiccan ritual joining of people in love into committed partnership before the Goddess and/or the God. Handfasting usually lasts for a pre-agreed period of time. The handfasting commitment may be renewed or ended at the will of the parties involved. Handfasting, without a marriage license, is not legally recognized by the United States government.

Handfasting doesn't require a state-licensed clergyperson or official; the ritual may be private or presided over by a Wiccan Priestess or Priest. Handfastings are performed for both same-sex and opposite-sex couples.

Do Wiccans raise their children in Wicca?

At a child's birth or adoption, Wiccans may hold a ceremony to name the child and place her or him under the protection of the Goddess and God, as well as the Wiccan community. The vast majority of Wiccans do not consider this practice to be a dedication or initiation of the child into Wicca.

Some Wiccans share their beliefs with their own children and some allow their children to take part in age-appropriate activities, for example, coloring eggs at Eostar (the Wiccan spring holiday). However, Wicca encourages self-determination and promotes freedom of choice. Some Wiccan parents educate their children in a variety of spiritualities and let them decide which path to follow when they become young adults.

What happens when Wiccans grow old?

Wiccans perform Croning or Eldering rites to honor older members of the Craft who have gained wisdom, skill, and knowledge. For many Wiccans, an *Elder* is a man or a woman in the Craft who has reached his or her late 50s or older. Many Wiccans consider retirement age to be the time for an Eldering ceremony.

The term *Crone* usually applies to a woman who has reached menopause. Crone is a term of respect, and is also the term for the third aspect of the Goddess (Maiden, Mother, and Crone).

Eldering and Croning are rites of celebration and recognition, and mark the past achievement and future potential of the Elder or Crone.

Finding Wiccan Resources

Wiccan books have become very popular. This popularity means that more books are being published all the time. Some are excellent resources; others are unethical, are sensationalistic, or don't accurately reflect Wiccan beliefs and practices.

What are the best resources about Wicca?

The following are a few books that have become classics. Many people were introduced to Wicca by these volumes. Each offers a look at the general beliefs and practices of Wicca. You may want to turn to these books for basic knowledge.

- ✔ *The Spiral Dance: A Rebirth of the Ancient Religion of the Great Goddess* by Starhawk (1979, 2nd revised edition 1989, 3rd revised edition 1999)

- ✔ *Dreaming the Dark: Magic, Sex, and Politics* by Starhawk (1982, 1988)

- ✔ *Truth or Dare: Encounters with Power, Authority, and Mystery* by Starhawk (1987)

✔ *Drawing Down the Moon: Witches, Druids, Goddess Worshippers, and Other Pagans in America Today* by Margot Adler (1979, revised and expanded 1986, updated 1997)

✔ *Wicca: A Guide for the Solitary Practitioner* by Scott Cunningham (1988)

✔ *Living Wicca: A Further Guide for the Solitary Practitioner* by Scott Cunningham (1993)

Which books are credible?

Check out the classic introductory books listed in the preceding section. After you know more about the subject, you can decide what type of information you want to pursue and narrow your interest (for example, books from a feminist perspective, scholarly books on Wiccan history, or books from the perspective of a specific tradition). Getting some general information enables you to be better equipped to judge the credibility of other books.

Avoid the following:

✔ Books or other material that violate the Wiccan ethical principles explained in this book. Don't purchase any book that advocates doing harm to others, or aiming magic at someone who is unwilling or unaware. For example, don't buy a book that promises to give you 50 great curses and hexes.

✔ Books that promote the idea that Wicca is only a magical practice. Buying a book on practice, such as a book on divination, is fine, but the author should acknowledge that Wicca is not limited to that practice; Wicca is a full spiritual path.

✔ Books or other sources (particularly individuals) that offer tabloid-style material, for example, teachers or books that promise to help you hit the lottery. No spirituality is going to be carefully and accurately represented in material displayed in the checkout lane of the grocery store.

✔ Books or teachers that promise to reveal the one, true way and all its associated inner workings. Wicca is about self-discovery and growth; it's not about secrets and it's not about putting down other beliefs to build up our own.

✔ Material that focuses on blending Wicca with other religions. You are certainly free to pursue that interest later; I'm only suggesting that you get a good overview of Wiccan spirituality before considering this possibility. You can then have a better foundation for deciding whether mixing Wicca with another belief system is viable or desirable.

Appendix B

Magical Properties of Colors, Herbs, and Stones

*I*n this appendix, you can find suggestions for selecting colors, herbs, and stones for use in working magic. For magic to be most effective, the unconscious mind must participate in bringing about the desired change or outcome. Ancient and primal images, sounds, smells, and textures help to activate the unconscious mind.

Individual colors, herbs, and stones may have unique properties and affect the unconscious mind differently. Most Wiccans make an effort to choose the components of a spell that are most appropriate for his or her magical goal.

Magical Herbs, Not Medicinal Herbs

WARNING!

The herb lists in this appendix are for use in magic and ritual *NOT* medical treatment.

Do not eat or drink herbs or apply them to the body (in poultices, ointments, creams, lotions, oils, and compresses) without seeking the advice of a competent, well-trained health professional. Using herbs safely and effectively as medicine requires dedicated study and knowledge in order to understand the appropriate uses, the potential benefits, and the possible side effects. Like any medicine, herbs can be toxic and can produce unintended and sometimes dangerous effects, especially if used incorrectly.

If you use herbs topically (you apply them to your body) in your ritual or magical work, for example in anointing oils or bath solutions, purchase products made for that specific purpose and labeled as safe for external use. If you make your own herbal products, consult a reputable source (person, book, or Web site) for information about the use and handling of the specific herb.

Don't leave herbs where children and animals can reach them. Some are poisonous.

In this book, the word *herb* refers to all parts of the plant: the root or bulb, stem, leaves, dried flowers, seeds, fruit, berries, bark, juice, and so on. Physicians, herbalists, and researchers use much more precise terms and definitions for the various types and parts of plants.

Choosing Colors, Herbs, and Stones

The following lists provide common magical goals and colors, herbs, and stones that may be appropriate for that specific work. However, these are only recommendations to provide examples for you to consider for your own use. In magic, the best approach is to follow your own intuition. The items are listed alphabetically within each heading, so don't worry about needing to use the "first" item as the best.

Courage, personal strength, and will power

Color: red

Herbs: basil, black cohosh, borage, dragon's blood, gentian, mugwort, mullein, poke, St. John's Wort, thistle, yarrow

Stones: black tourmaline, jade

Creativity and art

Colors: gold, orange, red, silver, violet, yellow

Herbs: lavender, valerian

Stones: amazonite, aventurine, chrysocolla

Dreams

Colors: blue, blue-green, gray, green

Herbs to induce dreams: bay laurel, chamomile, hops, jasmine, lavender, linden, mugwort, pine, skullcap

Herbs to prevent nightmares: chamomile, rosemary, wood betony

Stones to induce dreams: chryosite (peridot), emerald

Stone to prevent nightmares: holey stone (hag stone)

Education and study

Colors: brown, orange, white, yellow

Herbs: bluebell, caraway, clove, fennel, fern, licorice, periwinkle, pomegranate, rue

Stones: aventurine, carnelian

Emotional health and healing (fighting depression and anxiety)

Colors: aqua, black, dark blue, gray, green

Herbs: hawthorn, lotus, marjoram, morning glory, mushroom, purslane, sea holly, seaweed, St. John's Wort, sunflower, wintergreen, yarrow

Stones: bloodstone, carnelian, garnet, moonstone, sardonyx, topaz

Justice and politics

Colors: black, brown, deep blue, red, royal purple

Herbs: hickory, High John the Conqueror, St. John's Wort

Stones: amethyst, green tourmaline, hematite, pink tourmaline, tiger's eye

Love, sex, and attraction

Colors: green, orange, red

Herbs: acacia flowers, apple, cherry, cyclamen, gardenia, geranium, jasmine, lavender, meadowsweet, mint, mistletoe, myrtle, pansy, rose, thyme, valerian, vervain, violet

Stones: moonstone, opal, rose quartz

Luck

Color: green

Herbs: allspice, clover, fern, hazel, heather, Irish moss, purslane, violet

Stones: amber, fossilized sea urchin (shepherd's crown), fossilized sand dollar, holey stones (hag stones), jet

Mental abilities, memory, and focus

Colors: pastels, white, yellow

Herbs: clove, eyebright, lemon balm, marjoram, nutmeg, parsley, rosemary, rue, sage

Stones: carnelian, clear quartz crystal

Money, prosperity, and financial security

Colors: green, gold, silver

Herbs: clover, High John the Conqueror, honeysuckle, mandrake, may apple, sunflower, wintergreen

Stones: amber, black obsidian, bloodstone, carnelian, green tourmaline, malachite

Peace

Colors: light blue, violet

Herbs: loosestrife, morning glory

Stones: amber, clear quartz crystal, rose quartz

Physical health and healing

Colors: green, light blue, orange, black

Herbs: All medicinal herbs also have magical properties for healing.

Stones: amber, clear quartz crystal, fluorite, green tourmaline

Protection of home and property

Colors: blue, silver, white

Herbs: aloe vera, basil, bay laurel, betony, bladderwrack, bloodroot, feverfew, garlic, High John the Conqueror, juniper, laurel, marjoram, rosemary, vervain

Stones: amber, fossilized sand dollar, garnet, malachite

Psychic abilities

Colors: black, blue, silver, white

Herbs: bay laurel, bistort, dandelion, marigold, mugwort, nutmeg, wormwood

Stones: amethyst, black obsidian, clear quartz crystal, fluorite, jet, lapis lazuli, turquoise

Purification

Colors: gold, orange, red, white

Herbs: anise, bloodroot, broom, chamomile, eucalyptus, fennel, hyssop, lavender, lemon, myrrh, pine, rosemary, saffron, verbena

Stone: clear quartz crystal

Spirituality

Colors: white, transparent

Herbs: African violet, geranium, mistletoe, myrrh

Stones: clear quartz crystal, lapis lazuli

Wisdom

Color: blue

Herbs: calamus, mulberry, sage, sunflower

Stones: clear quartz crystal, jade, lapis lazuli

Index